"Patricia Roush is not just a heroine—for her efforts on behalf of abducted American children and women in Saudi Arabia—but a storyteller who recounts her personal drama in *At Any Price* with great charm and skill."

—DANIEL PIPES
Director of the Middle East Forum,
Prize-winning columnist, *New York Post* and *Jerusalem Post*

"Having signed the Convention on the Rights of the Child in 1996, whose nondiscriminatory article 2 is clear, and whose article 9 declares that 'State Parties shall ensure that a child shall not be separated from his or her parents against their will,' Saudi Arabia is duty bound to adopt measures to bring its national practice into conformity with these international standards. May this book's moving personal testimony describing the actual practice in Saudi Arabia—currently one of the 53 Member States of the UN Commission on Human Rights—be a stimulant in 2003."

—RENÉ WADLOW
Main Representative of the Association for World Education
(NGO to the United Nations in Geneva)

"The costs of America's 'Special Relationship' with Saudi Arabia grow more obvious each passing day. The story told by Pat Roush in *At Any Price* is but one more example."

—DOUG BANDOW
Senior fellow at the Cato Institute
and syndicated columnist

"*At Any Price* is a moving testimony to a mother's love. Hostage to the racist-religious laws of a state that endorses child abduction, Patricia Roush courageously fights an evil conspiracy that united American political opportunism with a theocracy under shari'a law. A truly indispensable book for our time."

—BAT YE'OR
Internationally renowned author and authority
on jihad violence, shari'a, and dhimmitude
Author of *Islam and Dhimmitude: Where Civilizations Collide*

"Pat Roush is a remarkably resilient woman whose perseverance will inspire you and whose book, At Any Price, will move you. It is only because of her abiding faith that I believe her daughters Alia and Aisha will breathe freedom again."

—JOEL MOWBRAY
National Review Online contributor
and TownHall.com columnist

"That the Kingdom of Saudi Arabia is the most intolerant Islamic regime in the world is more or less known; that the government of the United States is prepared to sacrifice young lives of its kidnapped citizens in order to appease that regime should become known thanks to this important book, At Any Price. Whenever you read of another weekend our president spends with the Saudi ambassador at that Texas ranch, remember Patricia Roush's daughters, now clad from head to toe in black abayas for life. Whenever you hear Mr. Bush's good friend Tony Blair declare that 'Saudi Arabia is a good and dependable friend to the civilized world,' remember that he talks of the country that is the source of most al-Qaida fighters and funding, the instigator of Islamic agitation all over the world, an Islamo-fascist freak show in which the only expanding industry is that of Islamic extremism. Patricia Roush's daughters remain, for now, victims of Washington's 'special relationship' with the Saudi kleptocracy. Their case indicates urgent need for America and the rest of the West to set themselves free from the need to pander to Saudi whims, including the nonexistent and unreciprocated 'right' of its government to bankroll thousands of mosques and Islamic 'cultural centers' around the world that teach hate and provide the logistic infrastructure to Islamic terrorism."

—SRJDA TRIKOVIC, PHD
Author of *The Sword of the Prophet: A Politically Incorrect Guide to Islam*
Foreign affairs editor for *Chronicles* magazine

AT ANY PRICE

How America Betrayed My Kidnapped
Daughters for Saudi Oil

PATRICIA ROUSH

WND BOOKS
A Division of Thomas Nelson, Inc.
www.WNDBooks.com

Published in Nashville, Tennessee, by Thomas Nelson, Inc.

Scripture quotations are from the NEW JERUSALEM BIBLE. Copyright © 1966 by Darton, Longman & Todd Ltd. and Doubleday & Company, Inc. Used by permission.

Library of Congress Cataloging-in-Publication Data

Roush, Patricia.
    At any price : how America betrayed my kidnapped daughters for Saudi oil / Patricia Roush.
    p. cm.
    ISBN 0-7852-6365-9 (hardcover)
    1. Roush, Patricia. 2. Kidnapping, Parental--United States--Case studies. 3. Kidnapping, Parental--Saudi Arabia--Case studies. 4. Mothers of kidnapped children--Biography. 5. Intercountry marriage--Case studies. 6. United States--Foreign relations--Saudi Arabia. 7. Saudi Arabia--Foreign relations--United States. I. Title.
HV6598.R68 2003
362.82'97--dc21   2002155722

Printed in the United States of America

03 04 05 06 BVG 6 5 4 3 2 1

To my Flowers, Alia and Aisha

And to all American women and children
who are unable to leave Saudi Arabia

Contents

Preface   ix

1. East Meets West (June 1975–January 1985)   1

2. 1,001 Nightmares (January 1985–May 1985)   22

3. Free to Be, but Not for Long (May 1985–January 1986)   38

4. Hope That Is Not Seen (January 1986–March 1986)   47

5. Two Women (March 1986–December 1986)   53

6. Miracle on 34th Street (January 1987–January 1988)   70

7. Silkworm Missiles and Lies (January 1988–December 1988)   90

8. Allah and Little Girls (January 1989–June 1991)   106

9. Soldier of Fortune Flytrap (July 1991–September 1994)   123

10. Tomorrow—It's Only a Day Away (September 1994–June 1995)   142

11. The Princes and the President (June 1995–June 1996)   166

12. Dark Night of the Soul (June 1996–December 1997)   187

13. Chronicles (January 1998–December 1999)   206

14. Burton's List (September 2001–October 2002)   228

15. Freedom and Liberty   266

16. The Journey   274

Afterword   287

About the Author   289

PREFACE

Our government lives on long lies. It was ten o'clock in the morning and I, unknowingly, was about to witness another one. I was in my kitchen with a framed painting in one hand and a hammer in the other, searching for that right spot on the wall. As I was climbing down the ladder, the phone rang.

"Ms. Roush? This is Bill McCullough from American Citizens Services at the Department of State. I have some news for you."

I braced myself against the refrigerator as that pitting feeling in my stomach returned. "Is something wrong? Did something happen in Saudi Arabia?"

"Assistant Secretary of State Burns has asked me to tell you he will not be able to meet with you personally but will be sending you a letter sometime in the future."

"I never asked to meet with him personally. I just asked him to negotiate for the release of my daughters from Saudi Arabia."

"Ms. Roush, I have something else to tell you, and you are not going to like what I have to say. Your oldest daughter was married last week."

I was shaking. My body became numb and limp.

"What? What did you say? You bastards! You waited so long and now she has been destroyed! After all these years of pleading with you for help, and now it is too late! I want to talk to Burns. Why didn't he call me? Why did he have you do his dirty work for him? For sixteen years, I have waited for that special call from someone with the State Department telling me that my daughters were coming home. And now this—my worst nightmare, come true?" I hung up the phone and fell to the floor.

After nearly two decades of continuous effort spent in lobbying four secretaries of state and four U.S. presidents, spending every bit of money I had on three teams of mercenaries to covertly rescue my children, working for major changes in state and federal legislation, and hounding the press for coverage, my twenty-three-year-old daughter was sold by her Saudi father into an arranged marriage.

The child I had cherished and loved beyond belief who had been ripped away from me was now in a harem inside Saudi Arabia. A letter, signed by twenty-three U.S. senators, had been hand-delivered to Secretary of State Colin Powell just three weeks before, asking for his intervention with the Saudi king "in the most urgent terms for the release and repatriation of Alia and Aisha Gheshayan." One of his subordinates wrote the usual Washington "kiss off" response. Now Alia's fate was sealed.

A daughter's wedding day should be one of the happiest moments in her life, shared with her mother, and I was not even aware of it. I found out about this sacred rite of passage from a secondary consular officer at a governmental office. It was as if I had been erased from her life.

Overwhelmed with grief, I had to get out of the house. I got into the car and drove to the beach. The waves calmed me like a lullaby. My mind drifted to happier days. I could see the girls in the water, laughing and playing with me. Three-year-old Aisha was on my back in the shallow water. As I waded along the shore with her arms tightly wrapped around my neck, Alia, six, swam alongside us and shouted, "Mommy, watch me! I can swim underwater . . . Watch!"

She swam like a fish with her little blue-polka-dot bathing suit clinging to her small wet body and her long, dark brown hair wrapping around her head and neck like kelp. She had learned to swim at summer camp and enjoyed showing off her new skill.

My eyes blinked and I was back on the beach—alone.

Returning to the house, I opened the front door and went straight to my office. Tracings of sixteen years of work lined the walls: a kidnapped children's poster displaying the faces of my daughters; awards; pictures of me with senators, mayors, celebrities, the girls; Aisha's framed finger painting from preschool; neatly framed articles from print media; and file cabinets and storage boxes filled with documents and papers.

I slumped into the chair near my desk in front of my computer and penned a letter to Secretary of State Colin Powell requesting that I be granted an immediate visa to the kingdom of Saudi Arabia to see my daughters and this man, whomever he might be, who had just married Alia.

Then, in an almost obtunded state, I wandered into the kitchen, made a cup of tea, and made my way to a white Adirondack chair on the deck. I allowed my head to come to a comfortable rest on the back of the chair and looked skyward. *Now what?*

I had one last thing to do for them.

Walking back into my office, I grabbed my laptop and returned to the deck. Placing it on top of the glass table, I began:

Dearest Alia and Aisha,

I have missed you so much all these years and love you beyond heaven and earth. I want to give you this gift. The only treasure I can give that will be of value to you—the gift of the truth. So I am writing the story of what happened—your story and mine—and hope that one day, you will come to know how much your mother loves you . . .

I

❧

EAST MEETS WEST

Your whole past was but a birth and a becoming.
—Antoine de Saint-Exupcry

"Batricia"

It was June 1975, about eleven o'clock at night, and the thumping sound of the disco beat reverberated off the walls of the student union at the Catholic university known for its once-famous basketball team—the University of San Francisco. I wasn't a student at this institution—couldn't afford it—but was there for this Saturday night gathering. It was a diversion from my grueling schedule at San Francisco State and my job and responsibilities.

The room was filled with a mixed ethnic assortment of students and their friends—Asians, a medley of Middle Eastern males, young white males and females—listening and dancing to the sounds spun by a student disc jockey. I was sitting alone on an overstuffed chair in a corner, sipping a 7-Up, when a young Middle Eastern male approached me. He pulled up a folding chair and started to talk.

"You go to school here? I didn't seen you before?"

I hesitated. He had unusual eyes that instantly captured my attention. They were large, almond-shaped vessels filled with liquid black coal that could penetrate to the other side of your soul.

I responded slowly, "No. Just visiting. Where are you from?"

His head tilted back slightly as he laughed. "Saudi Arabia."

I wondered about the cast on his left arm. "What happened to your arm? Broken?"

"Yeah. I fell. I play soccer in front of Hayes-Healey Hall. That's the place over here where I have my room. I just came to United States few months ago. So now I study English here at this school. My family is big family in Saudi Arabia. My government sends me here to study criminology. Want to dance?"

"No," I declined. "I have to go. It's getting late."

"I can call you? What is your name? I like to talk to you again."

"Pat."

"Bat?"

"No, Pat. Patricia."

"Batricia. Batricia. I like that name. Pretty. I shall call you, Batricia."

We spent another hour chatting about Saudi Arabia and the United States. He told me his name was Khalid Gheshayan, the oldest son of a wealthy Saudi whose family ties were well connected to the ruling Al-Saud monarchy. He stated his grandfather had ridden camels and horses with Ibn Saud, the desert patriarch who had united the Arabian peninsula after WWI and whose descendants now control the oil rich kingdom. As an anthropology major at San Francisco State University, I was intrigued with his stories. Perhaps I had seen *Lawrence of Arabia* one too many times, but as the evening came to a close I gave him my phone number.

Kapsa with Rice

We began having long phone conversations. I had been divorced for several years and was struggling with being a single mom, going to school, working part-time, and grieving the recent loss of my father. Khalid seemed to have a naïveté about him, an unsophisticated, uncomplicated, carefree approach to living, and I was overburdened with life itself.

He introduced me to his friends Salam and Abdul Rahman. They had an apartment on Geary Boulevard where many of the Saudis in Khalid's group gathered socially. The smell of *kapsa,* a Saudi stew made with lamb, curry, cardamom, and hot peppers, filled the air. It was the one dish they all seemed to know how to prepare. They were very lighthearted, friendly, and generous. They enjoyed each other and joked easily—making fun with an easy, almost childlike playfulness. The camaraderie was unlike what I had seen among American men. They would sit on the floor in a circle, drinking sweetened tea from demitasse cups and talking, playing music, and amusing themselves with anecdotes and tales about their country.

They were never without courtesy and hospitality. I was always treated like a "guest of honor" when invited to their many dinners where everyone would sit on the floor—Saudi style—eating kapsa, rice, and salad with bare hands. Khalid's attentiveness to me was almost obsessive. This was his first journey outside the strict Wahhabi Islamic backdrop of his native Saudi culture. He was like a kid at Christmas, opening one present after another with delight at each surprise. At first it was refreshing for me to see this kind of savage "innocence" firsthand; my interest in the ancient Middle East and antiquity colored my judgment. I processed the cultural differences as being exotic and a remnant of the peoples of the past that were coming alive before my very eyes. But then I began to see how Khalid was having difficulty adapting his cultural beliefs and background to all the "fruits" of the open society he became a part of when he took that flight to America.

He drank and experimented with different types of alcoholic beverages which is strictly forbidden by Islam. He and his friends smoked hashish or marijuana at times, but drugs were not a large part of his life. He liked hard liquor.

He called me several times a day. At first I was flattered. I loved the attention and the romantic idea of being pursued. A twenty-nine-year-old woman with a low self-esteem who is lonely, insecure, and vulnerable is easy to wear down. I was that woman.

Esther's Daughter

"Daddy, you're here! Daddy! Now the kids can't tease me and say where is your father?"

I stood on the running board of my father's 1952 Pontiac and wrapped my arms around his neck. I dug my fingernails into his skin. I wouldn't let him go. As I kissed his cheek I could feel the scratch of the beginnings of a five o'clock shadow and could smell the unmistakable odor of my—yes, my—father! He was here in Cicero, Illinois, in front of *Bella Papa's* house on Fifty-fourth Avenue.

Bella Papa, my mother's father, was dead, but we all lived on Fifty-fourth together—my mother, my sister, Bobbie, my mother's sisters and their husbands, and my cousin Marie. This was *la famiglia*.

My mother, Esther, second daughter of Italian immigrants Enrico and Maria Stancato, was named after a Jewish woman whose bed was alongside my grandmother's in the medical ward the women shared at Cook County Hospital in Chicago in 1918.

Maria was pregnant with my mother and had had a difficult labor. The Jewish woman requested that my grandmother name her baby Esther, after her. This was asking a lot, but my grandmother was a very religious woman with a caring heart and honored her friend's request. So even from the beginning of her life, my mother had a distinct identity separate from her family—a little Italian girl with the name of the ancient Jewish queen of Persia.

My grandmother, Maria Cerza Stancato, had a short life filled with infant mortality and physical pain caused by tuberculosis of the bone in her leg. My mother used to tell me that she always remembered her mother in bed saying the rosary and her prayers in Italian. She died at age thirty-three, leaving Bella Papa with four young daughters to raise. His oldest daughter, Julia, sixteen, was left to raise her younger sisters—my mother, Esther, another sister, Amelia, and the youngest sister, Harriet, whom everyone called "Baby Doll"—while he worked on his small vegetable farm to support the girls through the Great Depression. It was a happy household filled with many relatives and friends. Enrico Stancato was a poor Italian farmer with a generous heart who shared whatever he had with anyone who came to his door. They struggled, but in that house filled with music, singing, dancing, and love there was a oneness of spirit.

When World War II broke out, my mother got a job in a defense plant making parts for U.S. aircraft. She met a tall, blond, blue-eyed man with a soft voice and easy Cary Grant charm and wit—my father, David Roush.

Chicago in 1944 was bustling, and "Rosie the Riveter" types like my mom were keeping the war effort together. My father, unable to get medical clearance for military duty because of an injury to his optical nerve in a childhood accident, came to Chicago from central Indiana seeking employment after the depression. Esther and David were passionate about each other and became inseparable. They were very much in love. There was only one problem—Esther had a husband.

She was married in 1941 to a man she said she never loved, Bob Labut. Soon after the war began he was shipped to the South Pacific and did not return until 1946. When my mother met my father she was emotionally torn about what to do, but her love for my father couldn't be denied. She remained in conflict because of her Italian family and her Catholicism and then became pregnant with me just as the war was ending and the troops were returning home.

Many years later she told me, "Pat, I was pregnant and I didn't know what to do. My father didn't know, and Bob didn't know and he was coming home from the war."

When her husband returned home from the navy, Esther was four months pregnant. She told him but couldn't face Bella Papa. So she disappeared with my father and lived on the South Side till after I was born. Bella Papa wasn't educated, but he wasn't stupid.

He said to Julia, "Where is Hesta?"

"Papa, Esther had a baby girl."

"Where is this baby? Bring her to me."

From the moment Bella Papa saw me, I was his darling. This old Italian man, who was barely five feet tall and walked with a slight limp from an old stroke, carried me around in his arms from the time I can remember. So my early years were spent with a loving grandfather and my adorable aunts, who cared for me with all the love and attention I could possibly desire. Esther never resolved her guilt about Bob and my father. She continued to seesaw between them and, oddly enough, they both loved her very much and tolerated this situation.

Bella Papa said to her, "Hesta, maka uppa yo min'. You cantta hava both. Bob or Davie. Decide."

She finally did. She told them both to leave. She had a baby with Bob before it was over—my sister, Bobbie. And then Bella Papa died. I was devastated. My safe little world ended.

On Our Own

With the death of my grandfather and the marriage of all my aunts, things changed quickly and would never be the same. I spent the rest of my childhood with Esther and Bobbie. We moved to a new house away from the family. My mother, five foot two with green eyes and a temper to match, was unpredictable and unflappable. She successfully opened a restaurant, did carpentry, could cook a seven-course meal in an hour, fixed cars, and tackled the most difficult challenges. Once she even hitched up a twenty-eight foot trailer to her '51 Hudson and pulled it from Chicago to Florida with Bobbie and me in the back seat with our dog, Bonnie. She was courageous and fearless—a nonstop little tigress that never let go of something she started.

Bobbie and I took piano lessons, dance lessons, art lessons, drama lessons, and went to Catholic schools. She always wanted me to be a medical doctor. She would tell her friends, "Pat's going to be a doctor. She's so smart. I just know she's going to be a doctor." I did love books and biology was one of my favorite subjects. I would spend hours reading the encyclopedias and books from the science reference set she bought for us. She tried to give Bobbie and me the things she'd never had, but what we really wanted was her time and her love. She worked hard at her job and at home and put in long days. She was a single mom in the fifties, and it was not an easy life.

I took care of Bobbie and did the housework. My mother was either working or sleeping, exhausted from all the long hours she put in. There was no money from my father to ease her burden. She grew bitter and angry. My father married when I was seven, and the new wife was extremely jealous of my mother and me. She took my father to California. He repeatedly tried to see me after Bella Papa died, but Esther would turn each attempt he made into a scene from a horror movie.

One day he approached the house and Esther let him in.

"I just want to see Pat. I don't want any trouble, Esther. I just want to see my little girl."

We were in the kitchen and my mother was at the sink. I was sitting on a kitchen chair, and my father was standing near the back wall. She was screaming at him at the top of her lungs. Then, suddenly, my mother ran up to my father and threw a glass of water in his face. He just stood there while she cursed at him. I cried. I just wanted to see my daddy.

It was never to be. My childhood and later my teens would be a lonely journey. I amused myself with my books, piano, and fantasies. I retreated into a world where I couldn't hear my mother scream at me and deliver curses: "You're just like your no-good father. You can't do anything right. I should have given you away when you were born."

Her profanity and verbal abuse would haunt me for years and emotionally damaged me in ways she could never know. At the same time she could turn around and be the most caring mother in the world. She had a dual, alcoholic-style personality, even though she didn't drink. I loved her, but she could never accept that love or the love of anyone else. She alienated everyone close to her and, sadly, never received the healing that she needed until she was upon her deathbed.

I found out that my parents had never been married when I was fourteen—the summer before freshman year in high school—and it put me in such a spin. I didn't speak for two months and was severely traumatized for most of my life because of this. My Catholic upbringing didn't fit with this reality. I took it hard and hated my mother for lying to me all those years. I told her that I didn't want to live with her any longer. She refused to allow me to go to southern Illinois and live with my father's brother and his wife whom I loved very much. Instead, my mother cruelly beat me in front of several of our relatives. I called my uncle and aunt and they got in touch with my father whom I hadn't seen in six years. He came to Chicago and wanted me to go to California with him and his wife.

So without my mother's permission, I left with my father and lived with him and his wife in southern California for seven months. I thought at last I would have my father all to myself. I was wrong. His jealous wife would hardly allow us to have a conversation together. Her antics and lies made it impossible for me to live there so I had to return to Chicago—back to Esther. She greeted me with anger and hostility and continually taunted me about my father and his wife. I had no one and nowhere to go. I dreamed about getting away from her screams and madness.

Jerry

When I was fifteen, my mother's best friend, Stella, invited us to the Polish wedding of one of her relatives. I asked if my friend Carole could come along.

We were dressed! It was 1961 and bouffant hair was in. Carole and I spent hours in front of the mirror that day backcombing and spraying our tresses. A careful application of white lipstick was made after we slipped into our five-inch heels and poured ourselves into our dresses. We were ready for the party.

After the dinner the band played and I noticed a six-foot-four Troy Donahue type of guy standing near the bar looking at me. Our eyes met. He was surrounded by other young men who were laughing and drinking. Little did I know that they were all members of the "Marquis," a social and athletic club of suburban Chicago. He said his name was Jerry Veverka, an architectural student at the University of Illinois.

We danced and talked until it was time to leave. He asked if he could call me. I was too young for Jerry at that time. We exchanged phone numbers and talked on the phone a few times, but he was a college man, and I was still in high school. No matter how mature and sophisticated I thought I was, I was still a teenager. I grew up acting much older than I was because I had so much responsibility and never really had time to be a child. I raised myself and my sister and always felt so alone and different. I could never quite understand this difference, this calling, but much later in my life I would come to know its meaning very well.

A few years later, after Jerry graduated from the university, he called me and we began to date. I was seventeen at that time. He came from a good Catholic Polish-Czech family, got a well-paying job in architecture after graduation, and bought a new sports car. I was living with my mother, who was still struggling hard. She had a catering business and worked from sunrise till sundown. I was driving then and had a part-time job after school. I was independent, and Jerry opened for me new worlds of art, jazz, sophistication, and an intellectualism that I enjoyed.

Later that year Jerry landed a job with a well-known architectural firm in Michigan, and soon after I graduated from high school we were married. As with many girls who grow up without a father, I found myself in an early marriage as a way out of the house. I had finally accomplished my goal of getting as far away from my mother as I could. Jerry and I soon had a son, Eric, and a daughter, Daina. Now I was free from both Esther and David. I had my own family.

But I had not grown up emotionally. I still didn't have an identity. It was the sixties, a difficult time to be young, with social unrest everywhere. Post–World War II baby boomers like me found themselves in an American social revolution that they were not prepared for.

After Jerry and I traveled to Europe, we moved back to Chicago, and then in 1968 we decided to move to San Francisco. He worked and I was enrolled at City College of San Francisco and later San Francisco State University as a part-time student. There were student strikes, televised student demonstrations and confrontations with the university president, S. I. Hiyakawa. Riots. Unrest. Turmoil. There was a constant churning of politics mixed with the newly unleashed sexual revolution, women's liberation, drugs, rock 'n' roll, "God Is Dead," flower power, and war protests. We lived right in the middle of it all.

San Francisco was a new experience for us—a culture shock. We were not ready for that kind of change, and our marriage began to suffer. We grew apart and couldn't seem to put it back together. In 1972 we separated. It was difficult, but we were very amicable and worked out agreements concerning the children. We lived within two blocks from each other, and the children easily went back and forth. It was a workable divorce with no anger or recrimination.

I was unhappy with America and the establishment. I kept hearing news that many of my former classmates from elementary school and high school were dying in a war in Southeast Asia that was orchestrated by men in Washington with no vision. McNamara and Nixon were rationalizing the war on the six o'clock news each evening and Watergate broke soon afterwards.

I majored in anthropology and became interested in antiquity and the classics. I wanted to go to the Middle East and work on archaeological digs. I romanticized it. I wasn't happy with what was going on at home in America and longed for a better world—a new culture. I was an idealist looking for a utopia that didn't exist.

Disregarded Omens

Jerry and I had been divorced for several years, and I was almost finished with my degree at San Francisco State when I met Khalid. I still had the idea that I was going to go off into the blue and somehow work in the Middle

East. I planned on working in the Arabian Gulf United Arab Emirates so that I could make enough money to be able to explore the ancient ruins of the Middle East.

The year after I met Khalid, I actually went to Dubai for a visit. Daina and I went for several weeks just to scope it out. After three weeks I knew it was not for me. I couldn't live in a country where women were wearing black veils from top to bottom. It bothered me to see the women in black walking in the hot sun with a trail of children behind them while the men wore white and were as fresh as a daisy. That was one bubble burst.

Khalid was still in San Francisco and not doing much. His scholarship was poor; he couldn't concentrate and was drinking. I was working for an insurance broker (so much for my anthropology degree), and seeing him off and on. His parents had moved to San Francisco and intended to stay for one year while a new home was being built in Riyadh.

His mother, Fatima, was married at the age of twelve. She gave birth to ten children—eight survived. Khalid was the oldest. Fatima's health was poor, and she had multiple medical problems. The father, Hamad, worked for King Faisal for many years. When the king was murdered by a deranged relative, Hamad quit the government and came to the United States for cardiac surgery at the Cleveland Clinic.

Hamad was an old-fashioned bedouin who did not drink or smoke. He had one wife and lived a quiet life. He was well dressed, liked order, and appeared calm although Khalid mentioned that he had been very abusive to Fatima when the children were growing up. Khalid moved into his parents' apartment in San Francisco and continued to drink heavily. He quit school and played with his brothers during the day and went to the bars at night. I was not with him and saw him rarely but somehow couldn't make the break with him. It was as if there was a karmic destiny between us that had to be fulfilled. He often manipulated me into doing favors for him and feeling sorry for him. One night he was in the car with me. I was driving, and he had been drinking.

Looking at him in the passenger seat I said, "Khalid, why don't you get some help and stop this track you're on? Your parents are here now and maybe they can help you."

Without warning he reached over and pulled the car keys out of the ignition. The car stopped in the middle of the streetcar tracks. It was night and other cars were behind me. He opened the door, jumped out, and threw the keys down a grate into the sewer. Then he ran to his parents' apartment a few blocks away. I was stranded. I walked to the apartment, rang the bell, and asked for Hamad. When I explained what had happened, he just shrugged his shoulders and closed the door in my face. This scenario would be repeated over and over again. Khalid would put me in jeopardy, run for safety, and they would protect him.

I did not know at that time that I was pregnant. When I found out, it was too late. I should never have told him and just disappeared and raised my baby, but I didn't. I always felt I could handle anything. I was overly confident and didn't fully realize the danger I was in with this man. My false sense of control and confidence was to be my undoing.

Rosemary's Baby

The large dome of San Francisco City Hall served as the canopy for my wedding to Khalid Gheshayan. I was not enthusiastic. No one was invited; even I didn't want to be there. It was a formality, and I went through the motions because I couldn't reconcile not being married when my baby was born because of my background and religion. I was scared and sick.

My pregnancy was difficult. I continued to work until I reached my eighth month, when I was ordered by my doctor to quit. My blood pressure was high, my legs and feet were swollen, and I had symptoms of eclampsia (a dangerous condition of pregnancy characterized by seizures). Bed rest was ordered. Hamad and Fatima and their seven other children had returned to Riyadh one month before the wedding. I had the interior of my house repainted and bought new furniture and supplies for my baby. Then I tried to stay in bed.

Khalid was never home. He was always out with either his Arab friends or his newfound American drinking pals. I had few friends and became quite concerned because I had no one to be a labor coach for me. Khalid came with me to a childbirth class one night and walked out before the class was finished. I was embarrassed and frightened that I would have to face the delivery alone. I was thirty-two and had a history of difficult deliveries. The doctor was telling me that I might have to undergo a cesarean section. My mother wouldn't speak to me after I married Khalid and she found out I was pregnant.

"Pat, how could you? How could you lower yourself to this level? That's it. Forget you even have a mother!"

She hated him, and she was right. He was no good and would lead me to hell and back. I was alone and had to figure out what to do next.

But I was always good at that—too good.

When I was eight months pregnant, I asked Khalid to take me to Berkeley for my checkup appointment because I felt too sick to drive. He refused— he said he was busy. So I squeezed myself into the car and made it across the Bay Bridge. When I arrived at my doctor's office the staff was up in arms; my "husband" had called every five minutes for the last hour wondering if I had arrived yet and if I was all right.

A few weeks later, the end was finally near. My amniotic fluid broke and labor was induced. Khalid took me to Alta Bates Hospital in Berkeley where I endured a "natural childbirth," which was the mode in 1979 wholistic Berkeley. I went through seventeen hours of pain with no anesthetic. I hired a labor coach—a student from a wholistic health program—and Khalid disappeared when things got tough for me. I later learned that he had sneaked back into my hospital room and drank my roommate's bottle of champagne while I was delivering our baby.

Alia was born at 11:37 in the morning on Friday, January 5, 1979. "Give her to me," I said as soon as she was delivered. The moment I saw Alia, I fell in love with her. She was the most beautiful creature I'd ever seen.

I couldn't believe this beauty could come from his seed. I was worried throughout the entire pregnancy about the baby—what would his baby be like? I pressed her to my breast and just marveled. She and I were one spirit. I gave her the warmth of my body and we melted together.

Khalid had my car when I was in the hospital and without my knowledge used my apartment as a place for his friends to crash. My anxiety rose as I dressed Alia in her pink sweater set to make the journey home from the hospital. I felt safe and supported when I was in the hospital but knew I couldn't stay there forever.

He arrived late to pick us up. I was weak and had black circles under my eyes from the difficult labor and delivery. As I opened the apartment door I could see pillows from the sofa thrown on the floor, and the living room smelled of cigarettes. It sickened me. I hated cigarettes and never allowed any smoking in the house. Now I had to bring my new baby home to this.

During the next few weeks I regained my strength, and one night while I was rocking and nursing Alia in the living room the door opened. Khalid stumbled in, tripping over himself. I could smell the alcohol and cigarettes from across the room. He was accusatory and began cursing me. He had a gallon of wine in his hand. I got up with Alia in my arms and walked into the bedroom. He followed me.

"Don't think I don't know what you are going to do, you bitch. I'm sick of you, and I'll show you who's in charge here."

He pushed me, with Alia still in my arms, against the wall. She was three weeks old.

"I'll fix you. You're not making any calls." Then he went to the telephone and pulled the cord out of the wall. After losing his balance a few times he left the apartment with the gallon of wine in hand.

I called the police. They found Khalid at the end of the street at the Oar House, a local bar he frequented. They arrested him and found he had a few other charges pending. He'd had an accident with his father's car while his parents were in town. He beat up the other driver and drove away. They accused him of hit and run and battery. His student visa had expired, and he did not apply for his immigrant visa after he married me so the police turned him over to the Immigration and Naturalization Service.

He was detained in a holding cell at the INS in downtown San Francisco. They called me and asked what I wanted them to do with him. Did I want him in the country or should they deport him? I knew the officer well. She was a pleasant black woman who had helped the Gheshayan family when they entered the United States.

"Deport him."

Blackouts and a Broken Nose

Alia and I had a honeymoon; I had her all to myself in peace. I bought her a new pram and we took walks every day. My daughter Daina helped me with Alia's bath, and each day before Daina went to school she would peek inside the room and give Alia a kiss. I had enough money saved to stay home for a few months and be a full-time mother.

Khalid stayed in Riyadh only three months and then took whatever money he could raise from relatives and flew to Vancouver, British Columbia. He called me from Canada. He was staying in a hotel while waiting for his visa to be approved by the U.S. consulate. I didn't want him to come back and should have stopped that process, but I was under the illusion that he could do no real harm. I always thought his problems were related to his alcoholism, and if he would only stop drinking, he would be different. When he was sober he could be charming, congenial, and soft-spoken. At that time I did not understand the culture of the Middle East. My Western personality was very transparent—I said what I felt and what was in my heart was openly expressed. This is not done in the Middle East. Theirs is a world of secrecy, deception, and manipulation. Khalid Gheshayan was an expert at all three.

Because I was used to coping with a mother who had violent temper tantrums and then could be the most loving and caring person, I had developed a manner of living with trauma and chaos in the house. I never wanted my friends to come over because I didn't know what my mother was going to say to them. I coped with her all my life. I accepted the way she was as normal behavior, even though I did not like it. I was a child codependent to my mother, and I became a model codependent to this dangerous man. My war cry was, "If only you would stop drinking." I didn't see what was buried beneath the drinking—evil.

Alia was three months old when Khalid convinced me to visit him in Vancouver. I was reluctant and didn't want to see him, but I gave in. As soon as I saw him at the gate at the Vancouver Airport, I wanted to turn around and go back to San Francisco, but it was late and there were no more flights for the day. He was gaunt. If he stood sideways, the sunlight would pass right through him. His skin was as yellow as Dijon mustard, and his breath smelled like an old wine barrel. The tissue surrounding his eyes was black and blue, his aquiline nose was misshapen and swollen. He told me one of the Canadians from the bar had punched him in the face during a fight and had broken his nose.

We got into a taxi and went to the hotel where he was staying. It was not the Hilton—more of a boardinghouse with regular residents. I walked upstairs with Alia in my arms. I carried her travel bed with one hand and threw her diaper bag over my shoulder. It was late and we were tired. Khalid kept introducing me to the various men who shared the establishment as we walked along the hall and up the stairs. I was embarrassed to be seen with him.

The air in the room was saturated and sticky. I threw open the windows and turned on a fan. Of course, there was no air-conditioning. After nursing Alia, I placed her in her travel bed where she soon fell asleep. Khalid was drinking a beer on the bed; I was sitting on a chair looking at the airline schedule I had pulled from my purse. He lunged toward me and pulled me close to him, trying to kiss me. I freed myself from his grip. "Stay away from me," I said. "I am leaving in the morning."

"You're my wife."

"Get back and don't touch me."

He turned around, stumbled over Alia's travel bed on the floor, and fell on top of my sleeping daughter. I screamed, picked up Alia, and opened the door and ran. As soon as I got into the hall men came spilling out of their rooms—some wearing nothing but the underwear they were sleeping in. They were not used to hearing the screams of a woman in their residential hotel and circled me and my infant.

"Are you all right?"

"Is the baby okay?"

"I'll take care of this guy for you, ma'am . . ."

They took my things and escorted Alia and me down the stairs to the office of the owner of the hotel.

He was a fiftyish Sicilian who offered to take me to his family for the night. I accepted. "What I can see is, you and this baby are the only good things about his guy. He has been nothing but trouble since he got here. In fact, I am going to tell him to leave."

The next morning Gianni, the Sicilian, took me back to the hotel. I told Khalid I was leaving and he should leave, too. He should go back to Saudi Arabia. There was nothing for him in Canada and he should be with his family. He could hardly walk. He was malnourished, and the one hundred and ten pounds he was carrying barely covered his five-foot-six frame.

He was sober and crying. "Don't leave, Pat. You know how much I love you and Alia. Don't leave me here like this."

I drew a bath for him and helped him into the tub. I washed his back and told him I would settle him into a different place and then I had to go back to San Francisco. He must return to Riyadh. Gianni helped to move Khalid to a motel and then took me and Alia to the airport.

Alia and I had a few more months together before I had to return to work. She was almost one, and I was so glad I could stay home with her for that time. My savings eventually ran out, and I was forced to find child care for her when I went back to work in an insurance office. Khalid had returned to the States but was not living with us. I couldn't allow that again. He was in the vicinity and would come by once in a while when he was sober. I wanted to file for divorce but didn't have the money. He called often and kept telling me how much he loved us, but he never contributed any support for Alia.

Khalid's health was deteriorating and he spent a lot of time in and out of hospitals in San Francisco and Houston, Texas, where the Saudi Educational Mission was located, for alcohol-related problems. He would call me from one institution after the other and want to talk to Alia. Finally, he agreed to enter a twenty-eight day inpatient detox and rehabilitation program at Mary's Help Hospital near San Francisco. I drove him to the facility and we met with a counselor.

First, Khalid was given a quiz to see if he could be classified as an alcoholic.

He answered all the questions with a yes response—even the one that asks, "Do you have any blackouts?" The interviewer said that his alcoholism had accelerated very rapidly in the five years that he had been drinking. He had all the acute symptoms. He was in denial and said it was just a minor problem in his life that he wanted to take care of. His liver enzymes were high, and he was seen by a team of psychiatrists who diagnosed him as a paranoid schizophrenic with delusions and hallucinations.

Khalid was uncooperative and detached and refused to participate in the group meetings. He was sober and not liking it. He blamed me for all his problems and told the psychiatrist, "It is all my wife's fault."

He signed himself out of the hospital AMA (against medical advice) after twenty days. The Saudi Educational Mission paid for it, as they would pay for his multiple alcohol-related and psychiatric hospitalizations. They asked no questions, and the bills were always paid. He continued to receive his monthly check from the Saudi Educational Mission even though he hadn't attended school for several years. It enabled him to stay in the States but eventually that, too, dried up.

Brooks Brothers

Khalid returned to Saudi Arabia and we didn't see him for almost two years. During that time, I hired an attorney and filed for divorce. Alia was almost three and becoming prettier every year. With her white skin, dark eyes and hair, and red heart-shaped lips, she looked like Snow White. She was in the same preschool that Daina had attended, and our lives were full. I was struggling with finances and we had no money for extras, but I had peace of mind.

One night I got the call. "Hello, Pat. This is Khalid. I am with my father in Los Angeles. We are here on business." He was not happy about the idea of divorce. "If you divorce me, I will make trouble for you, Pat. You know how much I love you and Alia. I will never let you go, Pat. Don't do this. I will get my lawyer after you and take Alia away from you. I beg you, don't divorce me. You are my wife."

"I'm serious about this, Khalid. That's it."

"I have changed a lot," he protested. "I don't drink anymore, and I am working with my father. We are here to buy equipment for his business. He is going to make me a partner in his business. You should see me. You wouldn't believe how I have changed. I exercise and take care of myself. I am strong and healthy. Can we just come to San Francisco to see you and Alia? My father wants to see Alia. This is his first grandchild. Please don't say no to me, Pat."

"All right—just to see Alia."

Hamad and Khalid came to San Francisco and stayed at the St. Francis Hotel downtown. They were wearing their best $1,500 suits and took us out to dinner. They played with Alia and bought her all new clothes and toys. Hamad spoke to me.

"Come to Saudi Arabia. It is nice for you. Good place for children. Peaceful. No guns like here. Bring Alia and stay at my home. You are welcome. Khalid is good now. Drinking made him crazy. Now, no drink."

When Khalid was sober and wanted something, nothing could stop him. He was an artist. He did not want me to divorce him and pulled out all stops. He looked good, smelled good, and was charming. He brought me gold jewelry from Arabia, played with Alia, and turned on the charm. He reeled me in. And I was such a defenseless fish.

One Plus One

I was pushing my Prego baby stroller up the ramp at St. Luke's Hospital School of Nursing one balmy autumn afternoon to a reception for incoming freshmen. Alia was holding on to the handle of the stroller as my new two-month-old daughter, Aisha, wrapped in her pink knit blanket, slept peacefully. I was determined to get a nursing degree to support my daughters and be financially independent.

Khalid did not go into business with his father. Hamad gave him nearly $50,000 and he spent it all—none of it on us. He then left us when Aisha was four months old and returned to the safety of the kingdom of Saudi

Arabia where his father's villa and servants would take care of his every need. If he needed more money, he would ask his father or another relative. There was an unending supply. His daughters that he supposedly loved so much were left for me to support and care for.

As I entered the large room where the gathering was held, a woman smiled at me and said, "Women can do anything, can't they?" She would become one of my instructors at the school and a very good friend who saw me embarking on a nursing career with an infant and a toddler and knew what a tough journey it would be.

The course was challenging, and I had no free time between the children, school, and a part-time job. My mother had come back into my life and stayed with us for a while. She had to retire because of a health problem and was still a very unhappy, tormented woman. She was restless and had a difficult time focusing.

After one year Khalid got a job in the kingdom and was sending me $500 per month. It was a Saudi-style job with many tea breaks, which suited him fine. He called often. He came to see us one Christmas and my mother chased him from the house with a few choice words. I watched him walk down the street in front of my house after the incident, thinking, *I hope he keeps walking.*

It was at that time that my son, Eric, fell seriously ill with a chronic neurological brain disorder. He was hospitalized for several months and I was nearly out of my mind with worry.

Another year passed, and I had only one more year of nursing school to complete. The girls, Daina, and I were doing well; Eric was placed in a long-term facility and we visited him often. Summer break was coming, and Khalid called to invite us to visit Saudi Arabia. He said we could all go to London on the way back for an extended holiday. I was exhausted and welcomed a much-needed break.

We got to Riyadh in June 1984. Khalid was sober and civil. Five-year-old Alia never warmed up to his parents, and his mother always frightened her. She clung to me. Aisha was more outgoing and would go up to strangers and ask them their name. She spoke very clearly for a two-year-old. Khalid took us to the old *souk* (market) and to the camel auction. He drove us to the archaeological ruins at Dharea and Al-Kharj. I had been to the Sahara and the Gulf and admittedly had a natural attraction to the quiet, barren beauty of these arid regions. I was finally fulfilling my youthful dream of studying antiquity, but somehow this was not how I had imagined it.

I met his relatives and they were externally polite, but there was an undercurrent of contempt for me as an American woman. The gender bias and the treatment of the servants bothered me. I witnessed Khalid's mother slap the housemaid across the face. She was an old Filipina who worked seven days a week and slept in their basement on a cot. I mentioned the incident to Khalid and he said, "It is not your business. She has a right to hit her."

The girls and I returned to San Francisco after six weeks. I had two semesters of school to finish and was anxious to get it over with. Two weeks after I got home I began to feel sick. I was dizzy, nauseous, and weak. I had pains in my legs and couldn't eat. At first I thought it was the flu, but it didn't go away. I went to see a doctor and the blood tests revealed that it was hepatitis. I kept getting worse, but I had to keep going. My schoolwork suffered; I was unable to keep my part-time job. I could barely take care of the girls. Finally I could not go to school any longer. I had to drop out of the program one semester before graduation.

Khalid called. "Why don't you come here? We have the best hospitals and American doctors. We can help you with the kids. You need to rest. Come here and stay for a while. My father is inviting you. We'll take care of you."

I didn't want to live in Saudi Arabia, but I was so sick. My mother had gone back to Chicago and couldn't help me. Daina was away at college. Eric was being taken care of. I thought I might just go for a few months until I recovered and then return to school for the fall semester.

As soon as we arrived in Riyadh, my life and the lives of my young daughters would be changed forever.

2

❧

1,001 NIGHTMARES

JANUARY 1985–MAY 1985

I pray that I may never see the desert again. Hear me, God.
—T. E. Lawrence

Flying Carpets to Nowhere

"Any women not accompanied by their male relatives, and who have no sponsor waiting for them when we arrive in Dhahran, will be taken into the retaining room."

The flight attendant from Saudia Airlines was making the announcement over the speaker system as our aircraft prepared for landing. I watched the Saudi women on the plane put on makeup, fix their hair, and don the black *abaya* and *shayla*—their stylish clothing hidden from view except for a hint of ankle and designer heels. I had kept my cover-ups from the visit a few months before. At first, it was a novelty, a fantasy—like pretending I was a character from *Arabian Nights,* but I was soon to discover this was no fairy tale.

Unable to get a direct flight to Riyadh, the girls and I had to take a connection from Dhahran on the edge of the Gulf. Khalid promised to meet us because as an unaccompanied woman I could not travel farther into Saudi Arabia without a male to take responsibility for me. Since he was not present when I disembarked from the aircraft, I had to be escorted into a retaining area along with several other women whose "sponsors" were not available.

It was January 1985, about eight o'clock at night. Recovering from an acute illness, I was still weak and tired easily. As I sat with my abaya wrapped around me on the uncomfortable, hard chair, the girls draped themselves around me.

"Where are we going, Mommy? Why are we in this room? I'm thirsty."

"I don't have any riyals, sweetheart. They won't take American money. I'll buy you some water as soon as your father comes. It shouldn't be much longer."

A young man neatly dressed in a military uniform approached me. "Patricia?"

"Yes."

"I am Majik Al-Gheshayan, Khalid's cousin. I am here to help you get through the airport security checkpoints and board your plane to Riyadh. It is nice to meet you."

He was dressed in a crisp uniform with shining boots and officer's stripes—a lieutenant colonel. Khalid had spoken proudly about this pilot in the Saudi Royal Air Force. "Where's Khalid? I thought he would be here."

"He wanted to come, but could not get a flight. He called, and I offered to help. No problem . . . shall we go?"

Eleven years later he would not be so friendly to me, and Khalid would be at the center of his wrath.

The jerky, kidney-crushing ride along the semi-barricaded, deeply potholed roads in Hamad's Ford Bronco took us to our new home on a parched parcel of land along the road to Mecca. On the outskirts of Riyadh, past the small gas stations that sold cold drinks and cigarettes, was Hamad's folly. These ten acres of sand and rocks were a hybrid mixture of his various dabblings. After becoming enamored with American recreational vehicles, he imported RVs to Saudi Arabia. Lined up in the back of the property was a medley of various new types of campers, a thirty-foot-long catering truck complete with stove and refrigerator, motor homes, and trailers.

Just in front of this array, side by side, were two sixty-foot-long, prefabricated Coachman homes furnished with American GE appliances. A long, narrow, concrete-block building perpendicular to these structures served as living quarters for the three Sudanese servants and as Hamad's office. Behind this was a forbidden area—the site of the shanties where the thirty-some men that Hamad had brought from the Philippines lived. A twelve-foot-high concrete wall surrounded the whole area except for the Philippine quarters—they had their own wall separating them from the rest of the property. A water tower stood in the middle near the RVs, and a water truck used to replenish the water sat in the parking area. About twenty suluki dogs ran wild, barking and breeding prolifically. A camel and her baby were penned behind the RVs, and various goats and chickens roamed the premises.

This was home.

We lived in one of the prefab Coachman homes. Soon after we were settled, Khalid's brother Tarik, his wife, Fazia, and their toddler daughter moved into the other prefab structure.

Hamad would arrive early each morning in his red Chevy Blazer to begin the day's work. On his way he often stopped off at the Afghan breadmaker's stall on Dibha Road and brought us hot, flat, sesame-studded round loaves to eat with our *fool* (fava beans seasoned with lemon, olive oil, cumin, and green onion)—a breakfast dish.

Khalid had a job managing a residential "compound" for expatriates. These were apartments for employees of the King Fahad National Guard Hospital. Foreign workers had to be supervised and were housed by the Saudi sponsors that hired them. Their passports were retained by their employer/sponsor, who also controlled whether exit visas would be obtained from Saudi immigration at the end of the contract. Disputes happened often between employee and sponsor, but the Saudi always won. Any claim taken to the Islamic courts would be highly unfavorable to a Westerner, and the Third World workers would never dare question a Saudi. Their governments were even less likely to protect them than the U.S. Embassy would be to speak up for an American in either a legal dispute involving wrongful pay or a criminal charge.

"No Happiness Here"

A day at the office for Khalid consisted of a long tea break interrupted by a long lunch break with no questions asked. The Filipino men actually handling the affairs of the office referred to him as "Mr. Khalid." He would sit in a chair behind a desk with his feet propped up, watching closed-circuit television (old American movies played to lull the residents into a semi-comatose state), and drink endless cups of syrupy tea served in glass demitasse cups.

Back in the Coachman, the girls and I would busy ourselves watching Channel 2, the English language television station that carried the news in French each evening. We looked forward to reruns of *Skippy the Kangaroo* from Australia. *Get Smart* marathons were a treat. The only other station was the Arabic Channel 1—where we would see the image of the mosque in Mecca with thousands of people dressed in white circling the Kaaba. Each evening the Arabic news would show the various princes receiving foreign diplomats and shaking hands when these dignitaries disembarked from an aircraft or as they sat in the *majlis,* massive rooms whose walls were lined with overstuffed chairs, drinking tea or coffee and smiling. There was never any in-depth news concerning the United States or op-eds. Censorship has an anesthetic effect. It was as if I had been placed into the movie *The Stepford Wives.*

I was looking for a proper *madressa* (school) for Alia. Khalid drove me to the American school. I hoped she could go to kindergarten there. They could not admit her; it was against Saudi law. I said, "But she is an American." They told me that since her father was Saudi, she was considered a Saudi. "No Saudi can attend a non-Arab school."

"But she doesn't speak Arabic, and I want her to have American or British teachers."

The head mistress of the school was very suspicious of me, standing in my abaya with my Saudi husband in his white *thobe* (full-length gown) and red-and-white-checkered *gutra* (headdress). She spoke guardedly, choosing her words carefully. Her muscles tensed and the veins in her neck stood out as she said, "Mrs. Gheshayan, I am sorry, but we must abide by the laws of the Saudi government."

The Saudi government schools taught little more than cooking, sewing, and the Koran, and Alia did not speak Arabic, nor was she culturally a Saudi. The choices were almost nil—I finally decided on an Egyptian school that taught in English. Each morning I would put the lunch I had made for her in her little backpack, and Khalid would drop her off at school. At first she didn't mind going and then one day she came home in tears.

"Mommy. This boy came up to me and tried to cut my arm with a piece of glass. I had to run away from him."

"Come here. Did he hurt you? Did you tell the teacher?"

"Mom, I tried but she wouldn't listen."

I noticed most of the children were unruly and undisciplined. I had experienced this before when we were invited to a relative's villa. Khalid's aunt, Hamad's younger sister, had several young children. They were extremely wealthy and had many servants. One evening they had invited us to their villa for coffee and dessert. They wanted to take the children to an amusement park and asked me to go along. It was women's night and no men were allowed in the park. She summoned her driver and took several of her friends and her Filipina maid. My girls and I sat in the back of the van. As soon as we entered the park her children began screaming and ran in all directions. They joined the other children in the area and began to push one another to get to the front of the lines for the rides. There was no order, and no one said anything. Khalid's aunt and her friends were not with her children. As soon as we arrived at the park they quickly found a table and sat around it talking and drinking soft drinks. She turned the children over to the maid, who was walking around trying to take them on the rides at the park.

I took my girls away and quietly accompanied them to the attractions they chose. The Filipina maid standing near me whispered, "There is no happiness here—no joy. My husband and I have worked for this family for nine years, and we are leaving soon. We are going back home. Their children are spoiled and get anything they want. There is no love and no happiness here—only tears."

By this time I had made a full recovery from my illness and wanted to get a job, make some money, and return to the States for the completion of nursing school. Since I couldn't drive and was without transportation, I had to rely on Khalid to find a job for me through his friends and the Saudi network. I had a university degree and could qualify for any number of managerial positions, especially since I was married to a Saudi. Besides, life in Saudi Arabia was becoming intolerable, and I knew I would not be able to stay there much longer. It was spring and the temperature would soon reach 120 degrees.

Expats and the Kingdom

We were so isolated and alone; the boredom was stifling. Sometimes the girls and I would go with Khalid to his job and take the shuttle bus from the compound where he worked to Medical City, another compound that housed the expatriates who were employed by the King Fahad National Guard Hospital, just to talk to Americans or Brits. He allowed this at times. There was no sense in Alia going to school. She wasn't learning anything and was afraid to go, so I homeschooled her as best as I could with no supplies or books and kept her safe with Aisha and me.

One day I was pushing the girls on the swings of the children's playground at Medical City when I met an American woman and her two children. She was a nurse married to one of the pulmonary specialists at the hospital. Deena and I quickly became friends. Some of the perks that entice foreigners to work in Saudi Arabia are the facilities, tax breaks, and salaries. The workers are housed together in compounds, have orchestrated social activities and outings for the wives, swimming pools, gyms, potlucks, and escorted shopping trips to the market. Saudi Arabia doesn't really exist for these folks who live in a Western-style complex with limited exposure to the Saudi people or culture. Their parties, social events, and frequent travel outside the kingdom keep them pacified, and after a few years, they can return home with lots of money and Saudi souvenirs.

Deena invited me to her large apartment in one of the residential highrise towers. It was fully stocked when she and her husband, John, moved in. Even tea towels were provided. She was pregnant with her third child and bored with living in Saudi Arabia. They stayed because of her husband's salary, the ability to travel easily to other foreign countries, and the free education for her boys at the American school. She was a Vietnam vet, having met her medical doctor husband while serving as a nurse during the war.

I had no other friends and was glad to spend time with her. She knew my situation and was curious about my life with a Saudi family. Her life was quite different from mine, and she had no worries. She had little knowledge of Saudi culture except for what she saw at the souk. I told her not to pay full price for anything and taught her how to haggle at the bazaar. The camel races were coming up and she invited me to go with her.

Khalid agreed that I could take the children and go with the Medical City bus group. There were nurses, doctors and their wives, and others who worked at King Fahad Hospital. It was my first outing with the expats. The girls and I looked forward to it because it broke the monotony of our drab lives and gave us a diversion. I walked around covered in black with nowhere to go, nothing to do, and no one to talk to. I thought I would lose my mind at times. The highlight of my day was the radio broadcast of the British Broadcasting Corporation (BBC).

We packed a lunch and spent the day at the camel races. Young Arab boys about twelve years of age were high atop the camel saddles. They looked like they would fall off at any moment as they teetered back and forth. The command "hut-hut" was given as they lightly tapped the camels with their sticks. Only bedouin and Arabian Gulf boys served as jockeys. They were light in weight and blithe-spirited. The camels glided over the sand like a herd of Pegasus horses.

Uniformed men in the military garb of the National Guard performed a few songs in a marching band. I met a young doctor who was working in the emergency department at the hospital. He was kind to the girls and told me he had taught himself Arabic so he could treat his patients without a translator. The clientele at the hospital consisted of mostly bedouin who had enlisted in the National Guard. Protectors of the royal family and loyal to Crown Prince Abdullah, they were uneducated and lived mostly in the desert with their wives and children. The doctor revealed stories about serious machine-gun wounds to men and brutal beatings of bedouin women. He could do nothing but try to treat them and then send them back to their families.

Predictions of Doom

Khalid had a friend, also named Khalid, who also had an American wife. The man was very black and was probably a Sudanese/Saudi mix. His wife, Maureen, was from Minnesota. Her husband changed her name to Miriam, which sounds more Arabic. They had a two-year-old son, and she was pregnant with their second child. She told me she wanted the baby to be a boy—Saudis value boys much more than girls and it would be pleasing to her husband if she gave birth to another boy. They invited us to their villa for dinner one evening.

We rang the bell beside the metal door tucked into the thick wall surrounding their villa. Khalid opened the door and we entered the courtyard. The concrete-block building with small slits etched out for windows was typical Saudi architecture. It kept the villa cool and maintained the privacy the culture demanded. We slipped off our shoes outside the door and entered a large, dark room with thick oriental carpets misted with incense.

"*Salaam aleikum.*"

"*Aleikum salaam. Kef Halik?*"

"*Quayes. Hamda-allah.*"

The men exchanged greetings by embracing and kissing each other on both cheeks. Miriam and I went into the kitchen. She didn't have any servants so she had to do the cooking herself. She was making the usual kapsa, rice, and salad. Saudi cuisine is not complicated, and even with the advent of new supermarkets and foods imported from all over the world, traditional foods are still served. Miriam offered me a cool drink, then stated matter-of-factly, "You know you will never be able to leave with your children, don't you?"

I glared at her. "What do you mean?"

"I mean they can't leave. Even if you can leave, they stay." Her flat, dry speech was unsettling.

I knew that her husband and son had been in Saudi Arabia for one year before she arrived from the States. She also had left her young daughter from another marriage back in Minnesota. Now she was in Arabia, pregnant with another baby and giving me this mysterious warning. Could it be that her Saudi husband had taken the boy from the United States to Saudi Arabia and then forced her to go there to be with her child? I was starting to add it all up. She wore the black headscarf at all times, even inside the house. She wanted another boy, not a girl, and sat in the backseat of her husband's car. I always sat in front with Khalid and took the scarf off once I came inside the house. I remembered how she was always submissive and never laughed—always keeping her guard up.

I smiled and confidently said, "Oh, I can leave anytime I want, and my children go where I go. There is no problem here."

"Maybe one of them will be able to leave with you, but the other will stay here until you bring the first one back. That's how they do it. They hold one here as an insurance policy."

"My husband loves the States too much. He hates it here. He's crazy, but he would never do that. Besides, I'm an American and so are my children. We can always go to the American embassy if something happens."

She said no more and walked silently into the next room.

The more I tried to dismiss it from my mind, the more the shadow of that conversation haunted me.

Taking photographs in public, especially of women, is forbidden in Saudi Arabia. One day I was so intrigued by the colorful characters in the souk that

I hid my camera under my abaya and asked Khalid if I could take a picture of the African women walking by balancing large baskets on their heads. Khalid said it was fine. After the photo was taken one of the African women came running after me and tried to grab my camera. Khalid screamed at her in Arabic and she backed off quickly. He said, "They are nothing. I'm a Saudi. Let them call the police."

I wanted Khalid to take me into the heart of the souk where Westerners never went. We left the children at the family villa with his brothers and sisters, and I covered myself in black from head to toe like a Saudi woman, with not an inch of skin showing. I usually wore the abaya with a headscarf and sometimes the *burqa,* but rarely did I cover my whole face with no eyes showing. This time I had to go Saudi style. I could not look like a Western woman, and my green eyes were a dead giveaway under the burqa.

My love of the study of ancient peoples and times compelled me to explore untainted Arab settings as much as I could within my restrictions. Being married to a Saudi, I could penetrate the society more than other Western women. This time as we entered the old market near Headchopper's Square (the informal name given to the governor of Riyadh's palace, which was the site of public executions held each Friday), I dared not bring my camera. Daggers and swords, "hubbly-bubblys" (water pipes), and antique silver bedouin jewelry for dancing girls' ankles caught my eye everywhere I looked. Sweet smells of incense billowed around the heads of bearded, turbaned old men with missing teeth who sat cross-legged on oriental carpets, surrounded by their wares.

Good deals could be made for camel saddles and handcrafted belts to hold daggers. I walked behind Khalid and just observed. Nothing was said. No one could see me, and I was almost invisible under all that black. Whenever I wore the shayla, though, I had trouble keeping my balance. Walking with a piece of thick black cloth covering your eyes is an art.

As exciting and exotic as that trip was, day-to-day life in Saudi Arabia was far more humdrum. Khalid went to the compound every day, and the girls and I either went with him and took the shuttle to Medical City, stayed at the compound with him and watched television and drank tea, or we stayed in the

Coachman in the sweltering heat and watched Hamad's chief Sudanese servant, Ali, slaughter chickens in the yard. I was allowed to walk around within the walls of Hamad's property, but I could not venture out the gate. Ali spoke a little English and would offer me a cup of tea. He stood by the door with bare, black chest and a colorful sarong wrapped around his strong, broad frame. One day there was a beautiful white cat lying on the carpet in Hamad's office. I picked it up and it purred in my arms. I brought it into the Coachman to protect it from the sulukis. The girls loved him and we called him Jonathan.

I noticed that Khalid kept getting heavier and more muscular. He wasn't fat—he had definition to his arms and legs—his torso was fuller. Once in a while he would lift weights at the compound, but that couldn't be the cause of this new look. He was always buying "medicine" at the pharmacy. Anything could be bought at these establishments. There was no control over substances that they sold. One morning he was swallowing some capsules and I asked if I could read the label on the bottle. It was a steroid. That explained why he was getting bigger and stronger.

Broken Bones and No Way Out

It was seven o'clock at night and we had just arrived back at the Coachman. I was at the kitchen table unpacking groceries and the children were hungry, asking for something to drink and nibble on. The layout of the Coachman was similar to a mobile home, with a large open space used for the kitchen, dining and living rooms separated by only small, low partitions. Khalid was lying on the floor watching television. I told him I wanted to go back to the States with the girls and finish nursing school. I couldn't get a job, and Alia wasn't going to school. We needed to organize our lives.

We talked back and forth for a while about the girls and I leaving. He became very irritated.

"What do you mean, you want to leave? You have everything here. What do you want me to do? Get you a maid? I will bring a black woman from Nigeria for you, if that is what you want. No, you stay here."

I told him my family missed me and I couldn't do anything there.

Without any explanation, he jumped to his feet and sprinted toward me. I ran to the back bedroom and braced myself against the lightweight, hollow door. He bolted into the door and threw me to floor. The door closed behind him. As I looked up all I could see was the white of his robe and his glazed eyes and gnarled, twisted lips. The pounding of his bare feet thrusting against my chest was unbearable. I whimpered, "Stop, stop."

"I'll kill you. I'll kill you."

Alia was knocking on the outside of the door. "Mommy, Mommy, are you okay?"

After what seemed an interminable time, the kicking stopped.

I slowly stood up.

Oh, my chest. I was short of breath and gasped for air. The pain in the middle of my breastbone was agonizing. I couldn't lift my arms. Alia ran to me and wrapped her arms around my waist. "Mommy, are you all right?" She turned to her father. "What did you do to my mommy?"

"Khalid, you have to take me to the hospital. I think my lung is punctured. I can't breathe. Please, Khalid."

He scoffed at me. "You're faking it. There's nothing wrong with you."

"This is serious, Khalid. I need medical attention."

"You want me to drive all that way at this time? It's too far."

After about fifteen minutes he changed his mind. "All right, I'll take you to Al-Ali Hospital, but if you tell anyone what happened, I'll kill you. I could kill you right now and throw you out in the desert anytime. Who will help you? The Sudanese? Ali? He can't. He is under orders from me. They do what I tell them to do. Understand? You are lucky I don't kill you now. You cause me trouble all the time."

I could hardly put the abaya and headscarf on. Every time I moved my arms I wanted to scream out in agony. I climbed into the back of the Bronco with the girls on each side. Alia wouldn't let me go and softly sobbed. I walked up to the guard at Al-Ali Hospital a few miles from the property and told him I was having chest pain. They took me in the back while Khalid and the girls remained in the waiting room. Austrian and Syrian doctors staffed the facility. I was cloaked in my abaya, sitting on the edge of the exam table. An Austrian doctor approached me and pressed his fingers to my breastbone. I screamed. "Why are you screaming? What is the problem with you?" he said disdainfully.

I whispered, "It hurts. My husband beat me. I'm afraid. Can you help me?"

He pretended he didn't hear me, ignoring what I said. Khalid entered the room and asked what was going on. They sent me to radiology. I had a broken breastbone, several fractured ribs, and a cardiac contusion. They wanted to admit me to the hospital, but I refused. I didn't know what Khalid would do with my girls, and we did not want to be separated. I asked for some pain medication. They wrapped my chest with a binder and sent me home with Khalid.

For the next few weeks I was quiet and spoke few words to Khalid. The girls and I were obedient and kept ourselves out of the way. I did everything Khalid told me to do without a word. We watched Channel 2 and listened to the *Voice of America* and the BBC. Keeping a vigil at night, I hardly slept, wondering if this was the night he would kill me. I held Jonathan the cat with me in bed and could hear the eerie sound of the *athan,* or prayer call, from the mosque at dawn. Was there any way out of this hell?

After a few weeks Khalid said, "You know I didn't mean it, Pat. I said I didn't mean it—now that's it."

When he was at work one day I got enough courage to ask Ali if I could use the phone in Hamad's office. I called the American embassy.

"I need your help. I'm an American woman married to a Saudi. I have two little girls. We are in danger. He almost killed me. Can you help us get out of here?"

The consular officer said there was nothing they could do if my husband did not sign my exit visa. My children would never be allowed to leave because they belonged to their father. The embassy could not break Saudi law. I should do what my husband asked and maybe someday I would be able to leave. Would my husband agree to bring me into the embassy?

I couldn't risk asking Khalid to take us to the embassy. If he knew I was talking to them, I would have been in grave danger. We would drive around the streets of Riyadh, my ribs aching, and I would see the American flag flying high above the embassy. The site of it evoked such emotion. It was a symbol of freedom—but not for me.

Alia's Turn

One night we went food shopping in downtown Riyadh and had just gotten back into the car. The girls were in the back seat and I was on the passenger side in the front. Alia stood up and leaned over the front seat to tell me something. Khalid suddenly slapped her hard across the face. She screamed, "Mommy, help!"

I immediately opened the back door, took both girls out of the car, and we began walking into the street. It was night. I was wearing the abaya and headscarf, had no money, no friends, no place to go, no passports and no visa. I had just my two little girls by their hands—all of us in tears in the dark night.

Khalid began to follow us in the car. He drove slowly alongside the dusty pathway we were on with his arm hanging outside the car window. "Where do you think you are going? You have no place to go. Get in."

I knew if I ran into a store they would call the police and turn us over to Khalid. He had absolute power over us. He was our master. We were his slaves. He could do with us as he wished. My children and I could be killed, and as he told me, "No one would even know."

We got in the car. I sat in the back seat with the girls. He was raging and turned his head around and said to Alia, "And she stays here!"

Alia shrieked, "No! No!"

We lived in terror and submission as the next few months went by. I called the embassy once in a while just to tell them I was still alive. Their position had not changed. Nothing could be done. Khalid was getting bored with working and living on Hamad's property. His parents owned a lavish villa in town with servants and conveniences. He missed that style of living and wanted to move back with them.

In Saudi culture, even after sons are married, they bring their families and live under the roof of their father. It is a grand patriarchy, and the wives and children just become part of the property owned by the man and male members of the tribe. The way we lived, isolated with no one but his brother next door, was unusual. Saudis are rarely alone, and the consensus or opinion of family, tribe, and neighbors is very valued. They avoid scandal and gossip, and secrecy is a way of life.

During the holy month of Ramadan, fasting, which includes abstinence from food, drink, and sexual relations from sunrise to sunset, is demanded according to the Koran. Khalid used to drink and eat in private and be devout and sanctimonious in public. I asked him about this and he said, "I can disobey as long as no one sees me"—a tidy summary of Saudi society.

Home to America

As the monotony of our lives continued, Khalid's interest in taking full responsibility for us began to wane. He was tired of driving us around (I didn't have a male driver as do most Saudi women). The tea-break job he had afforded no stimuli. He was bored just going to the compound, coming home, eating, and watching us cooped up in the Coachman like rats in a maze. I carefully played on this situation. I stepped lightly. We began to have conversations about him getting the sponsorship back from the Saudi Educational Mission and returning to the United States. I knew he hated his life as it was. He was receptive to this idea. I suggested that we both go back to the United States and complete our education. I could be a nurse, and he could change his major to something he liked.

He finally agreed.

I asked if he would take us to the American embassy. The girls clutched my arms as we entered the consul general's office. I took off the abaya as I looked up at a large board on the wall with names written with a black marker. I asked, "What's that?" Stephanie Smith, the consul general, replied with a French accent, "Those are the names of the Americans in jail here."

She told me, "Do exactly as he says. If he changes his mind between now and the time you get on that plane, there is nothing we can do. He must go to Immigration and get your passport and the passports of your children stamped with an exit visa. Then he must accompany you to the airport and sign the papers with the Saudi guards allowing you and the girls to leave. Without that signature, your passports, even if you have an exit visa stamp, will not get you out of here. Do as he says and leave as quickly as possible."

Most international flights leave Riyadh at midnight. We arrived at the airport early. I was wearing the abaya, headscarf, and dark glasses. I was cautious and wanted nothing to go wrong at the last minute. We were at the first security checkpoint when I noticed a man in the corner watching us. It was Jim Bigges, a consular officer from the American embassy, whom I had previously called in distress from Hamad's phone and had met at the embassy along with Stephanie Smith. Khalid was taking care of the baggage and noticed me saying hello to him. He quickly scurried back to me and suspiciously eyed Bigges. "Who are you?"

I explained that he worked for the American embassy. Bigges remarked that he was just seeing a friend off on another flight. I later found out that he was stationed at the airport to be sure we got on the plane as planned. I could tell Khalid didn't believe him and my muscles tightened. After giving the consul an acid look, he walked away.

We got to the gate. The seconds dragged by—at last the call to board. The girls and I began to slip into the queue of passengers waiting to depart. Emotionless, Khalid rose from his seat, walked up to me and murmured into my ear, "Good-bye, Patricia. I'll see you in the United States. It won't be long now."

3

❧

FREE TO BE, BUT NOT FOR LONG

MAY 1985–JANUARY 1986

It is a sin to believe evil of others, but it is seldom a mistake.
—H. L. Mencken

Home Again

"Mom . . . over here!" I saw my mother standing on the other side of the roped-off area as we inched our way through U.S. Customs at the Chicago O'Hare Airport. She didn't know what we had been through. How could I tell her? I never wanted her to know the truth about what had happened to us in Saudi Arabia. We were free now. He couldn't hurt us anymore.

"Alia, look! There's Jonathan." We saw our white cat being carried in his cage by a uniformed customs officer. He cleared immigration just fine. I couldn't leave him in that desert so I had brought him home with us to freedom. My mother and I loaded our baggage into her Chevy sedan and headed for my aunt's house. We were destitute. The only money I had in the world was the $500 I had managed to save from grocery money Khalid had given me. My car was still safely parked at my sister's residence, but all of our belongings, except for what we'd brought from Saudi Arabia, were still in storage in San Francisco. I didn't care. We were together, free and safe. I would take care of the other matters in time.

It was May 1985. My aunt Mamie opened her home and her heart to us. "You are *mia famiglia*," she used to say. She gave us her guest bedroom, and the girls and I shared one bed. I got a job as a secretary, sent for my nursing school records, and enrolled for fall classes at another nursing school in Chicago. I signed Alia up for summer camp—the same one I attended so many years before. Aisha was almost three, and I enrolled her in a preschool where Aunt Mamie's son taught. It felt good; it felt safe. Thomas Wolfe was wrong. I did go home again.

After a few months I had saved enough money so that we were able to move into our own apartment in the neighborhood I grew up in—just a few blocks from Bella Papa's family home where my cousin, Marie, still lived. Alia was a first grader at Drexel School—our family's grammar school. I would take Aisha to the Cicero Children's Center before I went to nursing classes. Each morning she insisted on watching me from the window as I walked to my car. She and her teacher would be posted there, waving until I drove off.

My sister Bobbie's husband was an attorney, and I asked him to file divorce papers for me. Khalid did not know where we were, and we felt safe and secure. Alia was at a disadvantage in school because she'd missed almost the entire kindergarten year. But she was very strong-willed and pushed herself to catch up to the other students. At the Parent Open House she was proud to have me in her classroom; sitting in her desk, she would turn to look at me in the back of the classroom as she raised her hand to answer the questions the teacher asked. She was so happy when she joined the Brownies and wore her uniform proudly. She played Barbie dolls, practiced jump rope with her friends, and loved the movie *The Wizard of Oz*. She would say, "Mommy, I want to be just like Dorothy and go over the rainbow." Her favorite song was "Tomorrow," from *Annie*. She would go around the house singing, "Tomorrow, tomorrow, I love you tomorrow—it's only a day away."

It was almost Christmas and I took the girls to Aisha's preschool Christmas party. One of the dads was dressed up like Santa and Alia said, "Mom, is that the real Santa? I thought I saw black hair under his white hair." Aisha was dressed as Rudolf for a Christmas play the Children's Center was performing. She even had a special painted-on red nose and construction paper antlers. Alia wanted a new bike for Christmas and a Pound Puppy. She said, "Mom, they don't have anyone to love them. Can I please take one home?" Aisha wanted a red fire engine and a "Gabbage Gatch" (Cabbage Patch) doll.

Nothing Ages Like Happiness

But our joy was not for long. Just as our lives were finally becoming peaceful and happy, Khalid came to town. He had hired a detective and found us. One night someone tapped on the glass sliding door at the back of my ground level apartment. Jonathan was looking out the window. I opened the curtains and screamed. It was Khalid!

"Pat. I just want to talk to you. Open the door, Pat. I want to see you. I'm not going to hurt you."

I grabbed the girls and went into the back bedroom. I was shaking all over. I couldn't stop trembling. I was holding the girls next to me and crying. The girls were scared. Alia said, "Mommy, Mommy, is that my daddy? Is he going to hurt us?"

He finally left and called me the next day—and the next day—and the next day. His private detective had given him my phone number. It was two days before Christmas, and with a court date of December 26, my divorce was not yet final. I went to the Cicero police station and asked for a restraining order to be issued against him. They told me he hadn't committed any crime and I had no basis for such an order. Until a crime was committed there was nothing they could do. I told them he came to my home and harassed me and called me on the phone day and night. They said that was not sufficient cause to issue a restraint order.

The girls and I spent a cautious Christmas with my family. But there was a dark tide of fear flowing over us. Alia refused to ride her new bike in front of the house even if I was with her. She said, "Mommy, I saw my daddy in his car when I was walking. Please, Mommy, don't let him take me away. Please don't let my daddy take me away."

I appeared at Cook County City Hall in downtown Chicago on December 26, 1985 for my divorce proceedings. Khalid was not present. I was granted a divorce with full custody of my daughters. The girls were with me, dressed in their matching gray-and-white fur parkas with red mittens and little gray boots. After the proceedings, I showed them the beautifully decorated Christmas windows at Marshall Field's Department Store in the Loop, an area in the heart of downtown Chicago. They had never seen anything like it before.

A few days later my brother-in-law called. "He hired an attorney. They want to overturn your divorce and custody decree. He claims he was improperly served. I told this guy we just wanted to work this out amicably. What do you want me to do, Pat?"

"Ken, stop them. Go to court and don't let them do this. Do I have to be present in the courtroom? I hate to take a day off school for this. Can you handle it?"

"No. You don't have to be there. Look, I'll just talk to the attorney. We'll work something out. This is silly. Don't worry."

My brother-in-law had never met someone like Khalid and underestimated what was going on. He thought he could settle matters in a polite fashion among rational parties so he didn't go to court that day. The divorce was overturned along with my custody decree.

I couldn't believe what was happening. Little did I know that this was only the beginning—an omen of what would happen for the next two decades—a pattern of betrayal, lies, and deception.

Khalid continued to stalk me night and day. He went to Drexel School and asked for Alia. The principal called me: "Ms. Roush, there is a man here who says he is your daughter Alia's father. He wants us to release her to him. What should we do?" I requested that Khalid not be allowed near Alia and that she be kept inside during recess in fear that he would take her off the playground. "Mommy," she said, "It's boring staying inside when the kids are playing. I don't like it, Mommy. Can I go outside with the other kids?"

When I was a child there was a small store two blocks from Drexel School, Kay's Grocery. Sometimes after school I would walk there and buy candy on my way home. It was now an old building with a Palestinian family managing the store and living in the back. Khalid must have stopped there to buy cigarettes one day when he was driving around looking for Alia. He rented the apartments above the store—now he had a war room.

Preparation for a Kill

Khalid kept working on me nonstop. My pleas to the police were useless; as far as they were concerned, he was a law-abiding resident immigrant, and I was just a hysterical woman. One evening I had driven into my driveway and was unpacking groceries from the trunk when Khalid pulled up behind me. I was alone. He got out of the car and approached me. "Pat, why are you so afraid of me? If I wanted to take the kids, I would have never let you leave Saudi Arabia. I would never take them away from you. I wouldn't hurt you like that, Pat. I just want to see my kids. I haven't seen them for a long time. I'm gonna get the scholarship back. It's all set. I want to stay in Chicago and we can have joint custody. I miss the kids. Just let me see them this weekend. Please, Pat."

"Why should I trust you after all you have done to us?"

"I made a mistake. I said I was sorry. You know I don't want to go back to Saudi Arabia."

I was tired of the stalking, the phone calls, and the constant stress. I didn't know what to do. I knew he hated living in Riyadh. He loved the States. Maybe he would just go to school and visit with them one weekend per month. It was true, he could have kept us in Saudi Arabia if he had really wanted to. The delusion was kicking in. The it's-going-to-be-all-right story line that I'd fed myself since I was a child was happening again. He manipulated me and I allowed it. I weakened.

"All right. We will go back to court and get the custody decree reinstated, and you can have visitation rights."

"Can I just see them tonight or tomorrow night? I'll just take them out for dinner. Just for a few hours, Pat."

"Tomorrow. I'll bring them to your apartment at six o'clock."

The girls and I went to his apartment above the Palestinian store the next evening. I reassured them everything would be okay. I stayed with them for a while and then we all walked to his car and I buckled the seat belts around the girls in the backseat. It was a cold night—January in Chicago. As the car pulled away from the curb and I watched him drive away with the girls, I was left alone at the curb. A cold chill ran up my spine. Although he brought the girls back a few hours later, an eerie feeling still overwhelmed me.

I had some close Russian Orthodox friends who invited me and the girls for dinner shortly after Khalid came back. It was just after the New Year and they had also invited a friend who was a Russian Orthodox priest. It was their custom to bless the house each New Year, and after we ate, the priest brought out the holy water and did the official blessing. He was young and played with the girls. They adored him. Aisha teased him and said, "Don't get me wet," as he was sprinkling the water. We spent a very enjoyable night together. This priest would play a pivotal part in the coming months.

Our lives were getting settled so nicely, and the girls were happy again. Alia was excited about selling Girl Scout cookies and going to her first slumber party. The little invitation to the party was on her night stand next to her bed. Her best friend lived in the same building, and they played together after school and on weekends. And at last, I was finally able to afford to have our furniture and their personal items and toys sent from San Francisco. Planning a party for Alia's seventh birthday. As soon as the apartment was in order. Alia was a good student and loved our new life. Aisha just loved to be near me.

Day of Infamy

It was Saturday morning, January 25, 1986—the day before Super Bowl Sunday—and the Chicago fans were ecstatic; the Bears were going to play in New Orleans. Alia was invited to a birthday party the next day. Khalid wanted to see the girls. I told him he couldn't see them that weekend. He said he hadn't seen them in a while and would bring them back early Sunday morning so Alia could attend the party. Alia didn't want to go. "Mommy, please don't make me go. I want to stay home and play with my friends. Please, Mommy. I don't like him. All he does is stand around and smoke cigarettes."

"It will be okay, honey. It's just for a short time and then I will pick you up and we'll go to Becky's party. It's all right."

I dressed them in their little fur parkas and took them to the Palestinian store. Khalid was standing on the steps near the door smoking a cigarette. I brought the girls up to the landing. "Don't let them play outside. It's too cold. I'll pick them up in the morning about nine." After kissing the girls, I drove back to my home. I knew Alia liked the Palestinian girl from the store and thought she would play with her for most of the time.

I didn't feel good that day. I just couldn't concentrate and was very depressed. It was like I was in pain and I didn't know why. It continued the whole day. I never got headaches, but I had one that day. It was unexplainable.

The next morning I rose early and called Khalid. There was no answer. Where could he be? Did he take them out for breakfast? I got dressed and started to get the girls' clothes ready for the party. I took their party dresses from the closet and placed them on the bed with their lace socks and put their little patent leather shoes on the floor. Suddenly, I got a feeling in my stomach. "Oh no, they're gone. They're gone. My God!"

I ran to the car and drove to the Palestinian store. The man was standing behind the counter. "Where's Khalid? Where are my children? Where are they?"

He didn't say anything and shrugged his shoulders.

"Did you see him today? Where are they?"

Shaking and crying, I drove to the Cicero police station. I approached the desk sergeant and asked him to send a squad car to the Palestinian store. "We can't do that, lady. We have no reason to believe these children are missing. How long have they been gone? They're with their father, aren't they?"

I finally convinced him to just send someone to ask questions of the Palestinian. Two Cicero police officers came into the store with me. "Ask him where my children are. He knows. Ask him to let us go upstairs and see if their things are in the apartment. Ask him, please."

"Lady, we have no warrant," he told me before directing his question to the shopkeeper. "Sir, do you know anything about these children?"

The Palestinian stood behind the counter and with a half smile said, "I don't know."

His wife came through the curtains from the residence in back. "What is the matter? Why are the police here?"

I turned to her. "Does Khalid have my kids? Do you know anything?"

"Oh, no. What happened?" She looked at her husband and he looked away.

Unexpectedly the little girl that played with Alia came out behind her mother. I said, "Do you know where Alia is?"

Before her father could stop her, she quickly blurted out, "He took her away in a taxi yesterday and she didn't want to go."

Her father immediately screamed at her in Arabic, and she hurriedly went back into the residence with her mother. The police left and I went back to the police station.

I pleaded with the blue-uniformed man behind the desk. "You've got to stop them. The plane could still be in the air. Please . . . There is a Pan Am flight from New York to Riyadh every night. Call the airlines and see if he is on the manifest. Do something."

"You know, ma'am, you are overreacting. We can't really help you. They will probably be back in a few hours."

I went home and called Hamad's villa. Khalid's brother, Younis, answered, "They are on their way. Khalid will call you when they arrive."

Four days went by. I didn't sleep or eat and could only hear the haunting sound of the train whistle in the middle of the night. I finally called Riyadh.

"How can you do this, Khalid? They love me."

"Well, they're going to learn to love me. Alia is not allowed to talk to you. She only stays alone in a room and cries for you. We took her to the doctor and he told us not to let her talk to you again. The only way you will ever see your children again is to come to Saudi Arabia and do exactly what I say. Alia and Aisha are never allowed to leave Saudi Arabia again. They will stay here for the rest of their lives. Your embassy cannot help you. Go ahead and get Reagan!"

4

❧

HOPE THAT IS NOT SEEN

JANUARY 1986–MARCH 1986

'Tis always morning somewhere.
—Henry Wadsworth Longfellow

The Campaign Begins

"Overseas Citizens Services. May I help you?"

"My name is Patricia Roush, and my daughters were kidnapped by their father and taken to Saudi Arabia. Can you please help me?"

"I'm sorry, but if their father is a Saudi national, there is nothing we can do." More ominously, the woman added, "You will probably never see your daughters again."

By this time I was crying and semi-hysterical. "What do you mean there is nothing you can do? They are American citizens—born in Berkeley,

California. Don't tell me there is nothing you can do. Am I supposed to forget my children because some maniac took them away on a plane?" I hung up the phone.

That was my first encounter with the State Department—Theresa Hobgood. She knew the script well, and sitting behind the desk at Overseas Citizens Services gave her many opportunities to rehearse her lines. The State Department made it clear from the beginning that they would not get involved. But my love for my children would never allow me to take no for an answer. I couldn't believe that my government wouldn't do everything they could to get my kids back.

I didn't know what to do. I just stayed in my apartment and cried and made telephone calls all day. It was almost impossible to keep from crying when I was trying to explain what happened. No one wanted to listen to a crying, half-hysterical woman—especially the men. And most of the people I called for help were men in positions of authority. My heart was bleeding and no one was listening.

I called the American embassy in Riyadh. I would set the alarm for the middle of the night so I could speak to them during their workday. I requested that they go to the Saudi authorities and make a formal request for the release of Alia and Aisha. The consul informed me that he couldn't do that. It was true that the girls were born in the United States, but because of their father, they were also Saudi citizens, and under Saudi law belonged to their father. I had no right to my daughters under Saudi law. He said he would call Khalid and ask if he would allow a welfare visit from the embassy. I told him I had federal, state, and international warrants for Gheshayan's arrest and to inform Khalid that I just wanted my daughters returned and these warrants would be dropped.

Consul Ron Kramer called me a few days later. "Ms. Roush, the embassy has spoken with Mr. Gheshayan, and he made it very clear that he will not allow any visits with your daughters. He informed us that he will never return his daughters to the United States and has no intention of traveling outside Saudi Arabia. He is not interested in your warrants. He further stated that he wants nothing to do with the embassy or you. The only thing

I can suggest is that you contact one of the Saudi attorneys from the list that was sent to you. They may be able to advise you in regards to filing a lawsuit in Saudi Arabia."

What chance did I have of winning custody of my children in an Islamic court? I had three strikes against me. I was an American, a Christian, and a woman. They would never give me a fair trial.

"We have found that the Islamic courts are very fair," Kramer assured me. "You would have a good chance of getting custody of your children. Unfortunately our involvement in these matters is very limited."

"Well, what is the purpose of the embassy if not to help American citizens in need in foreign countries?"

"Our primary purpose is to further the interests of business and commerce."

"I can't believe this. These are two little girls who were taken away from the only person they've loved, trusted, and known all their lives, and you are telling me that you can't do anything to help them?"

Between the crying, lack of sleep, and not eating, I was like a character straight out of *Night of the Living Dead*. I don't know how I managed to continue nursing school. I just had to finish—only three months to graduation. I marched through it in pain.

In February 1986 I began a letter-writing campaign and attached the last picture taken of the children (in front of the Christmas tree wearing their Rainbow Bright nightgowns and with Pound Puppies on their heads). I wrote to President Reagan, Mrs. Reagan, Vice President Bush, Secretary of State Shultz, my two U.S. senators from Illinois, Alan Dixon and Paul Simon, and the entire Illinois delegation:

> All this was just a deception to get my daughters, and he did take the girls January 25, 1986, to the airport and they have not been seen again . . . He told me my oldest daughter "only cries for you." He is holding my two little girls in that country against their will and away from the only person that they have known all their lives—their mother. They don't know their father. They don't know his family. They don't speak Arabic. They don't think Arab or act Arab. They are not going to school. He broke U.S. law by taking these

little girls. I know exactly where they are, and I cannot get them out of Arabia without some help from the U.S. government. These girls are American citizens. They were taken from their home, put on an airplane, and are being held as hostages. This is a real story, not some hype on the six o'clock news. Everyone I call says they cannot help me. What should I do— just forget my children? How can I go on living without my little girls, who are being sacrificed by this Qaddafi-like maniac?

The Illinois State Police held their first Missing Children's Convention at the Chicago Hilton in March 1986. I was told it would be a good place for me to make some contacts. I sat in the Grand Ballroom of the Hilton in a row near the front. A young woman whose two daughters had recently been found after being gone for seven years was at the podium. Another angry man had taken away her babies. She was also a nurse. The pain etched in her face from years of grief was too much for me. I sobbed throughout her whole testimony. Her children were found in a neighboring state—they had been only two hundred miles from her all those years. The neighbors had recognized them when their pictures were broadcast on a national missing children's television program. Her nightmare was over. Mine was just beginning.

When I got home there was a message on my answering machine: "Hello, Ms. Roush, this is Sarah Pang from Senator Alan Dixon's office. I received your letter and want to help. Please call me."

Sarah Pang was the bright twenty-six-year-old graduate of Yale who worked as Senator Dixon's executive assistant in his Chicago office. She grew up in Rockford, Illinois, with a Chinese dentist father and Polish mother. Savvy, intelligent, wiser than her years, intuitive, and confident—she became my partner in the quest to free my daughters. She didn't do casework, and purely by accident or divine intervention became involved in my plight. We immediately connected and were always "on the same page," with an uncanny synchronicity to the way we thought and planned our strategies. I would call Sarah several times a day with ideas and suggestions; she would then go to the senator for feedback and, if possible, implement my suggestions. We worked like that for three years. If it weren't for Sarah Pang, I don't think I would have been able to survive that grief-laced period.

One of my first suggestions was that Alan Dixon contact the Saudi ambassador, Prince Bandar Bin Sultan. Dixon immediately sent the prince a letter and followed up with a phone call. Bandar had been in Washington for only two years at that time and was concerned about senatorial opinion. Dixon wrote, "I need your assistance with this matter. The actions of one individual should not be allowed to jeopardize the very strong relations our two countries enjoy. I urge you in the strongest manner to assist us with the safe and speedy return of Alia and Aisha to the United States."

I continued with my letters and pictures—this time to everyone in the U.S. Congress. Electronic mail was only a fantasy at that time. I turned my living room into a war room with photocopies, Pound Puppy pictures, envelopes, and yellow legal tablets I used for note taking and strategy planning.

My mother and I tried to find another source that might be able to give us some information concerning the girls. We asked around, and someone suggested a private detective in the Loop. We met him in a small office in an old downtown building. He said he had some contacts inside Saudi Arabia and asked us for a retainer of fifteen hundred dollars. We paid him the money and never heard from him again.

In the meantime, I was still calling the State Department and was repeatedly referred to the Saudi Desk. David Ostroff was in charge of that unit at the time. I kept asking him to do something and in his response he would faithfully refer to the Saudis as "our clients." I said, "If they are your clients, who am I?"

Early Manifestations

Father Andrew, the Russian Orthodox priest the girls and I had met two weeks before they were kidnapped, started to openly pray for Alia and Aisha during each Sunday liturgy at St. Panteleimon, in a southwestern suburb of Chicago. I was a cradle Catholic and the girls were baptized Catholic, but I needed to hear their names spoken in prayer and have a community of believers collectively pray for them. God doesn't ignore such devotion. It comforted me to hear the petition each Sunday: "May the children Alia and Aisha be safely returned to their mother." So I started to attend Sunday services at that small Eastern Rite church.

It was Orthodox Palm Sunday, and all fifty members of the congregation were present for the liturgy that morning. I was sitting in one of the middle pews of the church, which was more like an intimate chapel, with icons and the smell of incense surrounding me. The liturgy had not yet started. Two elderly women were sitting on either side of me. There was a stillness in the air. Suddenly, I received a hard slap on my left shoulder. I couldn't believe it! Who was this? I turned around and there was no one there. At least I could not see anyone. The older women in the pew in back of me looked surprised when I turned around. They had no idea what had happened. The two women on either side of me never blinked an eye. I faced the iconostasis screen and my heart raced. *Am I going to die here in this church like this? What is happening? Is God trying to tell me something?*

Two weeks later I was playing tennis and was in the middle of the court. When I brought my racket back to make the shot, it hit someone or something on the court with me. I immediately dropped the racket and ran to the net. I knew then I was not alone.

5

TWO WOMEN

MARCH 1986–DECEMBER 1986

We can do anything we want to do if we stick to it long enough.
—Helen Keller

The First Hero: Alan Dixon

I asked everyone in Congress to make telephone calls and send letters and telegrams to the Saudi embassy in Washington. Sarah knew that one of Dixon's friends, a judge in Chicago, had a daughter who worked at the Saudi embassy. Mimi was the personal secretary of Prince Bandar. Sarah called her and asked if they were getting much of a response from Congress. She acknowledged that letters were pouring into Bandar's office. Sarah and I were excited.

Vice President George Bush was planning a trip to Saudi Arabia for a meeting with King Fahad, who had a close relationship with the president.

As was discovered during the Iran-Contra scandal, at Reagan's request Fahad secretly sent $30 million to help pay for the Contra war against the Sandinistas. The king also helped finance Nancy Reagan's war on drugs with a $1 million contribution. I asked Sarah if we could brief the vice president before he left. She contacted Bush's assistant in the Old Executive Office Building, Lieutenant Colonel Doug Menarchek.

In April 1986 George Bush received a full briefing about my case. Dixon asked Bush to make a plea for the release of the girls during his meeting with the Saudi king. The vice president was a guest at Ambassador Bandar's palace while he visited the kingdom and had a solid relationship with the Saudis. His many business dealings with them would be revealed during the coming years. But when he returned to Washington, Dixon's office was informed that the vice president did not have the opportunity to discuss the matter of my daughters with the Saudis.

Disappointed with Bush's showing, Dixon addressed the case on the floor of the U.S. Senate at every opportunity:

I believe the Saudi government can and must do something about these two young American girls currently being held hostage in Saudi Arabia. In the spirit of comity and the spirit of goodwill, I believe the ruling monarchy in Saudi Arabia can restore these two young United States citizens to their mother, in whose custody they belong according to the United States courts.

This particular case involving Saudi Arabia is especially egregious, Mr. President. I intend to focus on this matter continually on the Senate floor. The tragic case of these two young girls, their mother, and their fugitive father, who today enjoys the safe haven and protection of Saudi "religious law," is absolutely incomprehensible and intolerable.

I hear all too often that we have a friend in this Saudi Arabian kingdom, that we have an influential friend in the Middle East.

I hear on the floor of this body about arms sales and other military agreements. I guarantee my colleagues that this case involving Saudi Arabia will receive a full hearing on the Senate floor.

By this time the story was becoming well known not only in Washington but nationally. One day I received a call from Bob Greene, syndicated columnist for the *Chicago Tribune*. "Pat, is there anything I can do for you? Do you need anything?" I told him Illinois Senator Paul Simon had refused to help and was uncooperative. A few days later I received a call from Senator Simon offering to help. I was quickly learning about the power of the press.

In 1986 former Reagan White House Deputy Chief of Staff Michael Deaver cashed in on his connections and opened his own public relations/lobbyist firm. He was known as a master image maker who had kept Reagan's profile high and bright. One of his new clients was the Royal Embassy of Saudi Arabia. I asked Sarah to call Deaver's office and suggest that a good PR image for the Saudis would be to bring these little American girls home to their mother. We would work it anyway they wanted. The Saudis could look like heroes—great humanitarians. Just bring them back. Sarah said they were very interested and told her they would recommend the idea to the Saudis and their Washington attorney, Fred Dutton.

Things were heating up, and I asked Sarah if Dixon would call Bandar again. The prince accepted his call and Dixon made a formal request that the girls be allowed to come home. It was spring 1986, and a sizable Saudi arms package was being debated on the floor of the U.S. Senate. Bandar was worried about Dixon's statements:

> Mr. President, the administration is seeking approval for a sale of sixteen hundred Maverick air-to-ground missiles to Saudi Arabia. I rise to oppose the sale. I believe this sale will not further the interests of the United States or the prospects for peace in the Middle East. On the contrary, this sale threatens to destabilize the fragile balance which exists in the region.
>
> The Saudi Air Force already has twenty-four hundred of the Maverick A guided air-to-surface missiles. The administration wants to sell the Maverick D, which has never before been exported to Saudi Arabia. This is an improved version of the Maverick, using an infrared guidance system which makes night attack possible, and doubling the range of target recognition.
>
> The Congress and the American people have repeatedly been told that

Saudi Arabia is one of America's "best friends" in the region, and that Saudi Arabia is "moderate" and acts to advance U.S. interests and peace in that vital part of the world.

We have been repeatedly urged to support one arms sale after another to Saudi Arabia—totaling more than $29 billion since 1981. These sales went forward based on the promise of Saudi friendship and support. The record, unfortunately, shows otherwise.

Dixon began to count the ways:

The Saudis have consistently opposed every American peace initiative in the Middle East. They still vehemently oppose the Camp David Accords. They have consistently refused to negotiate for peace with Israel, our most reliable ally in the region.

Rather than supporting the peace process, Saudi Arabia has helped to derail it. The Saudis reportedly pressured King Hussein into abandoning his peace initiative by threatening economic sanctions if Jordan should enter into direct negotiations with Israel. They pressure the Lebanese to abrogate the 1983 Lebanon-Israel Accord, and have refused to use their leverage to persuade Syria to pull out of Lebanon.

The Saudis have also repeatedly opposed other U.S. interests in the region, including our effort to curb the outlaw Qaddafi regime, U.S. attempts to defend its strategic presence in the Persian Gulf, and attempts to isolate and weaken the terrorist activities of the Palestine Liberation Organization and Syria, both of whom enjoy enormous Saudi financial support.

Given the downsides of the U.S.-Saudi relationship, Dixon also challenged the notion that we were getting our money's worth, driving home his point by pointing to my daughters:

The United States has sold billions of dollars' worth of arms to Saudi Arabia in what we are told are "litmus tests" of American fellowship. America has proven her friendship. Regrettably, we have not seen the same result from the Saudis.

In 1981, the Saudis raised the price of oil by $2 per barrel just one day after the Senate AWACS vote, forcing the price to an all-time high of $34 a barrel. Within a month, they gave more than $28 million to the PLO, and participated in an urgent campaign against Oman's agreement to cooperate militarily with the United States.

Closer to home, Mr. President, is another particularly upsetting example of our truly poor relations with the Saudis. I speak of the case of Illinoisan Patricia Roush. I have been attempting to secure the release of her two children, who are being held illegally in Saudi Arabia by her divorced husband. Although U.S. courts have awarded the custody of the children to Ms. Roush, and charged the father, a Saudi citizen, with kidnapping, the Saudi government refused to take an active role in securing the return of these American children to their mother.

Are these the actions of a friend? Are these the actions of a country helpful in the search for peace? Clearly they are not!

Sarah said it was far out of character for Alan Dixon to have so much conviction involving a human rights issue like mine. He was a moderate Democrat—an attorney from southern Illinois who was primarily interested in agriculture and banking. He was outraged about what had happened to me and my daughters and spoke about it every chance he could—at press conferences, on the Senate floor, at the White House, during TV interviews (he was even on *Geraldo* with me). Alan Dixon became a champion.

At last, there was movement from the Saudis. Bandar had started the process, and the American embassy was being contacted by the Saudi authorities. I received the following letter:

June 3, 1986

Dear Ms. Roush:

Ambassador Cutler is away from Saudi Arabia at present. I wanted to take this opportunity to let you know the current situation regarding the children.

We have been in touch with Senator Dixon's office and, as you may have learned from the senator's staff, the Saudi Ministry of Foreign Affairs (MFA) answered our initial diplomatic note concerning you and your children with a request for more information. We supplied the information concerning your ex-husband's whereabouts in a follow-up diplomatic note on May 19, and repeated our interest in seeing the children. We will continue to press for your rights and to raise the issue for the children's custody.

Everyone concerned with your case is heartened by the conversation Senator Dixon had with the Saudi ambassador in Washington. We hope the prince's recommendations to the Saudi authorities will lead to the outcome you desire. We all wanted to hear something before May 28 because the MFA, as practically every other Saudi ministry, has shut down until June 14 when the post-Ramadan Eid holiday is over.

We hope that the Saudi authorities will take some action on Prince Bandar's recommendation immediately after the holiday.

We are all very much aware of your acute distress in the present circumstances. I sincerely hope that when we next contact you it will be to inform you of some positive developments in the case.

Sincerely,
Edward S. Walker Jr.
Charge d'Affairs, a.i.

Everything seemed to be changing positively for me. I was reaping the results of my consistent, focused efforts to free my daughters. My case was highly public now, and more and more people were joining me in my crusade. The U.S. Congress gave unprecedented support, Senator Dixon was constantly working for a resolution, important media were calling, and I had just graduated from nursing school. My classmates and instructors gave me a standing ovation at graduation. I tearfully received my diploma onstage; I had worked toward that goal so I could support my daughters, and now they were not there to rejoice in this achievement with me. But I didn't have time for self-pity. The girls weren't home yet and I couldn't allow the pressure to die.

Congresswoman Lynn Martin from Rockford, Illinois, a close friend of Vice President Bush and later secretary of labor, called. She wanted to help. I asked her if she would personally take a letter to the vice president. She agreed and over time would personally deliver three letters to Bush from me, pleading for intervention. Each time he received one of these letters, he refused to offer any assistance and sent his "deepest sympathies about these tragedies."

The Cutler-Hejailan Connection

Since the State Department had never witnessed such an outcry concerning two American children taken to a foreign country, they did not know how to politically handle the situation. Their primary purpose was economic and military gain, and they used diplomacy to further their interests. Keeping the Saudis appeased and happy was one of their goals. They continually referred to the Saudis as their "clients" and did not know how to contain this new problem I was instigating. In July of 1986 the U.S. ambassador to Saudi Arabia, Walter Cutler, finally asked for a meeting with Prince Salman, governor of Riyadh and powerful brother of the king. I requested that he ask the prince, in the strongest terms, that the children be returned on humanitarian grounds and that Cutler exercise his authority as a representative of the United States to negotiate with Salman. Cutler was a seasoned foreign service diplomat who had been posted at Tunisia, Algiers, Iran, Seoul, Saigon, and Zaire and did not want to put his job in jeopardy. He was tentative and cautious with me.

At that time the girls had been gone for six months. I was never allowed a telephone conversation with them. I repeatedly called Hamad's villa, and Khalid's mother, Fatima, would answer, hear my voice, and hang up. I could hear the voices of my daughters in the background and my heart would ache. One time Khalid answered and told me, "The only way you will ever see them again is to come here." He put the phone near to Alia and told her what to say to me. She whimpered softly in a scared, frightened voice,

"Come here." If I had boarded a plane and gone to Saudi Arabia to join my daughters, I know I would have been put to death or worse.

Prince Salman's answer to Walter Cutler's request came back within forty-eight hours of the meeting. I called Sarah Pang, and she had just received the word from the State Department. The only solution was for me to go to an Islamic court. I was devastated. The day I received the news I was taking the state examination from the Board of Nursing for my RN license. Despite this news, I still completed my examinations and passed.

I called the embassy and asked Consul General Dick LaRoche about the State Department list of attorneys in Saudi Arabia. I asked his opinion about one particular name on the list, Saleh Al-Hejailan. He said, "No, not that one. Too pompous . . . likes to play both ends—the Saudis and the embassy . . . I know one thing—he's well connected. Maybe that's what you need—his connections."

Hejailan was eager to get involved. At the time, I didn't know that he'd been engaged in another case in Saudi Arabia involving the kidnapping of an American child about five years prior. He was very smooth. "I would only take this case upon a humanitarian basis, Ms. Roush. I would not want any financial compensation—only for the benefit of all concerned. I know Prince Salman and am a member of his court. Of course, we will work this out quietly. I can tell you, Ms. Roush, in an Islamic court, you will not have a clear way to see the results you may desire, but if everyone is very agreeable, things could go very nicely for you."

I continued to press every button and knock on every door. This was the year that Americans were taken hostage in Beirut. Father Lawrence Martin Jenco had been released and was recuperating from his ordeal at the home of a relative in a Chicago suburb. I had spoken earlier with his sister, Sue Franceschini, and she gave him a message from me. He then hand-delivered a letter to Speaker of the House Tip O'Neil. Dixon talked to White House Chief of Staff Howard Baker. And I met personally with Robert Asher, president of the American/Israeli Political Action Committee, in his Chicago apartment—the meeting was arranged through Dixon's office. I met with the executive assistant to Cardinal Bernadine of Chicago who wrote a personal letter to Secretary of State George Shultz. I worked on this night and day—with little sleep in between.

Salman and Hejailan were looking for a way to settle this quickly and quietly. They did not want me to go to an Islamic court because they knew I would not win. Salman was forced to tell Ambassador Cutler I had to settle the matter in Islamic court to keep Gheshayan from going to the religious mullahs. Once Hejailan got involved and found out about the interest in the U.S. Congress, he went to Salman to work out a plan. Hejailan was very close to the royal family and one of his relatives had been the Saudi ambassador to the United States before Bandar's reign. His brother was the Saudi minister of health. As the consul general of the U.S. Embassy stated, "he was well connected."

Hejailan did come up with a very doable plan of getting the children out of Saudi Arabia and satisfying Dixon and the Congress. First, he wanted to be appointed "honorary legal advisor" to the U.S. Embassy. He could have coordinated all the negotiations for the deal without this title, but he wanted to be recognized as grand pooh-bah by both the U.S. Embassy and the Saud princes, so he pressed the embassy for this title.

In October 1986 the American embassy sent a cable to the State Department asking for permission to bestow this title upon Hejailan:

> He considers it essential to the success of these negotiations that he represents the embassy rather than Ms. Roush. To demonstrate this, he has requested appointment by simple exchange of letters as "Honorary Legal Advisor" to the embassy.
>
> Al-Hejailan has asked for an appointment of indefinite duration, terminable upon notice by either party, and not limited to the Al-Gheshayan case. Al-Hejailan would provide legal advice gratis. The embassy, in return, would agree not to make unreasonable demands for service, and would permit Al-Hejailan to describe himself as legal advisor to the embassy for purposes of professional listing.

He may not get paid for the case, but Hejailan certainly planned on benefiting, and no doubt would have if the State Department in Washington hadn't given a no-go for legal and procedural reasons. Washington would not allow the embassy to go ahead with the plans outlined by Hejailan.

Cutler sent another telex to the State Department for clarification, noting in particular, "It is the view of legal experts here that if the case were taken to court under Sharia [Islamic] law it would be most unlikely that a resolution could be reached to the mother's satisfaction." Working with Hejailan, he said, might produce more favorable results:

It had been our impression and, indeed, we had been operating on the assumption that it was our duty to protect the welfare of U.S. citizens. As the Department is aware, Ms. Roush's former husband allegedly abducted the two children from the United States and a felony warrant was issued for his arrest. He is not a U.S. citizen, and according to official documents provided to us by Ms. Roush he has a long history of alcoholism, psychiatric problems, criminal activity, and failure at U.S. educational institutions. Under the circumstances we felt the interests of Ms. Roush and her children were our primary concern, and that it was our responsibility to do whatever we could, regardless of the odds against us, to help her regain custody of her two children.

Washington's reply was short and to the point:

Dept wishes to reiterate that Al-Hejailan may not represent the embassy in any fashion, whether formally or informally in the child custody cases of Alia and Aisha Al-Gheshayan . . . A consular officer's primary interest is in the protection and the welfare of the children, while recognizing implicit legal limitations.

The State Department legal, consular affairs, and human rights departments all concurred that the U.S. Embassy in Riyadh, Saudi Arabia, should not get involved in the negotiations set in motion for the release and return of my daughters to the United States. They repeatedly gave the same order to concerned embassy personnel to "remain neutral."

The embassy staff, including Deputy Chief of Mission Edward S. Walker Jr., knew that Hejailan was preparing a deal for the girls to come home. Hejailan proposed a meeting in Prince Salman's office to iron out the details for their release and requested Ambassador Cutler to be present at that meeting. Khalid Gheshayan would be asked to sign a document allowing Alia and Aisha to attend boarding school in London, thereby getting them neatly out of Saudi jurisdiction. I would be able to pick them up in England and take them home.

I was in constant communication with Walker during this time. We were aware of Hejailan's plan and confident we would get the girls out. A few days before the proposed meeting in October 1986 I telephoned Walker: "Mr. Walker, I'm just making sure that everything is going well on your end." It wasn't.

"Ms. Roush, I have some news for you. The embassy telexed Washington twice this week, and they will not allow the ambassador to go into that meeting."

"No, that can't be. Why? Why not?"

"I don't know. They have given us specific instructions."

"If the Saudis find out, they will drop the whole thing." Indeed, without the ambassador's support, the Saudis had little reason to think the case mattered to the United States. "Tell the ambassador not to tell Hejailan," I pleaded with him. "I'll call Senator Dixon's assistant and we'll fix it. It's Saturday and I might have some difficulty finding her today. But please, please don't let Hejailan know what happened."

"Yes, of course. I'll tell the ambassador."

The Saudi workweek is from Saturday to Wednesday, and the embassy keeps the same hours. Our weekend was in progress, but I called Sarah at home. "Sarah, we have to do something. The embassy has orders not to go ahead with that meeting. We will lose the kids if the Saudis find out. Can you find Dixon?"

"Pat, that's awful news. I think he's golfing. I'll try to find him and have him call the embassy."

The phone rang moments later. "Ms. Roush, Ned Walker. While I was talking to you, Hejailan called the ambassador. He knows."

I was shaking and started to cry. "My God! My God! They'll let it go. They'll know the State Department doesn't care. What am I going to do now?"

Dixon had an old friend at the State Department, Undersecretary of State Edward Derwinski, former congressman from Illinois. We called upon him, but Derwinski couldn't change department policy. Dixon tried to "fix it" by writing a letter to Bandar showing congressional support:

October 28, 1986

His Royal Highness Prince Bandar bin Sultan
Ambassador Extraordinary and Plenipotentiary
Office of the Saudi Arabian Embassy
601 New Hampshire Avenue
Washington, D.C. 20037

Excellency:

Once again thank you so much for your courtesy and concern over the fate of Alia and Aisha Gheshayan.

I became concerned over the weekend that confusion was developing surrounding the United States' feeling on this case. My reason for calling was to assure you that my colleagues in the Senate, the State Department, and the Embassy in Riyadh are all working together toward a humanitarian resolution of this serious problem.

I understand that a meeting is to take place in the very near future between Prince Salmam, Ambassador Cutler, Mr. Gheshayan, and Mr. Hejailan. It is also my understanding that the Embassy's role in this meeting was unclear to Prince Salman. My staff has spoken at great length with the State Department regarding this matter. Let me assure you that although the Embassy's role is not to decide child custody cases, it is absolutely understood that they are representing the interests of two young U.S. citizens: Alia and Aisha. The matter of custody, in the eyes of the U.S., was decided in Court.

Since the meeting may take place at any moment it would be greatly appreciated if you could assure Prince Salman that the U.S. government, as represented by our Embassy, is still very concerned and extremely supportive of Alia and Aisha.

> Kindest personal regards,
> Sincerely,
> Alan J. Dixon, U.S.S.

But the damage was done, and nothing Dixon could ever do would make it right again. Our moment was gone. Hejailan called me with a side of his character I didn't expect and some salt for my wounds. "Ms. Roush, your government doesn't want you, and your State Department will not help you. You will see your children if and when we decide."

Deliver Us from Evil

Hejailan then began what was to be an endless round of gamesmanship with me that would continue for almost two decades. This would begin with an overproduced videotaping of Alia and Aisha in Hamad's villa. While I was in an emotional whiteout after the State Department wouldn't allow the embassy to coordinate the arrangements for the return of the girls with the Saudis, Hejailan didn't waste any time in trying to create a celluloid piece of propaganda to be used against me.

Hejailan works with the international law firm of Clifford Chance, which has offices in London, New York, Geneva, Paris, and Riyadh. He hires American, British, French, and Dutch lawyers to work in his law offices in the Saudi kingdom, where much of the work is contractual and involves oil companies. When he interfaces in situations like mine, he frequently uses one of his expatriate workers as a screen to shield himself from view and to protect his image. Just as the Saudi government uses people like Hejailan, PR firms, and lobbyists, to represent them and keep their hands clean, Hejailan uses these foreign workers. Paul Simpson, a British lawyer working for

Hejailan, was used for the taping of this video while Hejailan remained off camera.

It was a November morning in 1986, and Consul General Dick LaRoche and Foreign Service National Mazen Shaban of the American embassy in Riyadh were invited to join Hejailan for a "visit" at the Hamad Gheshayan villa. Prince Salman's assistant, Ali Otaibi, was also present along with a camera crew, Hejailan, Simpson, Khalid Gheshayan, and Alia and Aisha. Altogether there were nine men and two little girls, according to LaRoche's description to me.

Saudi villas commonly have two living rooms—one Western style with rows of overstuffed chairs and sofas lined up along all the walls with small wooden tables in front of the chairs, and one Saudi style with a large oriental carpet and low-lying cushioned seating. The rooms are massive with high ceilings. Hamad and Fatima lived in a new villa in a middle-class area of Riyadh. The visit took place in the Western living room with Paul Simpson as interviewer. Hejailan acted as director and producer. He brought new toys for Alia, almost eight, and Aisha, four. The girls were wearing fresh dresses and were clean with neatly combed hair. They had the traditional black kohl lined around their eyes (Saudi bedouin type of makeup), and they spoke English; they had been living in the kingdom for about eight months.

Simpson was seated on one of the large sofas near Alia, who was unwrapping the gift brought by Hejailan. Gheshayan was sitting across from them on another sofa, and Aisha was standing near him. Simpson began, "Alia, you don't want to go back to the United States to see your mommy now, do you?"

Alia's mouth gaped open and her eyes were wide and glazed. "Mommy? Mommy? No . . . my mommy doesn't love me. She hates me! And my sister!"

"Alia, you don't want to leave Saudi Arabia, do you?"

She looked at Khalid before she answered, "I'm not going anywhere without my daddy." She then got up, walked to the sofa where Khalid was sitting, and sat down next to him. She was very upset and went to him for comfort. He never acknowledged her and did not even put his hand on her, cuddle her in her moment of need, or give her any word of solace.

Then Simpson turned to Aisha. He'd brought her a "mood ring," which has a stone that changes colors to show if you are happy or angry. He put it on Aisha's little finger and said to the camera, "Look, she is very happy. Very happy."

"Aisha, do you want to talk to your mommy on the telephone?"

Aisha actually answered "yes," but this tape was never shown. Hejailan went back the next day and made another copy after Aisha was coached and this part was edited into the original. In the second copy Aisha said, "No. Mama Fatima is my mother. Mama Fatima is my mother."

Consul General Dick LaRoche told me that the girls were very frightened by all of this, and when Hejailan first arrived and coached them on what to say, they refused and started crying. Khalid took them to the back room and threatened them and then they cooperated.

The next scene shows them with Khalid and the maid he hired to take care of them—a young teenage girl from Southeast Asia. She was the new mommy for my girls, and Fatima was their keeper. Alia feared Fatima and her wrath—now she was in charge of her and Aisha. I found out many years later that Khalid remarried one year after he kidnapped my daughters. His new wife did not want my children, and they remained in the home of Fatima and Hamad for several years until Khalid had several Saudi children with his wife. The American embassy never told me about this. I found out in 1991 from state department documents I received from the FOIA.

According to an unclassified cable from the embassy—signed by Cutler—to the State Department regarding this videotaping, "Both children were able to recite from memory the opening verse of the Qur'an. The FSN present observed that in general, their comprehension of spoken Arabic was weak . . . Consoff asked the younger child if she would like to speak with her mother by telephone, and she said she would like to do so. The embassy's welfare mission was accomplished. The attorney's purpose in filming the visit and in making an additional film on November 27 is not clear . . . Our aim is to limit our involvement in this case to that of highly interested and sympathetic observers."

Hejailan couldn't contain his mirth after this masterpiece was completed. He called me: "Ms. Roush, I just visited with your children. They are both very beautiful girls and I know this is only because of the way you have raised them. It has nothing to do with Gheshayan. You did a wonderful job with your daughters. They are so polite and well mannered, and of course, beautiful."

He was using a common Saudi technique of complimenting your enemy while sticking a knife in their back. It was cruel and sadistic and would be only a preview of what was to come.

Another Miracle

My grief was beyond description. After I received a copy of that videotape from the American embassy, I was inconsolable. In early December 1986 a woman called from the St. Panteleimon Orthodox Church: "Hello, Pat. There is a weeping icon at an Albanian Orthodox church on the North Side. I thought you might be interested in seeing it."

I was a Catholic and not quite sure what a weeping icon was, but for some reason I went to the church—St. Nicholas. It was a cold, misty evening, and as I walked into the nave, soft sepia tones caressed the walls, incense permeated the air, and flames danced from the candles in their red glass containers. The room was filled with lay people and clergy slowly filing past the icon of the Theotokos on the left side of the iconostasis screen.

As I approached the image I could see wet markings from both eyes and from the upturned palm of her right hand streaking down the painting. An immense feeling of peace overwhelmed me. I felt as if I were floating and out of my body. There was no more anxiety or worry. I wanted to stay there forever. After standing near her, I sat in the front pew and just gazed at the miracle.

I returned another evening and this time brought my mother. Before the services I told her to go to the altar to receive the anointing being done by the priests with the tears from the icon. I spoke to one of the orthodox priests standing near the icon and asked him to pray for my daughters. He wrote their names on a piece of paper. My mother and I then sat in one of the front pews. After the evening services, a different priest hurriedly approached us and was anxious to talk to me. He was overly excited and joyful. "Are you an Arab?"

"No. My daughters are half Saudi Arabian. Why?"

He was tall and muscular with olive-skin, black hair, and a black mustache. With a broad smile and twinkling eyes he said, "I was standing near the icon, and all of a sudden I saw images of two little girls and my mother's name, Alia, came into my mind. Then Father told me about your daughters and their names. My mother is Syrian, and her name is Alia. My father is Greek. Did you know Alia was the name of an ancient queen of Syria? Why did you name your daughter Alia?"

"I know it is not a common name in Saudi Arabia. I just liked the name and thought it was beautiful. Are you the pastor here?"

"Yes, I'm Philip Koufos. I have a message for you . . . your daughters are coming home. Your daughters are coming home."

6

❧

Miracle on 34th Street

January 1987–January 1988

*I pray for my little girls every day. I talk to
God about the girls. I tell Him that they love me
and I love them. We are so close. How can this be happening?*
—Pat Roush, quoted by Bob Greene
in the January 4, 1987, *Chicago Tribune*

Trying to Change the System

After the double cross by the State Department and Hejailan's cruel video-taping of my daughters, I decided to start a media campaign. Bob Greene interviewed me, wrote an article for his column, and alerted a staff reporter for the *Chicago Tribune,* who wrote a front-page story: "Fighting for Her Kids, Her Life." The local Chicago television stations called and sent crews to my home. Sarah Pang and I planned a press conference in Washington with the senator for the first anniversary of the kidnapping. It was late in January and I arrived at National Airport in the middle of a snowstorm.

Senator Dixon and I stood at the podium in a conference room in the Dirksen Building. "The U.S. government must act to secure the release of the more than twenty-three hundred American children who have been kidnapped by one of their parents and are held in foreign countries," he began. Dixon called on Secretary of State George Shultz to "increase the scope of [his department's] activities" on behalf of abducted American children. After stating that a letter to Shultz would be circulated to obtain the signatures of additional senators, he asked specifically that the State Department actively seek worldwide ratification of the Hague Convention on International Child Abduction, negotiated in 1980, which deals with the problem of internationally abducted children. Dixon also requested that services be developed within the Department to adequately address international child abductions, and that existing diplomatic channels be utilized to inform foreign government officials of each abduction case, custody decision, and pending felony warrant involving their country.

"The Hague Convention is a toothless document right now, signed by only twenty-nine countries and actually ratified by only seven of those," he said. "Our government must use its influence in the world to convince other nations to sign the treaty and abide by its provisions. Internally, anything the Department does will be an improvement over what it does now—which is virtually nothing—for the families affected by these crimes.

"Right now, our State Department seems to function as the world's largest legal referral service, telling a parent whose child has been stolen away to contact a lawyer in the country to which the child has been taken. The Department should develop services including the training and counseling of personnel responsible for working with victimized families."

Dixon also released a "Dear Colleague" letter that would be sent to Prince Bandar asking for intercession in my case. "The Saudi government has told my office to show them that the American government cares about the Roush case, and that then perhaps the Saudis will do something."

He went right back to the U.S. Senate the same afternoon as the conference and brought the matter up on the Senate floor, urging his colleagues to signal their support for the girls. As he pointed out on the floor: "The prince in Saudi Arabia said, 'If your own State Department and your government and your country do not care, why should I get involved with one of my citizens to return those two children to America?'"

Dixon also took aim at State Department policy: "If our State Department simply maintained a greater level of active involvement on this issue by conducting a dialogue with the appropriate government officials of the country in question, nine out of ten times these civilized nations would, I believe, recognize the integrity of our court system and return these children. I give that challenge to the State Department and the distinguished secretary of state, for whom I have the highest regard."

After the increased press and media attention about my story and plight, Dixon's office received a flood of calls from parents whose children had been taken abroad by a former foreign spouse. The office was not prepared for such a deluge but quickly became a virtual clearinghouse for international abduction cases. There was no unit at the State Department for parents to turn to for assistance and no National Center for Missing Children at that time. Sarah Pang was overwhelmed. "Pat, I had no idea what a huge problem this is."

"We need a special section at the State Department that can handle this," I told Sarah, "with trained officers that will act as mediators with foreign governments. The only place I can turn to is the people at the Saudi Desk, who are very antagonistic and take sides with the Saudis. This country must stand up for its children. After these guys take the kids, they run back to their countries and hide out. We can't touch them. My warrants don't do me any good. They must be held responsible for these kidnappings. There should be a federal law making this a crime and an extraditable offense."

Sarah agreed. We continued to talk about this proposed special section at the State Department and a new law. I asked her to present these ideas to Senator Dixon. By this time he was thoroughly disgusted with the State Department and what they were doing to me. The fact that this was happening on an even grander scale to so many other people convinced him that something had to be done.

Hejailan resurfaced and baited me again. This time it was with a proposed phone call to my children. He promised me that under order of His Royal Highness Prince Salman, I could now have telephone access to my daughters twice per month with no restrictions. He orchestrated another staged performance and used my own daughters to stick more pins in me. Khalid prompted the girls to tell me they hated me and to say, "You're stupid"—statements my children would never have made. Hejailan told me he audiotaped the conversation. He took delight in taping these contrived sadistic scenarios. I would not be allowed to hear my daughters' voices again for ten more years.

Faith and Politics

My days were filled with telephone calls, conferences with Sarah, writing letters, and trying to find a way to get the girls back. My nights were agonizing—fighting demons in my dreams until the dawn. The same dream would reappear: I was in Arabia in a villa with huge rooms, high ceilings, and oriental carpets. It was filled with young children standing shoulder to shoulder. Wading through this sea of faces, I looked at each child to see if they were one of my daughters. Morning after morning I woke up exhausted after spending the night searching for them in my dreams.

Father Andrew at the Russian Orthodox Church held a service for the girls on the one-year anniversary of the kidnapping. The icon at St. Nicholas continued to weep as she had since December 6, 1986—the date of the Feast of St. Nicholas, the patron saint of children, or Santa Claus. People continued to call and offer their prayers. My mother and I became very close, and she offered her utmost support. She told me one day, "Pat, I was in the backyard and it was overcast, then suddenly a light was shinning on my shoulder. I wondered where the light was coming from because the sun was not shining. When I turned around, the light was gone."

As Mahatma Gandhi said, "Faith is not something to grasp, it is a state to grow into." I discovered it was not only I who was being drawn ever so slowly into the web of God's love, but my family was also caught in the embrace.

I kept track of arms packages and deals made with the Saudis. I cut out newspaper clippings and tried to use every bit of information to contact people who might be able to help me. Without the backing of the Central Authority, the top command at the State Department, it would be a futile pursuit. The Saudis were in control of my children and knew that I was alone without anyone backing me except for a few members of Congress who wrote letters and gave speeches. I couldn't give up and lived under a weight of pressure that rarely subsided. The Saudis were accustomed to negative press now and then and had a great deal of patience to sit back and wait till it all blew over. Today's news is soon forgotten, and I could not get enough sustainable pressure against them or convince the State Department to do anything to help my daughters.

Alan Dixon talked to Senator Bob Dole. He wanted to help and made a call to Bandar, but Bandar knew he had nothing to worry about and would take no action. The PR and lobbyist groups hired by the Saudi embassy knew how to manage damage control and advised Bandar on all issues. Fred Dutton, Bandar's hired right-hand man in Washington, was always willing to step in to do more dirty work.

Bandar was becoming the most powerful diplomat in Washington. He gave lavish parties and socialized with the Washington elite. He was the illegitimate son of Prince Sultan, Minister of Defense, and a Sudanese slave from Sultan's household. However, Sultan did not recognize Bandar as his son until he became a teenager.

Eager to prove himself worthy, Bandar became a high achiever: He graduated from the British Royal Air Force College, received pilot's training in the United Kingdom and the United States, and received a master's degree from Johns Hopkins University. King Fahad, his uncle and once a well-known playboy himself, favored Bandar and appointed him ambassador to the United States in 1985. With his charm, ambition, and greed he would become even more powerful and dangerous as time went by.

The Man from Boston

Answering the phone one night, I heard an unfamiliar woman's voice: "I read the article about you and your children in *Woman* magazine, and I'd like to help. There was a story about a little girl who was taken to Iran. Her mother hired a man and he brought her daughter back. It was in the St. Louis paper. Can I send you the article?"

It was April 1987, and I thought this might be the answer to my prayers. The man's name was Ed Ciriello, and he was from Boston. He had been successful in a "caper" when he lured an Iranian national back to the States with his six-year-old daughter. The woman sent the paper to me, and I contacted the mother of the rescued child and asked her about Ed Ciriello.

"Ed?" she replied. "He's wonderful. If it weren't for him, I wouldn't have Mariam back now."

"How did you find him?"

"I got a copy of *Soldier of Fortune* magazine and found him through the classified section listed in the back. I thought I had nothing to lose. Mariam had been gone for almost two years when I hired Ed."

The child was returned just six months after Ed Ciriello began the investigation. I called him in Boston, and he sent me a business card that stated he provided "an unusual service for unusual problems."

Ciriello had an impressive résumé with a background of someone in a Raymond Chandler novel. He enlisted in the U.S. Army and later worked in the Criminal Investigation Division (CID). Then he entered the U.S. Navy, and working his way into the Office of Naval Intelligence, conducting operations for ONI and other agencies in Cuba, Mexico, Korea, and Italy. When he resigned from the military he became an investigator for the Pinkerton Detective Agency and a licensed private investigator. He later worked for the CIA in Vietnam, kidnapping North Vietnamese and conducting operations in Southeast Asia. He continued to work on covert operations in the Middle East (mainly Iran and Saudi Arabia) and Indonesia. When I met him he was living on his sailboat, the *Private Eye,* which was docked in Boston Harbor.

After I spoke with him on the phone, he sent me the following letter:

Dear Patricia,

I want you to know that if we proceed with this you will have my full commitment and best efforts to recover your children.

We both know what's involved and as much as I believe I can help you, I will not hold out any promises. I can only promise you that I will do everything humanly possible. Your children will be home with you and I'll be there to see it!

When you are ready to meet, please call or write so we may begin. No one has the right to do this to another human being, and you have not only my deepest sympathy but my loyalty as well. Until we meet . . .

Sincerely,

Ed

Survivors

I didn't know what to think. I liked the sound of what he was saying. Where could I get the money for such an undertaking? Could he really do it? I was certainly fed up with the Saudis and the State Department. My faith was being tested to the limit, and the clock was ticking for my girls. I was emotionally drained and physically exhausted.

I was working as a nurse in the oncology unit at West Suburban Hospital in Oak Park, west of Chicago. Every day I would go to work and care for terminally ill patients. It was demanding, tiring, and at times depressing, but I met the most wonderful people just before they left this world. Their hope and courage were often an inspiration to me in my struggle. One evening a thirty-one-year-old woman with lymphoma called me into her room. She was a frequent inpatient on the ward and I knew her well.

"Pat, I want to give you a note, but please don't open it until you get home tonight."

Dear Pat:

I just want you to know how much I respect and admire you. I saw you on the Geraldo show and know how much you love your children. I got sick when my son, Vincent, was one month old. I saw how caring your eyes were tonight when I told you about him. He is the reason I know I will win this fight. You will win, too. We are both fighters, and I just want you to know that we will both win this battle.

With respect,

Cheryl Strack

She was later discharged to home, and then one day I saw her on the ward in her "street clothes." She had come to the hospital for some medication and stopped by the nurses' station to say hello.

"Cheryl, there is an incredible holy shrine on the North Side at an orthodox church. Miracles are happening there every day. Would you like me to take you there?"

"I'd like that, Pat. But we are moving right now. We had to sell our home in the country so I could be closer to the doctors, but as soon as we're settled, I'll give you a call."

A month later just before I was off duty for the day one of the nurses yelled at me, "Hey Pat, they brought Cheryl into the ICU."

I ran up the stairs to the Intensive Care Unit and met Cheryl's husband, Mark, in the waiting room and then went to her bedside. She was connected to a ventilator. I bent over the bed and held her limp hand. "Cheryl, it's Pat. Do you hear me, Cheryl?" Her frail, emaciated body lay motionless on the bed while air was forced into her lungs through a tube placed in her throat and taped in place around her head. She died two hours later.

She had lost her battle. Would I lose mine also?

Face-to-Face

For months there was no response to Senator Dixon's repeated requests to Bandar for a meeting. Dixon's friend, Undersecretary of State Ed Derwinski, intervened again. Bandar refused to attend the meeting at Dixon's office and instead sent two representatives: Adel Sembawa, Deputy Chief of the Mission, and Rehab Mahsoud, Second Secretary. They were accompanied by the ever-present counsel for the Saudi embassy, Fred Dutton. Sarah Pang and another assistant to Senator Dixon, Joe Clayton, were also present. The State Department sent the same people I was getting no cooperation from: David Ostroff, Saudi Desk, and Elizabeth Soyster, Consular Affairs.

It was a very emotional meeting, and the senator raised the issue of my daughters and Gheshayan and the fact that I had legal custody under U.S. law. He attacked the Saudis' stand on my case, considering Gheshayan's criminal record while he was in the U.S., and questioned why the Saudi legal system protected such a man and gave no weight to the U.S. custody decision. Fred Dutton spoke for the Saudis and tried to explain that the problems were rooted in a basic incompatibility of religious and secular laws of the Christian and Muslim cultures.

Alan Dixon faulted both the Saudi government for failing to solve the problem, and the U.S. Department of State for not allowing Ambassador Cutler to attend that meeting in October 1986 and therefore "botching the deal." He told the Saudis they should let their government know it was imperative they find a resolution to the problem; otherwise, he and his colleagues would raise the issue of my case and other Saudi consular problems on the Senate floor at every occasion, and in connection with every other Saudi-related subject in the future. The upcoming congressional hearing concerning Saudi violations of human rights would also be a forum, as well as State Department appropriation hearings.

Neither the Saudi DCM nor the political officer said more than a few words during the entire meeting, preferring to let their lawyer, Dutton, do all the talking—which annoyed Dixon, who in turn addressed all his remarks directly to the Saudis. While Dutton promised they would review the case again, Mr. Sembawa indicated the embassy had already done all it could do to resolve the matter and that even if Gheshayan were deemed an unfit father (highly unlikely in Saudi society), the children would never be given back to their mother, but rather to another male member of the Gheshayan family.

Sarah reported that Dixon then stood up, slammed his fist on the desk, looked at the Saudis and said, "I'm going to burn your ass for this. I'm going to burn you every chance I get." She had never seen Dixon like this before. He was outraged.

Then Dixon told them he was going to propose the creation of a special "department" to deal with child custody/kidnapping cases. Joe and Sarah asked if the State Department could try once again to arrange a meeting between Gheshayan, his father, Prince Salman, and Ambassador Cutler in an effort to demonstrate the high level of interest in the case.

Just as the Saudis and Dutton were walking out, Ed Derwinski came into the office. He put his arms around the shoulders of the Saudis and started walking out the door with them, saying, "Boys, we've got big trouble here."

David Ostroff then asked Joe and Sarah to urge Senator Dixon to refrain from bashing the State Department in front of foreign diplomats.

Dixon kept his promise to the Saudis and began an intense campaign to bring up my case every chance he got. On May 7, 1987, two weeks after the meeting in his office with Dutton and the Saudis, Dixon made a four-page statement on the floor of the U.S. Senate. He reiterated what the Saudis said in the meeting, described Gheshayan as an international criminal being protected by the Saudi Arabian government, and announced his plans to expose the details of this case over and over again:

This particular case involving Saudi Arabia is especially egregious, Mr. President. The tragic case of these two young girls, their mother, and their fugitive father, who today enjoys the safe haven and protection of Saudi "religious law," is absolutely incomprehensible and intolerable. Khalid Al-Gheshayan has violated the United States law by abducting two United States citizens to Saudi Arabia. It is as plain as can be, Mr. President . . . I will not accept the answer the Saudi Government has given, and I urge my colleagues to look closely at cases in their own States involving children abducted to Saudi Arabia. Today I am demanding from the Saudi government its respect for American laws and the decisions of American courts . . . Mr. President, I ask unanimous consent that the entire record—which is this thick—on the criminal violations and the misconduct of Mr. Gheshayan be printed in the [congressional] Record.

Dixon eloquently addressed this issue on the floor of the Senate for almost three years. He objected to incoming Saudi arms packages at every opportunity. While waiting in the "Green Room" on the set of a television program we were both to appear on, he told me, "Pat, I'm just one of a hundred senators. I can't do it without the cooperation of the other ninety-nine. All I can do is try my best."

454 Days in Hell

In June 1987 I was invited by the House Foreign Affairs Subcommittee on Europe and the Middle East to testify about my case, and the roles of Saudis and the U.S. Department of State. The topic of the hearing was violations of human rights by the Saudi government. California Congressman Tom Lantos called for the hearing at the request of a Palestinian businessman, Sam Bamieh, who allegedly was a former financial adviser to Saudi King Fahad. Bamieh, who had been inside the Saudi loop for many years, stated that the king was told Bamieh's mother was Jewish and quickly placed him under house arrest. Unable to leave the Saudi kingdom, Bamieh was placed under palace imprisonment for a few months until he signed a release. After boarding a commercial airplane in Riyadh, a Saudi government official came aboard and placed an envelope, said to be from the king, in Bamieh's lap. Fearing a trap, he did not touch the envelope until the plane left Saudi Arabian airspace. When he opened it he found a check for $400,000.

Upon returning to California, Bamieh filed a $58 million lawsuit against his two former Saudi business partners, who he claimed owed him money from business dealings. The attorney for one of the men was Robert Gordon, whom I would meet later in my dealings with the Saudi government. Fred Dutton, attorney for the Saudi embassy, was present in the San Jose courtroom for the proceedings. He was described by the *San Jose Mercury News* as "one of capitol's most astute lobbyists."

According to the January 5, 1987, issue of *Fortune:*

> The kingdom's practice of detaining businessmen, says Frederick Dutton, a Washington lawyer who represents the Saudis, is a "Third World way of beating the city slickers who went over there in the boom and slip out." As for Bamieh, says Dutton, "we're going to beat him in court."

The witnesses for the hearings included: Bamieh; Scott Nelson, an electrical engineer who worked for King Faisal Specialist Hospital; James Smrkovski, a linguist with Saudia Airlines; Henry Ramsey, an Aramco accountant; an American woman with children in Saudi Arabia who wished to remain unnamed, and me.

Except for Bamieh, the men had all been arrested and tortured by the Saudi authorities. Smrkovski, who had worked in Saudi Arabia thirteen years, was imprisoned for 454 days, from August 22, 1985, until November 19, 1986. When I met him at the hearings he had been out of prison for only six months and was suffering from post-traumatic stress syndrome. Although a Fulbright scholar, Jim was unable to give his own testimony because of his fragile psychological condition after the torture. The statement by his brother, Lonnie, a twenty-one-year veteran of the Michigan State Police, is very compelling:

> I learned of [the imprisonment] within a few hours after he was taken. He and his family were due to be at our home for a visit . . .
>
> I called his wife. I spoke to her. I realized he was missing so I immediately called the State Department and advised her to contact the consulate in Jeddah immediately.
>
> From that point on it became fifteen months of living hell for the whole family. It took twenty-six days to find out where he was and twenty to twenty-two days to find out if he was even alive. At one point from the State Department I heard this could only happen in the movies.
>
> My response to that was this was the longest movie I have ever sat in. I

heard such things as Saudis do not beat Americans. Would not jeopardize the AWACS or arms sales, but it happens.

. . . During the fifteen months my brother was held he was accused of spying for Israel and Iran, accused [of having] knowledge of smuggling guns and [being] involved in the sale of alcohol. He spent ten and a half months in solitary confinement. He was not allowed to speak to anyone for over a year, except interrogators. For the first six months he was confined to a three-by-six cell in a military dungeon thirteen steps below ground level. It would have been in Taif.

He spent those months in a mosquito-infested hellhole with absolutely nothing—no bed, no table, no chairs, no eating utensils. A light was kept on twenty-four hours a day. One night when he shut it off a guard sprayed roach bug killer in his face.

As a result he had fainting spells for several months.

I knew there was something wrong at that point because the Saudis delayed access to him for almost eight weeks. I demanded an explanation. I demanded they try to get a doctor to him because when he was seen I was informed that he said he was having fainting spells every time he stood up.

As a result of that, he had got some medication but he became nearly paralyzed from it. After he quit taking the medication he started to slowly recover. A sadistic "little Hitler" made him crawl for his food. Jim did not see the sun for six months. His legs were shackled, his arms in handcuffs; he was blindfolded each time he was taken someplace. We were under the impression he was being held at a prison in Taif. The fact was, he was not being held in a prison. Apparently, he was being held [at a] military installation in the vicinity of Taif.

To extract the alleged confession he was forced to sign a confession with his thumbprint. In Saudi Arabia it is customary to sign with a thumbprint. Jim was subjected to long hours of uncomfortable positions until he collapsed. Knee bends until he collapsed, beatings about his entire body and especially the feet . . .

Jim was subjected to the use of an electric prod [and] ultimately mutilation of six toenails.

Jim was equally psychologically tortured by threats of death, future tor-
ture, indefinite imprisonment, mutilation, and other inhumane treatment.
Whatever confession he was forced to sign remains a mystery since he knows
Arabic now, [but] at the time he did not. It was not explained to him.

Jim was moved several times after the first six months and on July 6,
1986, was again placed in solitary confinement. That gave him about four
months when he was not confined.

The beatings and interrogation resumed. He was held incommunicado
until September 1986. In October he was taken before a judge and allegedly
found guilty. We do not know for what.

Jim rejected the judgment, and again was placed in solitary confinement. Through the efforts of Senator Robert Dole, for whom I worked for
several months, Jim was finally released on November 19, 1986.

Nelson was imprisoned for thirty-nine days and released due to a call made
by Senator Ted Kennedy to King Fahad. Ramsey was held for approximately
seventy-five days and released for unknown reasons. Scott Nelson took his case
against the Saudis to the U.S. Supreme Court and lost, but it is reported that
he received a large undisclosed settlement from the Saudis. Ramsey's status is
unknown but Bamieh, although not receiving any compensation from the
lawsuit, did receive more than $20 million in a side deal with Bandar. Jim
Smrkovski, who had been tortured the most, never received compensation.

It was at this forum that I began to publicly decry the injustices of the
Saudi government and exposed the work of Hejailan.

"As long as the Saudi Arabian government allows this tragedy to go on,"
I said, "they are not allies of the United States and should not be treated as
our friends. My children are hostages in Saudi Arabia, and I won't rest until
they are brought back to me safely and until we are assured by the Saudi
Arabian government that they will not be re-kidnapped by any Saudi
national again."

I asked that the Congress demand that the State Department refuse to
issue visas to the Saudis who wanted to enter the United States, and Assistant
Secretary of State Marion Creekmore replied, "I don't think withholding

visas to the Saudis will solve anything . . . Our principal concern is that the children are being well treated."

From Foggy Bottom to the Watergate

The morning of the hearing I had an appointment at the Saudi embassy in Washington. It was the first time any representative of the Saudi government agreed to meet me personally. Several members of the State Department were set to accompany me in the meeting with the Saudi Consul General, Mohammad Hamiel: David Ostroff, Saudi Desk; Elizabeth Soyster, Consular Affairs; Theresa Hobgood, Overseas Citizens Services; and Irwin Pernick, Assistant to Undersecretary of State Ed Derwinski. They all walked with me from Foggy Bottom to the Saudi embassy across the street from the Watergate complex.

The block-long, multistory marble building with the Saudi flag flying above was a secured fortress with collapsible barriers. The tightly guarded entrance was our first stop. They searched my briefcase and confiscated my tape recorder. An assistant escorted us into the consul general's office, and the State Department crew quickly took the seats across the back wall while I sat immediately in front of the Saudi consul general's desk. He entered the room.

The conversation began with a few greetings. State Department officials said nothing, and I wasted no time in cutting to the chase. I took my daughters' two American passports out of my purse and laid them on his desk. "These are American citizens. They have a right to come home. When will my children be released?"

The diplomat leaned his stocky body over the desk as he smirked at me. "Well, you married him. Didn't you?"

"What does that have to do with anything? That is not the point. Your government is holding my American daughters as prisoners. I want them returned. This is not about Gheshayan. He's your citizen."

He just kept mocking me. The conversation went nowhere. Nothing was said by anyone from the State Department. Finally, I stood up, gathered the passports, looked Hameil straight in the eyes and said, "Go to hell!"

I walked past security, picked up my tape recorder, and left their bunker. The State Department peons, except for Theresa Hobgood, stayed behind with their Saudi "client" and apologized for my conduct. She was, remember, the first person I spoke with when my daughters were kidnapped in January 1986, who told me I would never see my daughters again. She followed me down the steps of the Saudi embassy, across the street, and into the restaurant of the Watergate complex.

This attractive, neatly dressed black woman wouldn't let me go. "Ms. Roush, Ms. Roush, please . . . can I talk to you?"

I turned around. "What do you want from me?"

"Ms. Roush, I just want to shake your hand. May I? You were great in there. I'm so glad you did that. He deserved it." I heard later that Hobgood resigned from the State Department.

Sarah told me I was becoming a kind of "folk heroine" at the State Department with the employees who couldn't speak the truth in fear of losing their jobs but secretly admired my pursuit of justice and freedom.

American-Saudi Princess

The next day I was a guest on *Nightwatch* with Charlie Rose. Sam Bamieh and the Smrkovski brothers were also on the show. Bamieh seemed to know a lot of people and I asked him to help. After I returned to Chicago I received a call: "I'm Princess Donna Al-Faisal. I saw you on *Nightwatch* last night and really admire your work. I'm an American who married a Saudi prince. Can you give me the names of the other women you are involved with? I want to coordinate a project with them."

"I don't know who you are. I can't disclose their identities. Give me your phone number and some references."

She quickly ended the conversation. I called Bamieh. "Who is this Donna Al-Faisal?"

"That one. She's on the payroll! She was married to some prince who was murdered at the Marriott in Washington a few years ago and now they use her—she gets about $10,000 per month. Bandar and Dutton must be getting worried. Let me call her and see what she is up to."

Another American woman, Joy King, had a kidnapped daughter in Saudi Arabia and went to Dutton after the hearing. She told him she just wanted to get into the kingdom and work as a nurse so she could be close to her child. She promised not to make any trouble and to stay quiet with no publicity. She parlayed her leverage with the Saudis with what I was doing with the politicians. Dutton let her in. She worked in Jeddah and had unsupervised visitation with her daughter, Sarah, one day per week—an arrangement never before made for an American woman under Sharia law. A few years later, when her daughter had started maturing, Joy found out the Saudi grandfather of the girl was molesting her. Joy and Sarah escaped from Saudi Arabia and went into hiding.

Hejailan came to his estate in Great Falls, Virginia, every summer and shortly after the hearing he called me. "Ms. Roush, you mentioned my name in front of your Congress. You will be punished for this and for going to the politicians and the press." Then he called Senator Alan Dixon and invited him to a dinner party, but Dixon refused and asked Hejailan to meet him at his Washington office. Dixon told him we intended to bring this matter up with the Saudi king. Hejailan smiled and left.

The embassy in Riyadh requested a consular visit with my daughters and Prince Salman complied. He sent his assistant Ali Otaibi with U.S. Embassy consular officers to Hamad's villa. The girls had been gone for eighteen months.

The following is from a State Department unclassified cable, July 1987:

Gheshayan continues to fear that the U.S. government intends to repatriate the children by whatever means it can, even by abduction if necessary. Mr. Al-Gheshayan entered the meeting feeling apprehensive and hostile. He said he had been directed to come by the Governorate and had had to force Alia, in turn, to be present because she wanted nothing to do with the embassy or its representative. He said he wanted to be left alone to raise his daughters in peace away from the disruptive influence of his former wife whether exercised directly or through the embassy. He was determined to cut his former wife off from further contact with the children. He said he would permit no further consular visits with the children because it upset them and insulted him. This was especially true with respect to their moral growth under Islam. Al-Gheshayan said that Ms. Roush's "sudden" concern for the children seemed insincere in view of "her past behavior."

He didn't know that he had nothing to fear from the United States government or his own government. I was the one looking from the outside in, and things would not change. Khalid's paranoia was symptomatic of his illness as described by the American doctors when he was a patient at psychiatric facilities in the United States. Now he could influence my daughters and teach them anything he wanted about me, our faith, or the United States.

Birth of the Hague Treaty

That same summer of 1987 Alan Dixon led the Congress into a ratification of the Hague Convention: "It is for Patricia Roush and the thousands of people in the United States who have had experiences like hers that I vigorously urge my colleagues to support this implementing legislation of the Hague Convention on the Civil Aspects of Parental International Child Abduction."

By this time Walter Cutler had been replaced as U.S. ambassador to Saudi Arabia and the incoming ambassador was to be another foreign service career diplomat, Hume Horan. He was a former ambassador to Sudan; an Arab scholar with an Iranian diplomat father and American mother. I asked Sarah if Dixon could meet with Horan before he left for Riyadh. The meeting went well, and Horan told Dixon he would bring up the matter with the Saudis. In September 1987, at Horan's reception before King Fahad, he was snubbed by the royalty and treated coldly during his ambassadorship.

Horan was constrained by the State Department from forcefully present-ing my case and later told me that he was under orders from the Department not to pursue it. Many years later he related that he was instructed by Prince Salman not to speak of my case again.

A Real Private Eye

By this time, my mother and I were nearly out of our minds. I called Ed Ciriello in Boston and asked him to come to Chicago for a personal meeting. He had sent me a story about another successful "operation" he was involved in to res-cue a little girl from Egypt. After sending him the airfare, I waited to meet this "sleuth" with great anticipation. As I stood at the arrival gate at Midway Airport in Chicago, waiting for a man I didn't know and couldn't recognize, suddenly this fifty-something, weathered man appeared. I wasn't sure if it was Ed so I watched him walk out of the gate area. He was slightly slumped and carried a duffle bag over one shoulder. His nose was a little off center. "Ed?"

"Hey . . . I haven't been to this airport for many years. Used to live in Chicago when I worked for Pinkerton. We got a lot to talk about."

First we stopped at the fish market and I bought some shrimp. We talked nonstop. He was Italian—Sicilian—and we got right into the Italian thing—pasta . . . cooking . . . my mother. He had two sons in the Chicago area that he'd walked out on when they were kids. He bummed around his whole life and wasn't the family type. This was a really tough guy.

It was a hot August evening. I had all the fans on and was standing at the stove cooking shrimp jambalaya. Ed talked about various possible scenarios for getting the girls out. He knew Saudi well and was smart in a way I'd never seen before. No, it was more than smart—he was "electric," with no politi-cal double-talk, just action! I liked it.

My mother came over and talked to him in Italian; she liked him, too. Then we got in the car and drove downtown to Buckingham Fountain on the lakefront. The colored lights kept changing as we walked around the spurting water. We stopped at the rail and looked into the falls. Ed said, "Pat, remember this night. I have a feeling we are going to get those kids back. Only time will tell, and I'm here to tell the time."

My mother and I did not have the money at that time to coordinate a covert operation with Ed. We needed time to raise the money but knew we would hire him to rescue the girls, if all else failed.

I flew to Washington in October to meet with State Department officials and Senator Dixon for the opening of the desk in Consular Affairs that would come to be known as the "Office of Children's Issues." Assistant Secretary of State Joan Clark and a few other parents were present. The Department tried desperately to stop the desk from being opened, but pressure from the Senate as a result of Dixon's rhetoric was overwhelming, and money was earmarked by Congress for the unit. At a press conference later that day Dixon said, "We want to elevate the profile of this problem until the State Department understands that we mean business."

A Merry Christmas

Hume Horan had been at the post of U.S. ambassador to Saudi Arabia for about three months. He was prevented from presenting my case on a state-to-state level with the Saudis by the State Department but sincerely tried to do what he could.

I was depressed throughout the holidays, beginning with Thanksgiving, through Alia's birthday on January 5, and on to the anniversary of the kidnapping on January 25. I decided to work at the hospital on Christmas Day. I thought if I worked and focused on the needs of the patients, I would get through the day easier. While I was caring for one of the patients, another nurse shouted, "Pat, you've got a phone call. It's the ambassador."

I was confused. "What ambassador?"

I went to the nurses' station and picked up the phone. "Ms. Roush, this is Hume Horan calling from Riyadh. We were just sitting here watching the old movie *Miracle on 34th Street*, and I thought about you. I just want to wish you a Merry Christmas."

7

❧

SILKWORM MISSILES AND LIES

JANUARY 1988–DECEMBER 1988

We doubt that the Sharia system that did not bend for the granddaughter of King Khalid would bend for Ms. Roush.
—Cable from U.S. Embassy, Riyadh, January 1988

Systems of Evil

The slight figure covered in black was brought into the center of the square, blindfolded, and left standing alone. The guards on the other side of the concrete parking lot lined up and faced the guilty woman, then raised their rifles, took aim, and fired. The audience applauded.

This was the death of a Saudi princess, King Khalid's eighteen-year-old granddaughter, whose only crime was falling in love with a young commoner. She broke the strict Wahhabi, the Islamic law of the land that her grandfather ruled. She knew the rules, but does the crime of being young and in love warrant a firing squad? The boy was beheaded in the square just before her sentence was carried out on that warm Friday afternoon.

A British citizen was in the public square the day of the execution and secretly took photographs with a hidden camera. After his return to England, the 1980 documentary movie *Death of a Princess* was produced. The Saudi government broke diplomatic relations with Great Britain, and tensions between the two countries increased. The Saudis countered by hiring an American filmmaker, Jo Franklin Trout, to narrate a three-part documentary about Saudi Arabia. She drank tea with the bedouin women in the desert, interviewed smiling princes, and portrayed Saudi Arabia as a very progressive and liberal country with high ideals and morals. They had their own customs and traditions but were moving ahead into modernity under the wise leadership of the Saud family.

Death of a Princess was aired on PBS in 1982. Gheshayan had just left me with a three-year-old daughter and a four-month-old baby. As I sat in my living room in San Francisco with my children, I never imagined that my two little girls would also be victims of that same regime. A Saudi king did not intervene to save his innocent granddaughter from a brutal death, and now I was asking his brother, King Fahad, to save my daughters from a life sentence in Saudi Arabia.

Senator Alan Dixon and U.S. Ambassador to Saudi Arabia Hume Horan had spoken on the telephone about what looked like my only chance for the release of Alia and Aisha—a direct appeal to the Saudi king. The State Department wouldn't allow the American embassy to negotiate with the Saud family princes for the release of the girls and referred to a draconian code of State Department policy that had to be adhered to. Rather than rescue young, innocent children from a perilous life sentence inside a dangerous medieval totalitarian regime, the State Department chose to sacrifice these two girls and at the same time espouse the rhetoric that they were interested only in the "welfare and well-being of the children." Once the State Department backed out of a Saudi proposal to get the girls safely out of the country and revealed to the Saudis their ambivalence about the importance of my daughters' lives, Senator Dixon and the Congress could not undo the damage.

In fact, the harder we tried, the more the Saudis resisted until my case became a type of "thorn in the side" to the Saudis. They just dug a foxhole and refused to budge. There were other cases of Saudis stealing American children, but since I made it an issue in the press and political arena and wouldn't take no for an answer, I was singled out and became an irritant to the Saudi government. I was forced into this position by the State Department's betrayal and refusal to make this matter a state-to-state issue with the Saudis. I had no choice. I was now pitted against two systems of evil—the U.S. State Department and the Saudi Arabian government.

The Saudi "Supreme Court"

Although Ambassador Hume Horan was constrained by the State Department from pursuing my case with the Saudis and could be no more than an "impartial observer," he was told that he could relay a congressional letter to the Saudi king. He recommended to Senator Dixon that there be a personal, humanitarian petition made by as many senators as possible. Horan emphasized that such an appeal should stress the humanitarian dimension of the case, and seek the king's guidance on how the question could be addressed in a humane and compassionate manner. All negative information about Gheshayan should be omitted. Horan said I should also write a personal petition to the king, and he would deliver it with the senatorial request. I was told that this action would be the equivalent of going to the Supreme Court and that if I failed, there would be recourse neither with the Saudi princes nor within their legal system. It was all or nothing.

The letter from Dixon was prepared and circulated for signatures among the senatorial offices. I called Fabbio Saturni, the desk officer for our new international child abduction unit, at the State Department and asked if President Reagan and/or Secretary of State George Shultz could call King

Fahad around the same time the letter was delivered. It was just one call that would mean so much. He didn't think that was possible.

Dixon's staff was able to convince fifty-four U.S. senators to sign the letter to the Saudi king. "We implore you to act on a humanitarian basis both on the facts of this case and in consideration of the long history of friendship our countries have shared." Four pages of signatures followed the letter, including those of John McCain, Joseph Biden, Thomas Daschle, Daniel Patrick Moynihan, William Cohen, John Glenn, Albert Gore, Bill Bradley, and John Kerry. My letter to the king accompanied this petition, which was delivered to the Royal Diwan in March 1988.

The timing couldn't have been worse. Not only did the Saudis dislike Hume Horan because of his Iranian background, he had used his skills in the Arab language to engage all kinds of Saudis—including the kingdom's conservative religious leaders who were critical of the ruling family. They didn't want someone so adroit at penetrating their closed society; he was continually being shunned by the royals. Worse still, a secret deal between the Saudis and the Chinese was uncovered. It was the worst moment of Saudi-American interactions between the 1973 oil embargo and September 11. Bandar was the central actor.

Though the Saudis were easily one of America's biggest customers for armaments, they resented the process they had to go through to acquire the most advanced U.S. systems. They survived showdown votes in Congress when friends of Israel opposed the sale of advanced aircraft to them. And on other occasions administrations had to evade congressional opposition to sell weapons to Riyadh. The United States refused to sell some kinds of advanced weapons to the Saudis, including missiles. So the Saudis bought from other countries, too, including Britain, France, and—in one deal that caught the United States by surprise—China.

The *Washington Post* reported that in secret talks begun in China in 1985, Bandar negotiated a billion-dollar purchase of Chinese CSS2-class missiles with a range of about fifteen hundred miles—far enough to reach Turkey and Israel from Saudi territory. The United States, and Israel, failed to discover what was going on for two years. When intelligence agencies in both countries realized what had happened, they were livid. The State Department instructed Hume Horan to see King Fahad and deliver a stern message expressing "surprise and disapproval of this action," as Horan recalled in an interview later.

Horan said he knew the king would be offended by the verbal spanking he had been ordered to deliver, so he called Washington to confirm that officials there understood the import of their instructions. Yes, he was told, deliver the message. He did so. When he returned to the embassy, he found a new telegram from Washington revoking the previous instructions—which he had just carried out.

Bandar had persuaded senior officials of the Reagan administration not to deliver an official protest to Fahad. Bandar reassured the Americans that the missiles would be deployed in a way that made clear they were no threat to Israel. They had a conventional warhead and were intended to deter Iraq and Iran, Saudi Arabia's traditionally hostile neighbors, and would be used only in retaliation, the Saudis said.

The administration sent Philip Habib, a retired undersecretary of state then serving as a special Mideast peace envoy, to Riyadh to try to mend fences with Fahad. Habib brought Horan to his meeting with the king. Fahad was clearly furious with the ambassador and asked Habib, in front of Horan, to have Horan replaced. When Habib raised the issue of the missiles, the king said angrily that he had told Horan "to keep his nose out of it." He complained to Habib about Horan's Iranian ancestry.

The Reagan administration decided to replace Horan with his predecessor, Walter Cutler. The decision was made so quickly that even before Horan could leave the country, the State Department asked him to seek Saudi approval for Cutler's reappointment as ambassador. According to the *Washington Post*, Horan stated this was a humiliating mission. He said, "They made us kowtow. The American ambassador's influence ended in Riyadh."

Successfully forcing the Americans to replace their ambassador gave the Saudis a palpable psychological edge in their dealings with the United States from that day on. And the Saudis have never had another Arabic speaker as U.S. ambassador.

The news of the expulsion of Hume Horan from Saudi Arabia, persona non grata, was devastating to me. They also refused to acknowledge the letter from fifty-four U.S. senators to the king and took a typical Saudi political stance, the posture of ice and silence. The U.S.-Saudi relationship was stressed, and I went to the Saudi "Supreme Court" and lost. Worse, I was not even given recognition.

The Cutler Affair

Walter Cutler was both the State Department's and the Saudis' man of choice to replace Horan. *Why?* I wondered. I called Sarah Pang. "If they want Cutler so badly, and haven't responded to our letters, why don't we stop them from getting him? What have we got to lose?"

Sarah went to Dixon, and he placed an objection to the confirmation of Cutler in the Senate. I wrote to Senator Jesse Helms, chairman of the Senate Foreign Relations Committee. His office agreed; they would stop Cutler because of what happened to my children. Then I called Hejailan in Riyadh: "Mr. Hejailan, there's been an objection to the confirmation of Walter Cutler by Senator Dixon and Senator Helms. He won't be coming back to Riyadh unless my daughters are allowed to return home."

"Ms. Roush, I think this can all be worked out quietly," he told me. "I will be in New York in two weeks and would like for you to be my guest at the Waldorf Hotel. We can talk about all of this at that time."

I had never met him. Now after all he'd done to me, I would stand face-to-face with my nemesis—in the same room with this man who had caused me so much pain. I now had something he wanted—Walter Cutler.

Then I called Assistant Secretary of State Joan Clark and asked if I could come to Washington to meet with Walter Cutler. I told her about Hejailan, and she stated a meeting with Cutler would be arranged after I met with Hejailan.

It was early May 1988 when I arrived at LaGuardia Airport, took a taxi to Manhattan, and got off at the Waldorf Astoria. I had only read about the

Waldorf in books and couldn't imagine anyone ever being able to afford a room there. I was early and didn't want to appear too eager so I stopped in the lobby for a cup of coffee and freshened my makeup. I looked pert in a black-and-white fitted dress, with a maroon briefcase and bobbed haircut. I called Sarah from the public phone. "Sarah, I'm here. I'm scared. What should I do if I'm alone with him and he offers me something to drink? He might poison me. Or put me in a box and take me out like a piece of luggage. Who would know?"

"Pat, Fabbio Saturni from the State Department is worried about you. He just called. He said you shouldn't be going in there alone. The senator's concerned, too."

"Don't worry, Sarah. I'll tell him everyone knows I'm here and let him know that if something happens to me, there will be questions asked. But I'm still not going to drink anything."

"Call me when you get out of there. Fabbio wants a call back, too."

I straightened my dress and walked to the counter to use the house phone. "Mr. Hejailan, this is Pat Roush. I'm in the lobby."

After a long pause, he said, "You're in the lobby?" Yet another pause. "In the lobby?"

"Yes, I'm downstairs. We have an appointment, remember?"

"Of course, Ms. Roush. Come up in about fifteen minutes. I'm in the penthouse in the tower."

I made my way to the elevator, and a neatly dressed man in a three-piece suit, carrying a black briefcase joined me on the ride to the penthouse. He scrutinized me, "Going to the top?"

"Yes."

"Who are you with?" he asked.

"I'm with myself. Who are you with?"

"Chase Manhattan. Going to see Mr. Hejailan?"

The door opened and we both got off and walked across the hall to the white French doors of Hejailan's suite. I rang the bell. Hejailan opened the door. "Ms. Roush, *Salam Aleikum.*"

"Aleikum Salem."

He quickly ushered me into one room and "Chase Manhattan" into another. "I'll be with you in just a few minutes, Ms. Roush."

Hejailan's right eye had a slight twitch, which was most difficult to ignore. An overweight, mid-forties, slightly balding, mocha-toned man with a hooknose—this was the picture of my adversary. His resemblance to Khalid was uncanny. I sat on a chair, and as I waited I noticed a pair of woman's high heels in the corner—well worn. I wondered who this woman was. Would she join us?

He appeared after about fifteen minutes and brought me into the living room of the penthouse suite. "Would you like something to drink? A glass of wine?"

"No, thank you."

I sat on the leather sofa, and he positioned himself across from me in an overstuffed chair.

I began, "I just spoke with the State Department and Senator Dixon—he sends you his best wishes."

"Thank you." He smiled. His eyes were like burning oil ready to ignite and devour me. His discipleship with darkness had brought him riches, power, influence, and control over the lives of people such as me. The fate of my innocent children rested with men like Hejailan, who played God with their lives. I had been placed in the position of a supplicant to get back what was manifestly mine—the bone of my bone and blood of my blood. I was forced to play a high-stakes game in a league, I was learning, had no rules. I wondered how much they wanted Cutler and how far I could push this.

"Are you traveling alone?" I asked.

"No. My friend is with me. She is Lebanese. She went shopping for a little while. You know, Ms. Roush"—he paused—"Prince Salman likes Walter Cutler very much. Things could go very well for you if Mr. Cutler were to return to Riyadh."

"Mr. Hejailan . . ."

"Please, call me Saleh."

"Right. Mr. Hejailan, you know what I want. We've been through this for two and a half years now. You know the truth and I know the truth. There's no one else in this room now but God, so we don't have to pretend what did or did not happen . . ."

He leaned back in his chair, looked at me, and nodded in agreement.

"I want my daughters back, and now you want Cutler. What are you willing to do?"

"Well, first of all, I will sponsor you into the kingdom—I will pay for everything—your ticket, hotel and meals, and arrange for a car. I will get some kind of temporary order so that you will be able to see your daughters immediately and have them for several hours each day. I will make arrangements for you to meet with many influential princes—Prince Sattam, Prince Salman, Prince Naif—and you can present your case to them. Then we will meet in the governor's office with Gheshayan. I am sure that we will have an agreeable meeting, and you will probably be able to leave with your daughters. But Walter Cutler must be in Riyadh so he can accompany us to these meetings. This is very important."

"What guarantees do I have? Once Cutler is confirmed you can do as you wish. Promises have been broken before."

His bulky body bent forward in the chair and as he threw his head back, he shrieked with a chilling laugh, "Ms. Roush, you have my word. That is all over now. We understand each other. What other assurances can I give you?"

He knew he had me. I had no leverage except Cutler and once he was gone, he couldn't be recalled if the Saudis didn't keep their end of the deal. I asked, "Why don't I go to Riyadh now and Cutler can go with me as a special emissary. We'll meet with the princes and Gheshayan and bring the girls home together. Then he can be confirmed and on his way in his ambassadorship."

"It won't work that way. No. Mr. Cutler must be the ambassador first. Besides, many of the princes are on vacation now."

"Well, I'm taking the shuttle to Washington tonight and will meet with Walter Cutler tomorrow at the State Department. I'll ask him if he will go with me to meet with the princes, if he is confirmed."

The door to the penthouse opened and a young woman entered the room. Hejailan stood up. "Ms. Roush, this is Leila."

The Sheep

I spent the night in Washington and rose early for my meeting at the State Department. Joan Clark, assistant secretary for consular affairs, shook my hand and escorted me into her office. Already seated around the room were David Ostroff, Elizabeth Soyster, Irwin Pernick, and Fabbio Saturni. Walter Cutler came into the room after we were all seated. After sitting on a chair next to me, he began to fumble with papers on his lap and kept shifting his eyes from one person to the other as he fidgeted in the chair.

I began the conversation. "I met with Saleh Hejailan, the Saudi attorney who works for Prince Salman, yesterday in New York. He has proposed a plan that involves his sponsorship of me into Saudi Arabia and a series of proposed meetings with princes to petition their intercession for the release of my children. He has offered to finance the trip and make the appointments, but he wants Walter Cutler to be in Riyadh so he can accompany me to these meetings. There was a meeting proposed by Hejailan and Prince Salman in 1986 that you were invited to, Mr. Cutler, but you refused to attend. I want to know if you will be able to attend these meetings."

Cutler quickly blinked his eyes and looked at me, then turned to Joan Clark, who was sitting on his left. "Is this legal? I want to know if this is legal."

Her neatly cut, short gray-blue hair framed a pale white face with lines that hinted of her sixty-plus years. Joan Clark was a seasoned foreign service diplomat who had risen through the State Department ranks. She scanned Fabbio Saturni's face for an answer; he nodded. "Ah, yes," she said, "this would be acceptable."

I looked directly at Cutler beside me and said, "You know that Senator Dixon and Senator Helms have objected to your confirmation in the Senate. Hejailan tells me Prince Salman likes you very much and things will go my way if you are confirmed. If I ask the senators to remove the objection and you go to Riyadh, will you make a strong case for my daughters' release? I have to know this, Mr. Cutler."

"If the Department says it's all right, then I'll go."

I questioned Joan Clark. "Miss Clark, do I have a commitment here?"

"Yes, that's fine."

We all rose from the chairs and as I headed for the door, I approached Walter Cutler. "I'll see you in Riyahd, soon." He didn't reply and timidly looked away.

While I was in Washington, I met an American businessman, Franklin Scharf, who was representing the interests of Rukmino Sukarno, the daughter of the former dictator of Indonesia. He told me he was doing business in Saudi Arabia and asked if there was anything he could do for me. I told him most of the story and about the letter to the king. He offered to ask Ms. Sukarno, whose father had been a good friend of King Fahad, for intercession. She sent a personal letter to the king and offered to be a "godmother" to the children if they were returned.

Hejailan Plan II

The American embassy was alerted to the new Hejailan plan and sent a consular officer to Hejailan's office in Riyadh for a meeting. Hejailan was there with one of his employees, an American lawyer named Robert Thoms. The American embassy stated in a cable:

> Following his opening statement on May 21, Al-Hejailan mentioned only once the possibility of Ms. Roush regaining custody of her children, and this was when he referred to her strong personality and her incredible initiative and "strength" in enlisting 54 U.S. Senators to work for her.
>
> When congen [consular general] referred to the difficulty of obtaining a visitor's visa for Saudi Arabia, Thoms assured her that it was not difficult for Al-Hejailan because he was a good friend of Prince Salman.

I told Sarah about the plan and said, "What if they renege? What guarantees do we have?" We both agreed—there were none.

Cutler wasted no time and walked into Dixon's office a few days after the meeting. He told the senator, "I can't do anything unless I'm there." He promised Dixon that if he were confirmed, he would do everything he could to get the girls back. Dixon trusted him and they shook hands.

Senator Helms's office was adamant about Cutler not getting the ambassadorship and asked me whether Cutler's presence in Saudi Arabia would assure that I could return with my children. I replied that I was not sure. Helms's staff said that without some indication of Cutler's "good faith" they could not support the nomination. I then asked what their feelings would be if Cutler went to Saudi Arabia immediately and returned with my children. They said he would then stand a good chance of being confirmed.

I called Hejailan and again proposed the plan for Cutler to go to Riyadh first, get the girls, and then come back for the confirmation—no dice. He repeatedly changed his mind concerning the finances and meetings. I had issues concerning my safety once I was in Saudi Arabia that were not being addressed honestly. The visitation with my children was constantly being circumvented. Hejailan talked in circles and vagaries.

Said the American embassy in a cable:

Al-Hejailan said he would contact Ms. Roush, and request a visa for her to visit her children in Saudi Arabia. However, he will require from her a letter of gratitude. He had two "small" requests from the embassy. One, he does not wish her to be "stationed" in his office. Second, Al-Hejailan prefers to wait for the arrival of Ambassador Cutler to start these procedures. He would like Ambassador Cutler to attend the meetings, particularly the one with Prince Salman.

He emphatically mentioned that Cutler had to be in Riyadh before anything would happen. After I told the embassy in Riyadh that I thought the whole plan was another Hejailan trick, they informed me, "This is the only apparent alternative."

I was stuck with Hejailan again.

He composed and faxed a letter for me to sign, his so-called "letter of gratitude," and said he wouldn't do anything unless I signed it. It put me in a position of a groveling supplicant on my knees in utter submission to him:

Dear Mr. Hejailan:

I am deeply grateful for your kindness and generosity in assisting me to arrange to see my children in Saudi Arabia. I recognize you are motivated by purely humanitarian considerations and that you have no obligation whatsoever to help me. I recognize that you are acting independently of the Saudi Arabian government, as a private lawyer working to the best of his ability to further the public good . . . I cannot thank you enough for your willingness to expend efforts and money on my behalf. I will never be able to repay your kindness, except in words which are heartfelt and sincere.

He detested my strength and endurance and wanted to break me. My mother was at my home one day when I was speaking to Hejailan on the phone about this proposed "visit." She went into my bedroom and picked up the extension and started to cry, "Oh, Mr. Hejailan, please help us bring my granddaughters home. Please, Mr. Hejailan, I beg you, help us." I quickly ended the call. "Mom, don't ever let him hear you like that again. That's what he wants. He wants us to cry and break down and plead with him. He gets a sadistic pleasure from that. Mom, don't give him that satisfaction, please."

I didn't know what to do. Hejailan had me by the neck, the State Department continued to placate the Saudis every chance they got, the embassy was prevented from showing any strong concern for getting the girls out, Dixon had taken the "hold" off Cutler, and Helms's office finally said they would go along with whatever I wanted regarding Cutler. I was forced to either sign this absurd, degrading letter from Hejalian, or, whatever the plan was, it would be nixed. I had no guarantees about anything, and the "deal" kept changing.

The icing on the proverbial cake was when Hejailan requested that I become a Muslim to be able to get my kids back. He said if I could prove that I was a good Muslim who practiced the Islamic faith and would assure that the children received Islamic teaching in the United States, I might have a chance.

I refused.

Anatomy of a Double Cross

I signed the "letter of gratitude" and sent it back to Hejailan. Cutler arrived in Riyadh in August 1988, and thereafter Hejailan refused to take my calls. I called the embassy and they called Hejailan's office. Robert Thoms took the call. He told the embassy, "Pat Roush is a difficult customer with unrealistic expectations."

Cutler refused to talk to me or Senator Dixon. He got what he wanted, the State Department got what they wanted, and the Saudis got what they wanted. I became despondent.

I went to see Father Philip at St. Nicholas. The icon had stopped weeping, but I could still feel a powerful presence in the church. I spent many hours kneeling in front of the Theotokos and started attending the Sunday liturgy at St. Nicholas after Father Andrew at St. Panteleimon was transferred to another church out of the state. Father Philip still insisted the girls were coming home.

I was crying and called my mother one day: "Mom, I don't know what to do anymore. I should just kill myself and end this madness. I can't take it. I'll never get the kids back. This pain is too much for me."

"Pat, if you kill yourself, he wins. Don't let him do that to you, Pat. Don't let him take your life, too. What would I do without you? You know, Pat, because of what happened, we are all different. Little trivial things don't seem to matter anymore and we are all stronger, better people because of this tragedy. You mustn't give up."

In October 1988 I called Stephanie Smith, consul general of the American embassy in Riyadh. She told me Khalid had gotten married and left the girls with his family in Hamad's villa because his new wife didn't want my daughters around. He had a new baby boy and didn't want anything to do with me. He was determined that I would never see my daughters again and refused to give me any photographs. I had no idea that he wasn't even living with my girls. He had five unmarried, younger brothers who lived in Hamad's villa, plus two married sisters and one married brother. There were multiple maids and servants and the young maid that was imported for the care of my daughters. The girls certainly couldn't identify with Khalid's cruel, illiterate mother, whom they disliked and feared. He had told me a story about how she had taken matches and burned his fingers when he was about four as punishment for getting into her things.

Now she was the keeper of my daughters. They had no mother to read stories to them and tell them she loved them each night before they went to bed. Why couldn't they be with me? I had so much love to give them and was fighting so hard for their freedom. They knew nothing about what I was doing and were only told that I had abandoned them and didn't love them.

Scharf and Sharia

My faith sustained me as I searched for something to break this evil grip. Franklin Scharf, the businessman I had met in Washington earlier that year, called and said he was planning a trip to Saudi Arabia. Would I like him to try to arrange a visit with my daughters through the American embassy? I told him yes and to please try to get some photographs.

Khalid swore he would not allow any visit with the girls, but a Foreign Service National (FSN) that worked at the American embassy was able to persuade him to allow Frank Scharf and embassy officials to meet with the girls at the home of this embassy employee. Khalid repeated that he would never relinquish custody of the girls not only because he loved them but because they had "a family, a tribe, and Islam." He said he was tired of being bothered by the embassy and, "If they continue, I will send someone to kill Patricia Roush." Frank Scharf asked Khalid if he ever beat me, and the response was that according to Islam a husband has a right to beat his wife if she does not obey him. After the second act of disobedience, he can divorce her (if she survives the beating).

Frank Scharf was not allowed to take any photographs of the girls but came back to the United States with a fervor to file a lawsuit for me in an Islamic court. I told him we had already been through that. I would never win. Nevertheless, he spent weeks preparing the case and called Hejailan to ask if he would file it for us. Scharf would represent me since, as a woman, I could not appear for myself. Hejailan agreed and we sent one copy to him and another copy to the embassy. Hejailan never filed the papers.

Finally, I'd had enough. I called Assistant Secretary of State Joan Clark and requested that she ask Prince Bandar if I could fly to Riyadh for two weeks and see my daughters. The Saudi embassy sent a letter back to the State Department with this response: "It would not be in the best interests of the children to see their mother . . . a contest of wills would surely develop."

That was it—I couldn't take it anymore. It was over. I was finished with politics. After three years of bare knuckle fighting for my kids with Washington and the Saudis, they wouldn't even let me visit them.

I called Ed Ciriello. "Ed . . . we're ready."

In a very Bostonian-Ciriello way, he said, "Kid, fasten your seat belt for 'Operation Saud-eye.'"

8

ALLAH AND LITTLE GIRLS

JANUARY 1989–JUNE 1991

Remember, no amount of aggravation, nonsense,
pride swallowing or just plain foolishness will deter us.
I'm not interested in winning every battle—just the war.
—Ed Ciriello, May 1989

The Key to the Kingdom

By January 1989 Ed Ciriello was working on trying to get a job inside Saudi Arabia that would allow him to obtain a visa into the country. This took some doing because he couldn't very well submit his real résumé, which would have placed him on the "Red Alert List" of undesirables to be excluded from the kingdom. So, we waited.

In June I got the call from Ed. He was in Texas on a job interview and was very excited. "Pat, I can't believe they went for it. I did it! God, they want me to leave within the month. Well, kid, we're goin' to 'Saud-eye.'"

I flew down the stairs to tell my mother, who was busy cooking at the stove. "Mom, it's Ed. He's going. He got the job in Arabia. Mom, we're going to get the kids back."

Ed got the necessary documents together and his visa from the Saudi embassy was finalized. He was hired by Metcalf & Eddy, a U.S. company that was involved in environmental construction projects, and was sent to Al Kharj, approximately sixty miles from Riyadh. Ed put together a résumé to fit the job description and without the firm checking his references, he was hired.

A few days before he left for Arabia, on the Fourth of July, he went out on Boston Harbor in his boat, *The Private Eye*. The beauty of the night sky aglow with fireworks was so emotional for him—so American. He told me he kept thinking about the girls and the mission that lay before him. While he was driving back to the pier a small craft came alongside his boat. He noticed the name on the back—*Aliyah*.

Will You Take Just One?

It was August 1989 and Ed was unpacked and ready for the first part of the mission—reconnaissance. Saudi Arabia is a mercenary/private investigator's nightmare. There are no street lamps to stand under, no unmarked, inconspicuous cars to hang out in on the street while you do surveillance, and no cheap, local informants you can safely buy.

Saudi culture is a closed society. Everyone watches everyone else. Saudis know their neighbors well. There are no pedestrians taking leisurely walks. No sidewalks and no house numbers. Mail is not delivered to private residences, and streets have no street signs. The Arabs know where they are going, but few Westerners, even if they speak Arabic, can find their way around without a guide.

High, concrete walls surround each residence or villa. There is usually a small, metal door in the front of each residence, which is tightly secured. Small slits in the concrete walls of these villas serve as windows. People spend very little time outdoors. Women in black are ushered in and out of these concrete mausoleums into waiting cars driven by a hired, Third World man possibly from Yemen, Pakistan, Egypt, or the Philippines to take them to the souk or to visit friends. There are very few other places women can go. There are no cinemas, no public assembly allowed, no cultural events, no public libraries, no public swimming pools or parks.

There are no outlets for the Saudi people. From a population of twenty million Saudis, 65 percent are under the age of twenty-five. Unemployment is high, and the youth have few channels to pursue—the women have none, except marriage at an early age and multiple pregnancies.

A non-Saudi or Westerner would be a red flag in a Saudi neighborhood and reported to the Saudi police immediately. And there are plenty of police around—secret police, religious police, and military police. A virtual armed camp. Ed was entering a dangerous situation and he knew it.

After Ed left for Saudi Arabia, I decided to move back to San Francisco to be near my daughter Daina, who was attending college. My son's condition had improved somewhat, and he had come to live with me in Chicago so I could care for him. When we returned to San Francisco I rented a comfortable flat near Golden Gate Park and got a nursing job. The city had changed in the four years I had been gone—first to Saudi Arabia and then to Chicago. AIDS had ravaged San Francisco and the smell of suffering and death permeated the hospital I worked in. It was extremely difficult to care for the increased numbers of dying young men who were undergoing intense pain and anguish.

Memories of the girls were everywhere: Golden Gate Park and Spreckles Lake where the girls wore their rainbow vests as they happily chased toy sailboats along the shore, the children's playground with the carousel, the beach, the house where we had lived—all brought up images of their little faces and sweet smiles.

Plan A

On a weekend visit to Riyadh, Ed happened to meet an old friend he had worked with from British Military Intelligence. They spent the day together talking about old times. He accompanied his friend to the compound where he lived with his wife. She was a Pakistani teacher who worked in the Saudi school system. Ed felt comfortable confiding in these two and told them about his mission. The man and his wife, Noora, were sympathetic. They offered to help. Noora would search for the girls in the Saudi schools.

Ed was encouraged by this and began to make plans to take the girls out through the Kuwaiti border. He bought a truck with a hidden compartment—just big enough for two small girls. He made a "dry run" and found a way out and across into Kuwait. Now he only needed the cooperation of the girls. They would have to calmly walk out of the school with the Pakistani teacher, get into Ed's truck, and hide in the compartment until they were safely across the border.

In the meantime, Noora had found the girls and began to cautiously talk to Alia, who was now ten years old. Would she ever like to see her mother? Would she like to go back to the United States? Alia responded, "Yes. I want to go back and be with my mommy, but Allah will kill my whole family if I leave."

Alia was scared to death by the lies of Gheshayan and his family. The wrath of Allah would befall everyone she had grown to bond with—the only safety net she knew. Would Aisha go? What had they done to her? Ed wrote to me and asked if I would take one child and not the other. I couldn't leave one behind. I couldn't make that choice . . . that "Sophie's choice." Oh no. Not the anguish of getting one to freedom and the other left to languish without her sister with Gheshayan as her master. Which one? Alia? Aisha? All they ever had was each other. If one refused to go, they must both stay until we could get them out safely—together.

Alia's Rainbow

After that I didn't hear from Ed for a while. I lived for any communication from him. Each time I ran to my mailbox and found one of his letters, I felt both joy and dread. Had something happened? Did he have good news? A new way out?

I lived like this for the entire two years Ed was in the kingdom. My life had stood still the moment my daughters were taken away from me. I had no purpose in life except to free them from the hell they were in, and no one knew that hell better than I. But I had no power to help my children, and the feelings of helplessness and hopelessness pierced my soul. I cried to God for help. I was aware of a "Presence" with me all the time and the signs I had been given were kept close to my heart, but the day-by-day and year-by-year buildup of torment and grief was almost too much for me to bear.

The sleepless nights and tortured dreams added to my throbbing, haunted memories of Alia crying for me all alone in a dark room while her father kept guard outside with the "mean grandmother," as she used to call Fatima. Alia would run to me to get away from her; now she had no one to run to.

My heart ached as I imagined my girls' even occasional exposure to the torridness of the Arabian sun. The penetrating heat caused exhaustion from the slightest exposure, such as walking from a building to a car. And the madness of being locked up inside the walls of a villa with nowhere to go, nothing to read, and no one to talk to. Sand and rocks with no green, no vegetation. And for diversion—nothing.

Alia loved the movie *The Wizard of Oz*. I bought a video copy of the old Judy Garland classic when the girls and I moved to Chicago. They watched it over and over again. One day Alia told me, "Mommy, I want to go over the rainbow just like Dorothy." She pretended she was Dorothy and her cat was Toto. And over the rainbow she went. Far away from her home and all she knew, into a strange land with strange people with a strange language she knew nothing about. There were no Barbie dolls or happy birthday parties there. (Saudis don't celebrate birthdays.)

There were no ruby slippers or good witches to protect her. I was fighting with all my might to bring her and her little sister home, but the forces were fraught with evil and had a tight grip.

One night I dreamed that Ed and I were trapped in a deep pit, each of us holding a little baby. Above was a high glass wall that surrounded the pit. Looking down on us from the other side of this glass wall was Khalid—smiling.

You Must Believe in Spring

It was April 1990, and the cycle of working in the hospital, waiting for some word from Ed Ciriello, and the cumulative effect of the last four years of constant worry and stress were taking a toll on my health. I developed a heart arrhythmia, constant attacks of low blood sugar, and chronic anxiety. A long-time friend thought my aloneness was unhealthy and I needed to become more active socially and start to enjoy my life. She wanted me to meet a friend of her friend's husband. He was a gifted musician who was recently divorced and available. I hesitated and thought, *That's the last thing I need—a man who is coming out of a seventeen-year marriage.* "No, thank you."

But my friend was persistent and invited me to her home for dinner and without my knowledge also invited David.

I walked into her kitchen and faced the French doors that opened onto the deck. The lights from the Bay glistened in the background. He was sitting at the table, looking through a book. When he raised his head, our eyes met and we were instantly engaged in a spell-like trance. His swarthy complexion, green-hazel eyes, and muscular strength were obviously attractive, but an indefinable inner essence jolted me off balance. I had never experienced that type of feeling before. It transcended any attraction I'd ever had for a man. It overwhelmed me and scared me at the same time.

The energy and oneness between us were so powerful that I couldn't refuse to see him. Among all my trials in my journey to rescue my daughters, now there was David.

Flying Carpets and Ali Baba

I found out years later that during this time, Ed was busy making contacts with a local drug smuggler in hopes of getting the girls out through either Jordan or Qatar. How does a fifty-seven-year-old former "spook," as operatives are known in the business, go about getting two young, scared, abused girls out of the Arabian desert?

This was a hostile Arab country with no good, clean borders, surrounded by water on three sides. Inside, high-tech surveillance systems monitor movement, keeping track of who's going where. These systems, bought from and supported by U.S. companies, make free travel impossible. How could Ed do this without either getting his head cut off or ending up spending the rest of his life in a filthy, three-by-six Saudi jail cell with rats and cockroaches for company?

He couldn't go around and ask the American military for help. He couldn't recruit the local Saudi boys or expats or Third World souls working as indentured slaves. They would surely turn him into the Saudi police for the fat reward. No, there was no one Ed could trust. He was alone.

Ed had savvy and guts, but more than that he had an unexplainable intuitiveness that had kept him alive all these years under intense circumstances. My faith and confidence in Ed never wavered. But this seemed a Mission Impossible that even Ed couldn't solve.

Meeting "Ali Baba" might prove the answer. Ali, a Saudi of about forty, knew the borders well. He brought items in and out and had a band of about six men who worked with him.

While working in Al-Kharj, Ed was searching for a way to meet the "bad guys" who knew their way around and could be persuaded for a sum of money to do a job. He began with another American and casually asked if he knew where some hashish could be bought. This led to the local drug dealer. After quite a long time of careful courting, Ed asked him if he knew anyone who could supply a larger quantity and a better quality. Ali Baba came on the scene at that time.

Ed and Ali and his band would meet in the desert and sit drinking cardamom-flavored Arabic coffee and talk. They pulled their vehicles over along the side of the road, took an Arabian carpet out, and spread it on the desert floor. Ed spent many hours with Ali before he could even approach the subject of whether Ali could get something across the border for Ed— something a little larger than hashish.

Protected Life

During this time I was grinding away with worry in San Francisco, receiving only vague notes from Ed from time to time. He couldn't dare tell me what he was plotting. It was delicate, and he didn't even know if Ali would go for it or if it was possible. I was working through the nurses' registry and one morning they sent me to Kaiser Hospital in Oakland. I had never been there before and was assigned to the post-op recovery room. It was very early, and no surgery patients had yet come back to recovery.

I was sitting at a desk in a large room with empty gurneys and IV poles when a very pretty young woman—another nurse—approached me. She was petite with dark eyes and short dark brown hair, dressed in a green scrub dress. As I stood up to greet her she said, "Hello, my name is Aisha. What's your name?"

This was the exact, verbatim expression my daughter Aisha would say to strangers we met in public. Unable to respond, I just stared at her, but the words didn't come out. Finally I heard myself utter, "Pat." She looked at me very strangely and walked away. I was trembling and short of breath. I went to sit down and wondered if I had imagined what happened. Where was she now? I looked across the room and couldn't find her. Was it an angel? Another sign? Was I finally losing my mind?

About ten minutes passed and she entered the room again. I decided to talk to her. This was too much of a coincidence. I had to know more. "Are you an Arab? Where are you from?"

"No. My father was Pakistani and my mother was Irish."

"I have a daughter named Aisha. Her father is a Saudi. In Arabic Aisha means 'life.'"

With a whimsical look she said, "In Pakistani, Aisha means 'protected life.'"

The next day the registry sent me back to Kaiser Oakland. It was lunchtime. I saw Nurse Aisha in the hall. She smiled and waved. It was funny, even her mannerisms were like those of little Aisha. I had my lunch tray in hand and sat down in a booth. I immediately noticed a small white, folded paper right next to me on the seat of the booth. Of course, I picked it up and opened it. It said, "Justice Shall Prevail 7-11." I wondered what it could mean. The ages of the girls at that time were seven and eleven. I kept the note. God was fortifying me. No matter what happens, Aisha is protected and there will be justice. But when?

The "A Team"

Finally I received some news:

5 September 1990

Dear Pat,

After what seems like an amazing and agonizing amount of time and effort, I have finally been accepted into the inner circle of "Ali Baba" and his forty thieves. Actually a Saudi with about six guys, but they seem ready to do business. I'm still not 100 percent sure they can do it—lack of guts mostly—but at the moment we almost trust each other.

The downside is of course money. Up till now we have been doing the usual Arab waltz. Coffee, talk, and more coffee. Now we have made it to the semifinals. Their price for a straight-out kidnapping is 200,000 riyals ($60K). Half up front. The balance after we cross the border. Understand, after I tell them the "whole" truth about what they must do the price will go up again. But for now they accept what I have proposed for the amount quoted.

Time is important. This "war" threat is the perfect cover. If there was ever a good time to do this, now is that time. In fact, if they go to shooting, it might even improve our position!

Too bad the State Department will not track his Arab ass for us. If he ever took them out of the country, the rest would be much easier than what we have planned here. Well, there is no chance of their help—never was—so we stay with what we have.

Money in large quantities with no guarantee of any results is where we are. No one but me wants to do this just because it needs doing. Money makes the best motivator for some and especially for smuggling and cattle rustlers.

Any ideas?

Ed

Iraq entered Kuwait as Ed and Ali were consolidating the "deal." We needed money and a lot of it. My mother and I got together what we could to meet Ed's request and sent him cashier's checks made out to "Cash" in small denominations of $4–5,000 each. Then we waited. U.S. troops were all over the region, and we were hopeful that there would be enough chaos to afford Ed and Ali the necessary cover. They planned and we prayed.

I called the U.S. Embassy in Riyadh and asked if they could intervene and get my daughters out of Saudi Arabia. I asked about the scud missiles I was seeing on the nightly news, the possibility of germ warfare and poison gas. And they told me, "Ms. Roush, we are perfectly safe here in Riyadh, and there is no need for you to be alarmed."

During this time I was on a television talk show and off-camera met a former marine colonel who worked for the CIA. They were busy sending supplies to Kuwait from Dhahran, Saudi Arabia. This man, whom I'll call Geoff, had rescued two American boys from Kuwait City a few months before and was interested in my story. I hoped he could help me.

A Window Opens

While Ed Ciriello and Ali were planning the details of the grab-and-escape, Geoff called me. He told me there was a "golden window of opportunity" to get the kids out, but it would be there for only a brief time. I had to act now. He was in touch with a few helicopter pilots and told them about my daughters. They wanted to help but would not grab the girls. They would get them out of Saudi Arabia but could not physically take them away from Gheshayan. If I could arrange with Ed to grab them and give them to the pilots, they would get them out. Geoff would arrange for me to get inside the country, and he would be with me when the kids were handed over to me. Together, we would get on the helicopter from Riyadh and be dropped directly onto the base in Dhahran. The kids and I would then be safely put on an American military cargo plane and taken to London.

My heart stopped. This was too wonderful. Ed had told me never to call him, but the mail took weeks to get through. I took a chance and called his company in Al-Kharj anyway. I left a message, but he didn't call back. He later told me Ali and the boys were not ready for the grab. They were not prepared, and it would have been suicide to do it at that time. I told Geoff the news. He was sorry. I was devastated.

In time, however, "D-Day" was set. I received the following letter from Ed:

November 12, 1990

Dear Pat:

The money was received from your mother and will be passed on to Ali Baba when we meet . . .

I fully expect things to go slower than I would like, but this is Saudi and nothing gets done on time. The actual grab could be as late as Xmas or even later.

When it actually happens someone will call you and give you the information you need. If things go all wrong you will be contacted and told.

I want you to understand and accept that if I get killed during this operation, I would have died with the full knowledge of what I was doing and you are to accept no guilt for it. None at all. I do this with my eyes wide open and will have no regrets if it ends in my death. I want you to have no regrets also.

These next few weeks are going to be very difficult for you, and all I can say is try not to worry more than necessary. Don't be hard on yourself. Just wait until you hear something. It will be before or slightly after 1 Jan. so grit your teeth and take it slow.

Everything is moving toward our goal and all is under control. With any luck at all the deed will be done, we'll all cross the border safely, and no one will be the wiser until it's too late.

Take care, Pat. Remember, no regrets and no panic. Just follow the instructions exactly, and hopefully this nightmare will soon be over.

Ed

D-Day

They were ready. I received a note that the day would be January 18, 1991. The "war" had broken out two days earlier. I was a little worried about this, but hoped maybe it would not matter or possibly even make things easier. I was nervous but had faith and hope that all would go well. The plan was for me to wait for the call and then take a plane to Qatar and pick up the girls. They would be waiting for me with Ed, and Ali and his band would be spending their money happily.

But it didn't happen that way. It was 6:00 A.M. on the morning of January 18 when the phone rang. It was Ed's friend Bobbe from Boston. There was trouble. Two men were killed and Ed was under house arrest. They were on their way in early morning to get the girls, and about six blocks from the Gheshayan villa they were caught in a police shoot-out.

There were three vehicles in Ed's caravan. What they call a crash car was in front, with one of Ali's men driving. Next was a van with Ali and his driver and all the "equipment" including several guns, duct tape, electrical tie wraps, and whatever else they needed. Ed brought up the rear in a Chevy Blazer.

The caravan was stopped at a traffic light in early morning when several Saudi police cars came speeding past them, firing at another unrelated vehicle. The crash car was already through the intersection, but Ali's driver panicked and began firing at the racing police cars. The police then shot back, killing the driver.

Ali got out of the van and ran to Ed's Blazer. Ed took out his gun and killed Ali on the spot because by getting into Ed's vehicle, Ali had implicated Ed in this shoot-out. Mayhem broke out. Police were all over Ed. There were two dead bodies. Some of the Saudi police believed Ed when he said he took the gun away from Ali and just defended himself against this aggressor, but one or two of them didn't buy it.

They took Ed to police headquarters, interrogated him, and then after a few hours let him leave.

After his release from jail, Ed sent the following letter:

20 January 1991

Dear Pat,

By now my friend Bobbe has called you and told you what happened. What else can I say?

Briefly here's what happened: On the way to the house a local police car somehow got involved and started shooting at the van where Ali and his driver were. I was behind him and did not see it start. The two are dead, the third got away, and I am under house arrest until the cops clear me of any involvement. At the moment they believe I was just in the wrong place at the wrong time, and I do not feel that I am in any real danger. For now there is nothing to be done except wait.

I'm not in the proper frame of mind to write the details of this . . . mess, but when I get out I will talk to you. Meanwhile, there is nothing left to do. I should tell you that Ali is dead because I shot him after he jumped out of the van and ran to my truck. The cops think I was just defending myself but since the Arab mind loves a conspiracy they, or at least a couple of them, want to tie me to him. I, we, can only wait to see if they can.

Stay tuned.

Ed

How Much Is Enough?

Once the police found out that Ali Baba was a drug smuggler, Ed was cleared of all wrongdoing. While I was waiting for the news of his release I had another dream about Ed. He was sitting in my living room smiling, and I thought about how wonderful it was to be able to talk to him and ask him all about what happened. I had received a box of Valentine chocolates that were on my desk. Another box was delivered to me by messenger, and after I answered the door, I put the second box of chocolates on top of the first box. The card read, "How much is enough?" It was signed just "E," the same way Ed signed many of his letters. Then I looked up at him; he was smiling at me, and I knew it was from him. Then I woke up. The interpretation was "Just how far are you willing to take this, lady? How far will you go to get these kids back?"

Ed returned to Boston. Then in June 1991 he flew to San Francisco to talk to me. He returned the photos I had given him to identify Gheshayan and the girls, along with Alia's rainbow vest, which he was going to use to identify himself to her as a friend sent by her mommy. I hadn't seen him since before he went to Arabia. His fifty-eight years were beginning to show. His friend Peter, a former British rock recording artist whom Ed met in Bangkok and who now lived in San Francisco, was with him. We all met for dinner on Union Street. It was awkward—a lot of small talk and then I confronted him about the killings and the girls. I at least wanted some information—like Khalid's telephone number and the location of my girls. Ed said Ali Baba had that information, and he was dead.

The Mystical Medal

It was now all over. Ed Ciriello was right. There are no guarantees and it is all about money. Since we had only limited cash, we had to rely on drug smugglers who were not professional enough to make it past Saudi police who were not even chasing them. But who knows what would have happened at the villa? They were going to go over the wall into the courtyard and overcome Gheshayan, his wife, driver, and maid. Something could have gone wrong. But something could have gone right. I felt this risk was worth it. There was no other way. For three years I begged the State Department for help and they refused. We were not rich, and we found someone willing to go and try. I would do it again under the same circumstances.

It was so unfair—Gheshayan with my girls. I struggled with my questions for God. I could hardly keep going. I was planning a trip to Chicago around Aisha's birthday, July 2. I wanted to see my mother and visit the Icon at St. Nicholas. Just before I left I was working at Kaiser again—this time in Redwood City. They sent me to the oncology unit—5 North. There was a cancer patient in one of the rooms—a woman in her mid-forties. She'd lost her hair due to chemotherapy, and the cancer was ravaging her body. I entered her room in response to a call light and noticed that she had a group of visitors around her bedside. Several of the men in the group looked Middle Eastern. I cringed.

Later in the day, as I was preparing to give my report and go home, one of the younger men came out of Joyce's room. He was standing at the desk at the nurses' station. For some unknown reason, I approached him and asked him where he was from. He was the patient's son and said his father was Iranian and his mother was an American.

The boy was tall, with dark hair and dark eyes, and he had a sweet smile. He reminded me of Alia. I don't know why. I just had a feeling. We talked a little and I mentioned to him that I had two daughters in Saudi Arabia, then I went home.

The next morning Joyce was assigned to me as my patient. I entered her room and she smiled, "My son told me about your daughters. I am so sorry."

The day went on and she had many, many visitors. Joyce had recently been diagnosed with metastatic cancer—it was in many organs of her body. Within two months it had devastated her. Her prognosis was bleak and she knew it. Friends had flown in from different areas to say good-bye. She had an ex-husband who had arrived from Iran, her two boys, and her male companion, who was very devoted to her.

It was afternoon and all the visitors had gone. She turned on her call light. I entered and said, "Hi, Joyce. Are you okay?"

"Pat, I want to give you something. Is that allowed?"

"It depends on what it is."

"It doesn't mean anything to anyone but me, and it is the most special thing in my life. I want you to have it. You listen to me, Pat. I am at the end of my life, and God is talking to me. I had my boys when they were little but will not be able to be with them now that they are grown men. I will not live to see my grandchildren. You didn't have your daughters when they were little girls but will have them as adults and you will see your grandchildren."

She was wearing a small, pewter medal on her neck with the words *St. Jude* written under the image of a man. It was old and on a silver chain. She took it off and placed it around my neck. While fastening the clip, she said, "My aunt sent it to me when I lived in Iran so many years ago. It brought me luck. You might not think so now, with the condition I am in, but it will be good for you. I don't mind dying, but I hate to be in pain and leave my sons."

"Joyce, we can keep you comfortable without pain, and you are not dying. Just this body is dying. Your spirit will not die and is going to God. Don't be afraid. Your boys are fine young men. They will be all right. How old are they?"

"Shaheen was twenty-five on December 16 and Sean was just twenty-two on June 11."

"Joyce, June 11 is my birthday! And December 16 is my friend's birthday! This is amazing; this can't be coincidence. Don't worry. Be peaceful, Joyce. You will be fine."

Just then the telephone rang in her room. It was her mother calling from New York. Our special moment ended and I left the room shaking. I went on my lunch break and called David (December 16 was his birthday). "You won't believe what just happened . . ." As I was talking to him, the silver chain holding the medal broke in my hands. I fixed it, put it back on my neck, and returned to the floor. About an hour later I looked and the chain was broken and the medal gone. I cried . . . *this must be a bad sign*. A dying woman had just given me her most valued possession, this special sacramental, and I'd lost it! I looked everywhere and couldn't find it. It was so small and the hospital was so big—if it was found, it would be a miracle.

I went home in despair. After going out for dinner with David, I came home to find a message on my answering machine—it was the nursing office: "You are working at Kaiser Hospital tomorrow and, by the way, some-one found your medal."

David and I visited Joyce at her home a couple of weeks later. Her sons were caring for her, and I took a picture of my girls and placed it beside her bed. "Joyce, don't be afraid. God is with you. Everything will be fine."

As I was leaving her home, her son, Sean, said to me, "My mother thinks you're very special. Meeting you has meant a lot to her."

Joyce died one week later.

9

SOLDIER OF FORTUNE FLYTRAP

July 1991–September 1994

Taylor told me this child abduction angle is the most lucrative,
moneymaking part of his business.
—Terry Douglas, Former Chief of Station, CIA,
stationed in Saudi Arabia

Beloved

David and I were having one of our "all-day dream days" when we would go from one activity to the other and laugh, tell stories, and melt into each other's eyes. He played piano, any kind of music you wanted—jazz, Latin, classics, oldies, swing—and I would either dance or stand by the piano and sing. Picnics at the beach, long walks in the surf, candlelight dinners, and listening to music by the fireplace were our favorite ways to spend time together. It was the kind of love I'd always wanted and could never find. He was everything I'd dreamed of in a man: handsome beyond description, caring, intelligent, talented, creative, and spontaneous. His visual disability gave him a kind of sixth sense. He was the only child of an Italian father and a Latin mother. They had lost several children in infancy and were very protective of their only child and gave him their undivided attention. His marriage to an older woman from Germany produced two daughters. After seventeen years, their marriage ended in a bitter divorce. When I met him he was forty and looking for a fresh start. He soon went back to college and became a special education teacher for the blind. He felt he had a calling for this because of his visual disability.

Music was his first love and he played in bands, trios, performed solo for all kinds of occasions—clubs, weddings, parties—and became accomplished enough to play with some of the well-known San Francisco musical groups. After his mother's death and his divorce, he moved into his father's house in a downstairs apartment. His father and I got along great and spent hours talking about Italy, politics, religion, and the state of the world. David's daughters loved my daughter, Daina, and we would have big family get-togethers. David and I would cook and he would play piano or accordion, which he played like a romantic dream—whatever he played, he played with feeling and soul. I loved him and he said he loved me. He would leave me notes all over my apartment—under my pillow, in the teapot, in my nursing bag— "Pat, do you know how much I love you? Sweet dreams, my lovely . . ."

We both loved the water and we spent much of our time together either in the water, on the water, or talking about the water. Hawaii was our favorite getaway destination. One day David and I were at Ocean Beach in San Francisco, lying on a beach blanket, when he said, "Pat, I want to marry you. I want to spend the rest of my life with you. I never thought I could love a woman this much. I get butterflies in my stomach whenever I'm anywhere near you. I'll never let you go."

His divorce was final on my birthday, June 11. Although I loved him deeply, I couldn't take that step. Something inside just said no. I had issues of trust after my shattered past and wasn't sure I could ever make that kind of commitment. I had days of deep depression and had no plan of how to get my daughters back. God was with me and I knew the signs were there, but everything I tried failed. What did God have in mind? Would this ever be over?

CTU

It was six months after Ed's mission ended in tragedy, and I was depressed about not having a plan to get the girls out. Then one day I was lying on the sofa reading *Time* magazine and noticed an article: "Rent-a-Rescue Commandos: Ex-Delta Force Operatives Hunt for Abducted Kids." I sat straight up. "Hey Dave, look at this! Ya think they'll go to Saudi? . . . They probably want a fortune . . . Ah, I don't have any more money, anyway."

Another month went by and I thought, *Why not just call them. What have I got to lose?*

They called themselves CTU, Corporate Training Unit, and were based in Fayetteville, North Carolina. Dave Chatellier, a former U.S. military-intelligence officer, answered the phone when I called.

I told him the story. He replied, "The worst thing is that your children have been gone for so long. We really like to take cases where the kids are gone for less than a year. Tell you what, send me the information on your case and I'll take a look at it and get back to you."

A week later Judy Feeney called me. Her husband, Don, a former member of the Delta Force, had founded the organization with Chatellier. She said they'd take my case and work out payment somehow, maybe signing over my rights to the story as they had done with another woman's case. They wanted to meet me personally. Every year there is a convention in Las Vegas sponsored by *Soldier of Fortune* magazine. CTU was going to have a booth and give evasive driving classes. Judy suggested I meet them there.

It was September 1991 and I was in the lobby of the Sahara Hotel, Las Vegas, Nevada. It was filled with men in camouflage military outfits, T-shirted, blue-jeaned fifty-something-year-olds with large stomachs and baseball caps, and an assortment of vendors selling anything from knives and guns to protection services. I left a message for Judy and Don from the house phone and went to the coffee shop.

As I was sipping my tea and savoring a slice of apple pie, I looked up and saw a blond, full-figured soccer-mom type with red-framed glasses standing over me. "Hi, Pat? I'm Judy Feeney." She called Don from a nearby phone and he walked in with Tommy Carter, a former buddy from the Delta. We sat at a table and talked. I had sent them the Hejailan tape of my daughters, and Carter said the girls were suffering from "Stockholm syndrome," in which prisoners of war start to identify with their captors. We talked a little more and then Tommy said, "If Donny says we go, we go." Then he left. Don walked out, and Judy and I went into the casino and I watched her play blackjack on the machine. She was optimistic about what they could do for me and told me they had access to radar in Saudi Arabia. She wished I had called them during the Gulf War when they had operatives on the ground in the kingdom. I promised to meet them the next day in the parking lot of the Sahara to watch their evasive driving class.

The next morning after breakfast I went to the open lot where cars were spinning in 180-degree turns at high speeds. Wow! These guys were really good! My confidence in them was increasing by the second. These were actual commandos! As I was watching Tommy Carter and Judy Feeney take turns teaching carloads of amateur, wanna-be mercenary types who'd paid $200 for a two-hour fantasy in the car acrobatic class, I noticed a tall, forty-ish, broad-shouldered man making his way toward me across the parking lot/race course. "Pat? I'm Dave Chatellier. We spoke on the phone. I understand Don has agreed to take your case. I just want you to know that I'm resigning from CTU and won't be a part of the operation, but I wish you good luck." He spoke with a charming country accent and I noticed he was wearing a hearing aid—probably the result of some military experience. Judy told me he used to wrestle alligators in Louisiana. I was somehow sorry he wouldn't be part of what we were planning.

When Don was discharged from the Delta he needed to transform his military expertise into marketable skills in the civilian world. He connected with Chatellier and CTU was born. Corporate Training Unit started out being a service offered to business executives to defend themselves from possible abduction or foul play. In the eighties there was a wave of kidnappings involving business executives, and CTU filled a need by teaching them defensive and preventive techniques.

They got into the child rescue business a few years after that when one of their men met a woman whose child was kidnapped and taken to Jordan. They succeeded in pulling off a very dangerous, dramatic rescue of the young girl and it became very publicized—a television movie was even made, *Desperate Rescue*, starring Mariel Hemingway. Feeney, Chatellier, and company were depicted in car chases across the sand and crossing over the Allenby Bridge into Israel with the child. They were also successful in another case of a pregnant American woman in grave jeopardy with her child in Tunisia. While visiting at the home of Betty Mahmoody who had escaped with her daughter from Iran, I met the rescued woman, Lorie Swint, after she was freed. Her parents were autoworkers from Michigan. They paid CTU $80,000, and signed over the story rights for the rescue of their daughter, granddaughter, and unborn grandchild.

Don Feeney was a forty-year-old tough Italian-Irish guy from Brooklyn who joined the army in his teens. I told my friend from the CIA—the one that tried to help me get the kids out—about Don, and he said, "Pat, stay away from him. He's got a reputation as a hothead and quick on the trigger." As long as even-tempered, methodical, seasoned veteran Chatellier was around he could balance any impulsiveness in Don Feeney, but Chatellier was getting tired of the constant interference by Don's wife, Judy. She left her three children with her mother and decided she was an "undercover agent." This irritated Chatellier, who wanted it to be a guys-only thing. He was used to the military and thought Judy should stay home where she belonged. Don continued to include her in all his plans and Dave Chatellier wanted out. There were other reasons he wanted to cut relations with Don, but I found out about all of those secrets after it was too late.

Feeney had problems with managing money, and as Judy's mother used to say, "Donny will borrow from Peter to pay Paul." Don and Judy liked the good life. Judy told me, "We like to fly first class because we fly so much." It's easy to fly first class when you're flying on someone else's money, but hard to justify it when your clients are working-class parents and grandparents of a kidnapped child. Feeney had gotten into trouble with the IRS, and Chatellier wanted his name off the books of the CTU. He was afraid he would lose his farm and everything else.

I spent months trying to get money together for another rescue operation. It turned out that they wanted the rights to my story plus money up front. In January 1992 my mother and I came up with $25,000. I called Judy. "That's wonderful, Pat. We have a plan, and Don and I will fly to San Francisco to meet you."

David and I met them in the coffee shop at the Doubletree Hotel near the San Francisco Airport. It was January 25—the anniversary of the kidnapping. They wanted the money electronically deposited into one of their accounts. I also brought $5,000 cash in a brown envelope and handed it to Don. He began, "We lost our contact with the radar inside Saudi Arabia so we came up with a plan to lure this guy out. How would he react if he found out that you died and left a lot of money to your daughters?"

"He won't go for that. He's too smart and he expects a trick. He's very paranoid to begin with."

"No, let's just say you had married a very rich man who left you a lot of money and then you suddenly got killed in a car accident. All your money is left to the kids and he has to come here with the kids to collect. Simple."

"It's a waste of time. Nothing can make him take those kids outside of Saudi Arabia unless a miracle happens."

"We can make a death certificate. We just bought some software that can make it look real authentic."

"No, I don't want to do that. I want you to go in and get my daughters out of there. That's what we talked about. Nothing else will work."

I told them that Khalid's father had had cardiac surgery at the Cleveland Clinic in 1975 and most certainly had been back to the clinic since the girls were kidnapped. Maybe we could set up a trap there. Did they have any way to get Hamad's medical records? I asked the FBI to get that information but the agent, Joe Dorley from Chicago, screamed at me, "Lady, what do you want me to do— take on the whole Saudi government?" Judy said they had a contact who could get anything we wanted from the clinic. As we said good-bye Don asked that they be able to meet my mother. When I asked why, he said that in an operation like this they wanted to meet with all relevant members of the family.

After a few weeks, Don agreed that faking my death wouldn't work. They came up with another plan. The year prior they were on another case involving an Arab who was being held against his will in Saudi Arabia. After getting him out of the kingdom they felt they could call upon him for a favor. They asked him to call Khalid in Riyadh and help set up a "sting" operation to lure him out of Saudi Arabia. He was able to locate the telephone number of Khalid's father's office and a dialog soon developed with Tarik, Khalid's younger brother, about buying some of the Coachman RVs that were parked on the property where I'd lived with my daughters. Tarik was eager to sell them—they were just deteriorating in the hot desert sun. Feeney's friend offered to meet him and Khalid in Cairo for business. Tarik said they never traveled and declined the offer—killing the operation. We did find out that Khalid's father was dead.

In the meantime, Feeney's contact in Cleveland, a Cleveland Police Department investigator, found some answers in the Cleveland Clinic. It was exactly what I thought: Hamad had been going to the clinic for years. His last visit was in 1988, and he was accompanied by his son Khalid. They entered the United States on diplomatic passports under the VIP sponsorship of the Saudi government. I had two State of Illinois felony kidnapping warrants, a United States federal warrant, and the strongest alert in place for Interpol—the Red Alert—all issued in 1986, two years before their diplomatic passports were issued. What good were my warrants if the Saudis could make a mockery of our laws and get everything they wanted? This agent viewed the records on microfiche but did not make a copy for me. So I knew it happened but couldn't prove it to the authorities. The State Department denied it happened at all.

Second Disappearance

It was at about this time that I took the St. Jude medal off my neck and placed it inside a small box containing little gold earrings that belonged to Alia and Aisha. It was a brown, plastic, two-inch-square box with Arabic writing on the outside that had held a purchase I made at the gold market in Saudi Arabia. The girls' little earrings from their babyhood and toddler years were very special to me, and I wanted the medal to be safe. So I carefully laid it on top of the earrings, closed the lid, and wrapped a rubber band around the box. I then placed the container in my large jewelry box on top of my dresser and thought it was secure.

When I went back to the box about a month later the medal was gone. It had disappeared. I took the earrings out of the brown plastic box and laid them all out on my bed—the medal was not there. I took all the jewelry out of the large jewelry box and looked for the medal—it was not in the box. Where could it be? I looked everywhere and couldn't find it. All the other jewelry was accounted for—only the medal was missing.

Don and Judy called and still wanted to meet my mother. I couldn't figure out why this was so important to them. She was a seventy-three-year-old woman living in Chicago—why should this be important to the rescue of my daughters? They persisted in this request and said they were on their way to somewhere and would stop in Chicago for a few hours to meet Mom. She picked them up at Midway Airport and took them out for breakfast in the old neighborhood. She ordered pancakes, and Don and Judy ordered steak and eggs. My mother offered to pay the check and said, "Let me pay for this . . ." Don looked at her and replied, "You already have."

Their appetites, spendthrift behavior, and senseless waste of money were to be their undoing and almost mine. My constant state of anguish and apprehension about my daughters, coupled with the never-ending grief that was nestled in my heart, thrust me into a chronic state of emotional anxiety that drove me to supplicate myself to people like Hejailan and beckon crooked covert operators like the Feeneys to save my children.

Running from the Devil

I called the Feeneys all over the globe. They had plan after plan that ended up in smoke. One minute Don and Tommy Carter were going in to get the kids and the next minute they were off to Bangladesh or London or Karachi. After the publicity they received in *Time* magazine and the television movie plus a book written about them called *Rescue My Child*, they were receiving hundreds of calls from desperate parents. In spring 1992 they disappeared for six weeks and I had no contact with them. Finally they surfaced and Judy had another "plan."

"Listen, Pat, I just got back from London and we met two British women who are security guards for Prince Bandar's mother. They have a way of getting us inside Saudi Arabia and are going to get all of us—including you and the girls—British passports. You'll be able to go in with us and be there when the actual grab is done. We'll all get out on British passports and fly directly to London. Donny is still in London and is not coming back. When everything is arranged, he will fly into Saudi Arabia and send for us after he finishes the recon and is ready to get the kids. Why don't you come down here to Fayetteville for a week and we can go over some things. I have another woman coming tomorrow—you'll like Sarah—and then we'll all drive to Marietta, Ohio, to meet Sarah Hill [another Sarah], whose little boy is in Pakistan."

Judy picked me up at the airport in Fayetteville in her van and as we pulled into the driveway of her home, a beautiful young woman with waist-length black hair and deep-set azure eyes ran out of the house to greet us. "Hi. I'm Sarah. You must be Pat. Can I help you carry your luggage? I have dinner waiting."

This was my first impression of Sarah Anderson Noman, a twenty-five-year-old, five-foot-one child in a woman's body, whose brutalization by her Yemenese husband ended with the kidnapping of her two young children to Yemen about one year before I met her in June 1992. Sarah was in a state of desolation over the loss of her children and unable to focus on anything except getting them back. She met Don and Judy and they promised to rescue her children.

The daughter of an Anglican priest and an oncology nurse from Tacoma, Washington, Sarah had suffered from dyslexia and attention deficit disorder as a child. An early marriage to a large, thickset Yemenese student who beat her petite body to a pulp caused her to seek recourse from the U.S. court system to protect her children, A'isha, who was two at the time, and Omar, six, from being taken to Yemen. Sarah requested supervised visitation for the children, which was denied by a family court judge. So they were easily whisked out of the United States to Yemen.

Once you met her, you would never forget her. She always had her guitar along and strummed a tune while she sang her original songs with a lilting voice—an entertainer who could stop the show. She attracted a lot of men—the wrong kind—who preyed on her naïveté and childlike innocence. She was always finding "Mr. Right." I teased her about her choices but couldn't prevent her from falling into the same traps. This was a fatal flaw for Sarah that would finally be the cause of her early demise.

After taking the tour of CTU, target practicing at the shooting range (I had taken shooting lessons and practiced my marksmanship regularly to protect and defend myself), and meeting Judy's family and kids, Sarah, Judy, and I were off to Marietta, Ohio, to pick up Sarah Hill. Her retired college professor father had refinanced his modest home to bankroll a Feeney rescue of her son in Pakistan. Don went to Karachi from London, and the "British Passport Plan" for my daughters' rescue was never discussed again. After months inside Pakistan, Don returned to Fayetteville. He was never able to get the boy away from his father or find a safe escape route. All of the professor's money was gone and another family was shattered.

The Feeneys kept telling Sarah Anderson Noman they were going to Yemen after Pakistan but they never went in. They continually gave me vague runarounds also. I became tired of story after story and after I heard about the failed mission in Pakistan, I became more and more depressed. I knew they weren't going to rescue my children, but I had no idea what to do next.

Early Warnings

David and I were together but I kept seeing things about him that troubled me deeply. One night I accompanied him to a private party that he was playing with his trio. On a break his friend Carl and I were talking and certain

Esther and Bella Papa—Mary Queen of Heaven Church (August 1941)

Esther and Pat—the prairie on 54th Street (1947)

Pat Roush and David Roush, Museum of Science and Industry, Chicago (1976)

Esther's seventieth birthday (June 14, 1988)

"Nonnie" (Esther) and Daina's son Ryan six months before her death (June 1999)

Khalid Gheshayan in San Francisco, shortly after arriving in America (1974)

Unknown Saudi, Khalid Gheshayan, and Khalid's brother Younis in San Francisco (1976)

Khalid's parents, Fatima and Hamad Gheshayan, in Riyadh, Saudi Arabia

Pat Roush and Khalid Gheshayan in San Francisco (1981)

Pat Roush—Riyadh, Saudi Arabia (1985)

Pat Roush—the Arabian Desert (1985)

Pat with Aisha in San Francisco at St. Luke's Hospital Nursing School reception (1983)

Alia at Aunt Babe's farm in Missouri (1983)

Alia and Aisha in Stratford-upon-Avon, England, looking at the ducks (1984)

Pat, Alia, and Aisha in San Francisco (April 1984)

Aisha as "Rudolph"—Christmas 1985 in Cicero, Illinois

Alia and Aisha with Pound Puppies—Christmas 1985 in Cicero, Illinois, one month before the girls were kidnapped

Alia and Jonathan in the Coachman, Riyadh (1985)

The Afghan bread maker on the road to Mecca (1985)

Khalid Gheshayan, his brother's daughter, and Aisha in the Arabian Desert (1985)

Pat Roush, Alia, and Aisha at the "Hamad Gheshayan Establishment" (1985)

Alia and Aisha at the souk in Riyadh (1985)

Khalid Gheshayan at a party for the expatriate employees of King Fahad Hospital in Riyadh (1985)

Pat Roush in Alia and Aisha's bedroom looking at photos of them (1988)

Alia left behind her school bag with her *Weekly Reader* and schoolwork

Aisha's "star" picture from her school that was kept posted by her teachers after her kidnapping

Ed Ciriello

Peter Aragon in his San Francisco garden

Pat Roush and David Baioni visiting Burney Falls near Lake Britton in Northern California

Pat Roush and Senator Alan Dixon—first press conference, Washington, D.C. (January 1987)

Pat Roush press conference on Capitol Hill (May 1997)

Pat Roush at a Saudi Embassy protest in Washington, D.C. (May 1998)

Pat Roush at the Saudi Embassy in Washington, D.C. (September 1998)

White House candlelight vigil by a parent coalition (1999)

Raymond Mabus, Former U.S. Ambassador to Saudi Arabia

Government Reform Committee hearing on June 12, 2002 (pictured are Miriam Hernandez-Davis, Dria Davis, Pat Roush, and Ethel Stowers)

Government Reform Committee hearing on December 11, 2002 (swearing in are Margaret McClain, Pat Roush, Michael Petruzzello, Jack Deshauer, James Gallagher, Morton Rosenberg, and Maureen Mahoney)

Pat Roush testifying at the Government Refrom committee hearing on December 11, 2002

Dan Burton with the CODEL and Saudi Foreign Minister Prince Saud Bin Faisal (September 2002)

Pat Roush in Assisi, Italy (2001)

Daina, her daughter, Nina, and Pat at Nina's
baptism (Summer 2002)

Pat (Marmee) and her grandchildren, Nina and
Ryan—Daina's daughter and son (Christmas
2002)

Pat with Freddie and Dolly

things came to light. "You know, Pat, Dave's doing all right for a guy who's always been waited on. His wife took good care of him, but you're a challenge for him. He likes things his way. I mean, it's okay to be traditional, but he's got this attitude—old world—kinda macho. I don't know how to explain it. It's strange."

I noticed that quality, too. And didn't like it. He was very angry about his visual impairment and didn't like to communicate honestly. He would become easily defensive. His lack of savvy in real-life issues and a childlike perception of the world coupled with continual neediness, a one-track mindset, and refusal to compromise bothered me. The fact that this longtime friend noticed the same things I saw made me wonder. That conversation gnawed on me, and turned out to be an omen of things to come.

Pieces of the Puzzle

I had quit my job at the hospital and started to work as a public health nurse in the San Francisco community. One day I had an assignment to go to the Mission District to visit a cancer patient who needed chemotherapy. After I parked my car on a steep incline I put my nursing bag over my shoulder and ascended the hill to the patient's house. I approached the modest, bright pink building and rang the garage door bell as the instructions had stated. A sixty-something-year-old man with a full head of curly gray hair and a shy smile, dressed in shorts and T-shirt, opened the door. He let me in and as I prepared to start an intravenous infusion into his arm, we began to talk.

The conversation excluded any small talk; we went right to the important mysteries of meaning and purpose of life and man's search for God. I soon found out he was a man of prayer and deep contemplation. He lived in a rented two-room space in the garage of a widow's home that was not unlike the cell of a monk. A hybrid of "Don Juan" from Carlos Castenada and St. Francis of Assisi, Peter Aragon had an unexplainable gift of wisdom. He avoided the accumulation of worldly goods and pleasures for himself. He lived simply and attended daily Mass at the local Catholic church, tended his garden, prayed, and read Holy Scripture. He'd had a spiritual conversion at age forty-two and had been celibate ever since. I returned to his residence to administer the infusion every week for several months. I looked forward to those sessions.

Peter seemed to possess a centering and peace that I had never seen before. He spoke of mysticism. I told him about my unexplainable experiences and raptures. He said these were manifestations of the Holy Spirit—God was revealing Himself to me, and I was being "called" by God for some purpose. I knew what he was saying was true—I'd felt it for many years, maybe since I was a young girl. I wanted something more . . . something I couldn't quite describe. I wanted to go deeper into the mystery.

The Grifters

There was no news from CTU. This, coupled with the annual holiday blues without the girls and the upcoming January 25 anniversary of the kidnapping, drove me into a downward spiral. I decided to take a solo trip to Hawaii for a week. My soul calmed with the soft trade winds, sweet smells of island flowers, blue water, and white sand. After a beautiful day on a Maui beach I went to my room and called the office at CTU in Fayetteville. Judy's mother answered. "Well, hello, Pat. Judy's not here. Donny got arrested in Iceland a few days ago and Judy's about to go crazy. He was on a case and they had this little girl with the father at the airport when security grabbed both the father and Donny. Judy and Jackie (one of the British women they met in London) were stopped in Europe with another little girl and were arrested but then they let them go. The Luxembourg police sent the little girl they had with them back to Iceland, and after questioning, released Judy and Jackie. Judy flew back here, but Donny is in big trouble now in Iceland."

All the calm and peace of the islands couldn't contain me after that. Another double cross from these people! I couldn't take it. Everything was gone. Now he was in jail for another failed rescue of someone else's children. They promised me so many things, took my money, and kept me on a string. This was my seventh year without my daughters. I had no life and my hope was fading fast. I felt so alone . . . so abandoned . . . so betrayed.

Judy Feeney crumbled without Don to lean on, and since they lived so well on other people's money and were in constant debt, with him in jail all the financial burdens fell on her back. She was, after all, just a country girl, a housewife who longed for the big time, and the golden goose that brought her into the fantasy world of the commando lifestyle was now being roasted in an Icelandic jail cell.

I called Dave Chatellier to tell him what I had found out, and he told me that was why he'd detached himself from Feeney. He also said that Don could easily have gotten those two children out of Iceland but became cocky and overly confident and instead went right through the airport where there was an alert on one of the girls' names. He gave me the number of another American woman who had given the Feeneys a large sum of money. Her two daughters were taken to Iraq. I contacted her and she said, "Yeah, I called Don and he said, 'Send me $10,000 and I'll do a recon.' So I sent the money and nothing ever happened. I wanted my money back and they refused. I told them I would take this matter to the State of North Carolina Attorney General's Office."

The Feeneys were international grifters. I wanted no part of them. I became so irate when all this came to the surface. All the past hurts, lies, and pain erupted and I called Judy, "I want my money back! You're a crook! You took my money, promised me you would get my daughters back, and lied every step of the way! I want my money back . . . I want my money back!"

She was curt. "Pat, I don't have your money. We owe the IRS $65,000 and if your money was here, the IRS would have it! Your money is in a bank account in England. I have to talk to Don about this. I will call you back."

"You'd better get my money back or I will take this to Senator Helms and have you arrested."

Weeks went by as I went through every emotion imaginable. Nothing could ease my outrage at these people. I heard that Feeney had escaped from the prison in Iceland but was recaptured while trying to leave the country. There was a trial and he was sentenced to one year in prison. *Dateline NBC* sent a reporter to the trial in Iceland and did a segment on the Feeneys, the foiled Icelandic caper, the bitter grandmother who had paid them $40,000 to rescue one of the little girls, and the father who was arrested with Don and later released. The picture they painted of CTU and Don and Judy Feeney sickened me and sadly confirmed what I had found out only too late.

I called Sarah in Tacoma and she told me she felt deceived also. She said she had a plan to rescue her children from Yemen. "I'm working on it, Pat. I'm gonna get my kids out of there; I can just feel it. I'll let you know what happens."

The Final Con

A few months and many threats later, Judy Feeney returned $13,000 of the $25,000 to me. I called Dave Chatellier to see if he and Tommy Carter, who had also separated from CTU, would go into Saudi Arabia for me. He thought about it and after talking it over, said they couldn't do it. "Pat, it would be like catching a tiger by the tail. We could get your daughters but then what? There is just no way out of that country with two kids who have been there for seven years. There are road blocks, police everywhere, and the best security system we could sell them. It's a virtual armed camp. I'd like to help you, Pat, but it can't be done."

I called him back a few weeks later. "Dave, do you know anyone else who is doing business in Saudi Arabia?"

"Well now, there is a guy . . . Mike Taylor. I have done some operations with him. Former Army Ranger—was in Beirut during the marine barracks bombing—speaks Arabic well, and married a Lebanese woman . . . I think her father is some executive for Pan Am. I know he is involved with security for the city of New York. You might call him. He's in Boston—North American Security."

Taylor was quick to respond to my call in September 1993. He said he could help me and had a lot of contacts on the ground in Saudi Arabia from the Lebanese connection. After his discharge from the Special Forces he'd put himself through Harvard University and opened his security company, the name of which was changed from North American Security to American International Security Corporation, located outside Boston. We didn't talk about how much money he wanted during the initial phone conversation. He knew Don Feeney and I later discovered he worked back and forth with him on various "deals."

In November 1993 he called me. "Pat, it's a done deal . . . a cakewalk. I know someone who is a former chief of station of the CIA in Saudi Arabia, and he is willing to help us get the kids out. I also have a very good friend—known him for years—who is in charge of all security for Saudi Arabian Airlines. He wants to help, too. I'll set up a meeting in Washington. Can you make it?"

"Sure, Mike. That sounds great."

"Oh, Pat. You know . . . I can't really ask these guys to come out and not give them anything. Think you could send a retainer of, say, $3,500 just to start this thing off?"

He made it sound so enticing: CIA chief of station—Saudi Airlines Security—city of New York. This guy wasn't like Feeney. No, this guy could be trusted. Well, if the city of New York trusted him, why not me? He wears a business suit, not army fatigues. Wouldn't catch him doing evasive driving classes for $200 a crack at some *Soldier of Fortune* convention. Michael Taylor is "legit," a real professional, a Harvard man.

Whenever I went to Washington, I would stay at the Ramada Inn in Old Town—Alexandria, Virginia. I thought the rates were cheaper and I could get away from the D.C. buzz and go down to the pier and have crab cakes and look out on the Potomac. It offered me a diversion and break from the depressing activities I usually took part in on Capitol Hill—trying to convince politicians to help me. I had been to Washington so many times: I could have been running for office, except I always had to pay my own expenses. This time, with Taylor, I paid not only for mine but for his and his pals'—including the lunch at the Ramada.

Taylor phoned me from the lobby. "Pat, we're all downstairs. We'll meet you in the restaurant."

The lunch buffet was on and we all sat down at a round table by the window overlooking the Potomac. I had never met Taylor before. He was about forty with sandy-colored hair and a slight frame, dressed in a black suit and carrying a briefcase—just as I had pictured him. The retired CIA agent, Terry Douglas, was six foot, fiftyish, and slightly gray with a mustache; and Burt Hutchings, the chief of security for Saudi Airlines, was a very round, jovial, red-faced sixty-plus-year-old. I should have known something was "rotten in the state of Denmark" when the meeting was scheduled for November 9, the anniversary of my wedding to Khalid.

Douglas was very nervous, hardly ate his lunch, and kept staring at me. After bringing out a typed questionnaire for me to fill out, he asked me about the story and situation with the girls. Hutchings kept getting up and going to the street to feed his parking meter. I felt apprehensive from the beginning but had already sent the $3,500 for this "meeting" to Taylor. It lasted for thirty to forty-five minutes and then they all stood up, Douglas gave me his card, and they left. Hutchings said as they were leaving, "I don't want to get a ticket."

I was paralyzed. That had cost me $3,500 plus the money for the trip. Taylor promised to call me that night but I never heard from him. I walked around the streets of Old Town, saw a movie, and went back to San Francisco in the morning. Several days later I called Terry Douglas at his home in Maryland. "Terry, this is Pat Roush. We met at the Ramada . . ."

"Oh yes, Pat. I was going to call you . . . ah . . . I just . . . ah . . . I can't do something like that. I wouldn't even try. I'm in business now and I don't want to take those kinds of risks. If Taylor wants to run around with those paramilitary types, fine. Let him. It's not for me. No Saudi could ever be trusted to help in a case like yours. Taylor told me this child abduction angle is the most lucrative, moneymaking part of his business. That might be true, but I can't get involved in it. I'm sorry."

I stupidly told Taylor everything Douglas had told me, and he defended himself and every Green Beret that ever lived. He then put his friend "George" on the extension phone. Taylor said he was a war-torn, multi-wounded veteran of the war in Beirut and was going into Saudi Arabia soon on another issue. George would do reconnaissance for my case while he was in the country and we could take it from there. He had so much to offer due to his background in the streets of Beirut and a brother who lived in Riyadh.

Taylor told me a lot of stories about what could happen. None of them materialized. I have no idea if "George" ever went to Saudi Arabia. I only know what Taylor told me and I'm sure that it was not the truth. He had me sign a contract basically letting him off the hook for everything. It was called, "The Search for Alia and Aisha." I foolishly sent him my last money—$11,000—and for one year, he lied and led me around in circles. I finally told an FBI agent in San Francisco about him. When he called Taylor, he said the money was for "expenses."

That was the end of the entire solider of fortune flytrap. I spent five years with Ed Ciriello, Don and Judy Feeney, and then Mike Taylor. I did everything I possibly could with my government to free my children and then was forced to resort to questionable operatives with credentials I had to accept. I lived in a continuous, desperate state, grasped at straws, and was like a drowning person who wouldn't quite die.

Beautiful Lady

It seemed that taking a trip always refreshed my body and soul after these letdowns—Chicago and Hawaii were my "hideouts"—but now my spirit was in need of replenishing. I was still working as a public health nurse and met a lovely, forty-two-year-old woman, Sandy, who had end-stage breast cancer that had metastasized to her bones. I made a visit to her home one evening and she was lying on a hospital bed in her living room, unable to move. We talked for hours while I was administering an antibiotic through an IV. She told me about her trip to Medugorje in Bosnia. It was a Catholic Marian shrine—five village children had visions of the Blessed Mother on a hill while tending their goats. Sandy said it was the most powerful experience of her life. Her husband took her there in a wheelchair despite the objections of her doctors, who said she would never survive the trip. She was so full of the Spirit—her face was glowing as she lay dying on her bed. Her husband and sixteen-year-old son ministered to her needs. She smiled at me and said, "Pat, I'm ready to meet my Lord. I'm not afraid to go to my God."

I told her about my girls and she encouraged me to go to Medugorje. After the Taylor saga, I had a small amount of money in my account and I decided to make that journey.

I got a package deal and landed in Dubrovnik in Croatia. Someone met me with a van and we drove for two hours to the tiny village of Medugorje in the Bosnian mountains. There were no hotels, but arrangements had been made for me to stay with a young Croatian family. I met a fellow traveler in this pilgrim household, an American pilot from St. Louis—Jim. My ten-day trip was filled with Mass at St. James Church in the village and hikes up Apparition Hill where the child visionaries saw the Virgin. Then one day Jim and I made arrangements to climb the holy mountain called Krizevac, where the local Catholics had erected a huge white concrete cross on the summit in 1938.

I wanted to be in Medugorje for Aisha's birthday, July 2. The day I planned the pilgrimage to Krizevac Mountain was a Sunday, July 1. We were to leave early before the sun got too hot. I knocked on Jim's door at eight o'clock in the morning—no answer. I knocked again. Maybe he had gone on ahead. So I just put my water bottle in my bag, grabbed my envelope with the "Pound Puppy" pictures of the girls, and took off for the mountain by myself.

At the base of the mountain I saw pilgrims descending from the rocks— loose soil in bare feet. The Stations of the Cross were placed along the path to the top. I braced myself and began the climb. It took me two hours to reach the summit. I touched the white cross and stood on "top of the world"—able to see all the neatly laid patterns of the earth and the five neighboring villages. The idyllic, pastoral landscape was refreshing, and its simplicity and intrinsic purity filled my soul. I stayed on the peak for several hours—just absorbing as much beauty as possible.

As I began to descend I took some pictures of the girls out of my envelope and placed them in a few spots along the trail. One Station of the Cross had a little wooden frame around it, and I thought it would be a good place for a picture. I stuck the corner of the image of my daughters under the wood of the frame so it wouldn't blow away.

When I got back to the village, I took a leisurely walk around the local cemetery (the anthropologist in me), photographed some Croatian women dressed in colorful folk outfits, attended the evening services at St. James, had dinner at a café, and then walked back to the Croatian family home.

By this time, it was dark and after midnight. There was a full moon and Jim, the American pilot, was waiting for me outside the house. "Pat, where were you? I missed you this morning. I guess I overslept. I went to Krizavac this evening and I saw your daughters. I saw your daughters." He was very excited and his speech was impassioned. I had seen this before—the night Father Philip had told me about the girls coming home. I knew God was revealing something to him.

"Pat, sit down. I have something to tell you and I can't explain it. You're going to see your daughters again. I went to the top of the mountain and saw all those pictures people put up but as I was climbing, I saw your daughters' picture on a station of the cross and suddenly I knew you would see them again. I don't know what happened and I can't explain it, but I just wanted to tell you about this."

"Jim, do you remember which Station of the Cross that was?"

"Yes, I wrote it down—it was the Twelfth Station—the Crucifixion."

10

❦

TOMORROW—IT'S ONLY A DAY AWAY

SEPTEMBER 1994–JUNE 1995

Let's go, Mommy, to the village of dreams
Away from the thorns.
Today we are invited by the whistling winds
So let's go, Mommy.
—Hindu Folk Song

Immovable Hearts

It had been almost nine years since my journey without my children began. I had walked a tightrope and lived on the edge for such a long time—I wondered how long I could continue. I was wearing out; the emotional roller coaster was aging me and taking a toll on all aspects of my life. All my money was gone, and the savings of my frail, elderly mother had been spent in aborted rescue missions and hoaxes played on us by exploitative con men. The State Department had betrayed me and forced me into a position of turning to paramilitary operatives who hoped to make a quick buck on people like me—desperate, heartbroken mothers who would do anything to get their children back.

Now I had no choice but to call the State Department once more. I was again at their mercy—maybe this time would be different. Just as Moses had repeatedly appealed to the obdurate heart of Pharaoh to let his people go, I had to once again go to the Central Authority of my government, the United States Department of State, to beg them to free my children.

The Desk at the State Department for Kidnapped Kids had expanded from one person to a fully staffed division of Consular Affairs at the State Department. I called Jim Schuller, the director: "It's been eight years since my daughters [were] kidnapped. I have no more money for mercenaries, and I need the help of my government."

"Pat, we are very concerned about your children. Fax us what you want us to do."

"To begin with, I want someone from the embassy to make a health-and-welfare check on my daughters immediately. We don't even know if they are alive. Can someone please take a photograph of my daughters? That's not asking too much." I began to cry. "I don't have any current information on my daughters. Why won't you help me? I can't do this anymore."

I called the American embassy in Riyadh. There was a new consul general—Gretchen Welch. Her husband, David, was the deputy chief of the mission. Raymond Mabus, a former governor of Mississippi, friend of President Clinton and political appointee, was the recently confirmed U.S. ambassador. I asked Gretchen to make the arrangements for the visit with the girls and to take photos.

She called back one month later. They were having a difficult time with Khalid. Mazen Shahan, the Syrian who worked for the embassy and who was present when Hejailan taped my daughters, was still working as a foreign service national (FSN) in the consul general's office. He offered the only continuity at the embassy. The American diplomats stayed in the country for only three years maximum and then were sent on to other assignments, but Mazen knew the history of the case and had contact with Khalid's relatives. Embassies always rely on native speakers like Mazen who know the local culture and customs. He was the only one at the embassy who seemed to know how to find Khalid, but this time he did not want to be found.

I was told that Khalid had changed residences three times since the kidnapping and wouldn't give anyone his phone number. The girls were now living with Khalid and his Saudi wife. They had three children of their own plus my two daughters. Mazen told me he had seen Khalid and my daughters at the local shopping mall a few years before and Khalid thought Mazen was following him. His paranoia was forever plaguing him.

My case worker at Children's Issues was Judy Rouse. I called her in October 1994 and asked if she had any news from Riyadh. "Mr. Gheshayan was extremely hostile and he absolutely will not allow you any contact with your children. The most you can hope for would be that the embassy will be able to see your children at different times. I know it is unfair, and a terrible tragedy, Pat, but we cannot force him and we cannot force the Saudi officials. It is their law and their country. The girls are Saudi citizens. There is nothing we can do."

I was so upset. After the call I had to compose myself enough to go to work at the hospital. I was shaking and emotionally drained. This was no different from nine years and three mercenaries ago. I don't know how I managed to get through the day and care for my patients. But Gretchen Welch called late that evening from Riyadh to tell me they went to Governor Prince Salman's office and spoke with Assistant Governor Sheik Abdullah Bleihed, who knew my case very well from the Hejailan plan in 1986. Gretchen said, "Pat, I told him, 'I'm speaking to you as a mother. This is not fair.' He agreed with me and said I will be able to meet your daughters and videotape them. I will also be able to take photographs of the girls, and you will be able to send them audiocassettes and pictures of yourself. You and your daughters will be able to write letters back and forth."

I had a package of clothes and gifts for my daughters that I was not able to send to them because of Khalid. Gretchen promised she would get it to them in some way. I asked her if she was going to stop with that or if she would continue to press them to free the girls. She said she would continue and then started to cry. In nine years no one from the State Department had ever cried or become involved with me on this level. A stone heart is usually what I got. I said, "Gretchen, can you do me a favor? Can you tell my girls that I love them and haven't abandoned them like Khalid has told them?"

"Pat, I will do it. I don't care who is in the meeting, either. I don't care if Bleihed is there; I will tell them."

Weeks went by and Khalid would still not cooperate with the Saudi officials for a visit with the girls. None of the promises made at the governor's office were kept. Gretchen received my package but couldn't give it to them. She stated, "There are such strong feelings about this case from everyone who has worked on it. I cannot promise you anything. We will continue to work on it, Pat." It was getting to her—Hejailan and Bleihed and the "Khalid shuffle." She was no match for them. They knew the routine too well.

It was about this time that I received a call from my friend Monica Stowers in Riyadh. Her two children were kidnapped and taken to Saudi Arabia. She had been able to get into the kingdom during the Gulf War and managed to stay. Her children were physically abused, sexually molested, and beaten by their Saudi father, Palestinian stepmother, and other relatives.

She called me to tell me her son, Rasheed, had just escaped from Saudi Arabia and crossed safely into Bahrain. She was afraid for her life and the life of her twelve-year-old daughter. Her former husband had just sold the little girl into marriage to a *mutawa* (religious policeman) who was thirty years old. He had paid the bride-price to the girl's father, which meant that he now owned the child.

Monica didn't know what to do. Under Saudi law the police could take the girl from Monica and give her to the man. I called Rasheed once he arrived at Monica's mother's home in Houston, Texas. He offered to have one of his friends marry Alia just to get her out of the country. He told me horror stories about his life inside Saudi Arabia. Khalid had sent my girls to the Saudi government schools, and Rasheed told me these schools taught nothing more than cooking, sewing, and Koran. He said at eighteen most of the girls are married.

I knew I didn't have much time before Khalid would be looking for husbands for my daughters. Alia was sixteen and Aisha was thirteen. The clock was ticking so fast, and my greatest fear was that my daughters would be sold into marriages with Saudis and forced to breed baby after baby.

Gretchen called. She had gone back to Bleihed's office and told him she would take the matter to Ambassador Mabus and Prince Salman if she did not get any results. She said, "Pat, I told Bleihed, 'It's been two months since we requested to see the Gheshayan children, and this is not a lot to ask.'"

Who Is My Mother?

The embassy got nowhere with Sheik Bleihed so Ambassador Mabus then sent a letter to Prince Salman. No one from the American embassy had seen my daughters for the past six years and Mabus stressed the need for "an urgent visit."

Salman's office began to try to locate Khalid and he once again manipulated everyone and would allow the embassy to see only Aisha, not Alia. He would keep her away from everyone and kept telling Mazen that Alia hated her mother and the United States. "She doesn't want to see anyone from the United States. I can't force her to come."

Finally one night I got the call from Mazen: "Pat, we will see Aisha in one hour in the lobby of the Marriott Hotel. He is not bringing Alia."

"Please tell her that I love her. Give her my letter and tell her to take it to Alia. I hope he lets her keep it. Ask Khalid if you can call me from the hotel and let me speak with Aisha. Please call me after the meeting."

This is the letter that I had given Mazen. It was translated into Arabic:

December 21, 1994

Dearest Alia and Aisha:

It has been almost nine years since you were taken away from me, and every day since that horrible day I have been in constant pain. I wake up thinking of you and knowing that this is another day of not being with you. I have tried so very hard to be able to be with you, but all my efforts to have you with me have failed. No matter what happens I want you to know your mother loves you more than life itself. I would die for you both. I remember when you were my babies and little girls, and long to hold you both again. I know you are young ladies now. Your childhood is gone, but you are still my girls and I want to be with you no matter how old you are.

I have sent some pictures of us together. I hope you remember some of the times we shared and I hope the love we shared is still with you. I pray that God is protecting you while I'm not able to be with you. If you ever want to find me, call the American embassy. They will help you.

I hope we can be together soon.

Your Loving Mother

I never got a call back from Mazen, but I called him. He stated that Khalid and Aisha were at the Marriott. Mazen and Myles Webber, vice consul, met them in the coffee shop. Aisha had the abaya on but took the shayla (face covering) off. He stated, "She is a sweet girl." She wanted to talk to them but she looked at her father and he looked at her and she just hung her head and couldn't say much. She speaks only Arabic, and Khalid spoke to Mazen only in English even though Mazen knew Arabic, so Aisha could not understand what was being said. Aisha had many questions about me and was interested in my life. Was I married? Did I have other children? What did I look like? Was I still a nurse? Did they have a recent photo? Despite her father's stern control, she still spoke out and told Mazen and Myles that she loved me and missed me. Khalid allowed the embassy to give her my letter but tore off the last sentence about calling the American embassy if they ever wanted to find me.

Aisha was so excited after reading my letter and wanted to take it and the photos back to show Alia. She wanted me to send her blue jeans and some type of coat. Mazen brought the paper for Khalid to sign giving me permission to enter the kingdom to visit my children. He refused to sign it and said he didn't like the way it was worded. He wouldn't allow the embassy to take any photos of Aisha. He gave the excuse that I would use the photos to have her kidnapped.

So, no Alia, no photos, and no letter allowing me to visit my daughters after nine years. And Mazen's tone toward me changed abruptly after that visit with Khalid. "He was very nice to us. He just doesn't want you to make trouble for him. He loves the children very much."

After that I went back to the press again. I called the *Washington Post* and the *San Francisco Chronicle* and did an article. I decided to write a letter to Ambassador Mabus and ask for his personal intervention. I stressed the interest of Congress and the press and the fact that the girls were reaching a marriageable age.

Hero No. 2

One night in January 1995 I received a call from the American embassy: "Ms. Roush, Ambassador Mabus would like to speak with you." Mabus was so supportive. He stated that he felt the children belonged with me and he couldn't imagine me not seeing them for all those years. He said, "Ms. Roush, this embassy is here for you to use anytime and in any way. Is there anything else I can do for you right now? . . . I'm looking forward to meeting you and hopefully we can get this thing settled once and for all."

Once Ray Mabus started his move to try to get the girls back, Hejailan came back into the picture. He knows the Riyadh scene very well and has dinner parties for the diplomatic corps. One of his best friends is Prince Salman, and I'm sure the word was out that I was trying to get into the kingdom again to see my children. Hejailan called me: "You have an image problem here because you went to the press. Now you have to come here and rebuild your image. You have to show us that you have changed."

I didn't want Hejailan involved again but there was no way around him. Gretchen Welch told me, "Everyone here is very rational. Hejailan is always right in his perception of what is going on. He is the lawyer for the embassy and handles all our legal matters in the kingdom."

I couldn't believe what she was saying. In 1986—nine years before—Deputy Chief of the Mission Edward Walker asked the State Department for permission for Hejailan to be the "legal counsel" for the embassy so he could negotiate for the release of my daughters. They telexed Washington twice for that permission and it was denied twice; thus, the Saudis dropped the matter and the embassy was told to "remain neutral and impartial." Now, Hejailan was the embassy's lawyer and handled all their legal matters. He was the darling of the embassy and guided them—whenever he said something, they listened. He lobbied for the princes and advised the American embassy. Did anyone notice a conflict of interest?

It was no different from when I was advised by the State Department that the only avenue left for me was the Sharia court. I was given the names of Saudi attorneys, and Hejailan was on that list. He blatantly worked for the Saudi government, yet my government, the United States, referred me to him to help get my children back.

Gretchen Welch went on: "The Saudis are convinced that the American press is out to get them, and you haven't helped matters much by going to the papers and media." Hejailan, obviously, had a great deal of influence with this woman. I only hoped that Ray Mabus could see through him and had the integrity and vision to proceed with what he knew was right and just.

Ten Years After

Ambassador Mabus had to make an appointment with Salman to ask permission for me to come into the kingdom to visit my daughters. Salman responded that he was aware of the case but was not current on the status. He said he would read the file and have Riyadh Deputy Governor Bleihed speak with Saleh Al-Hejailan to see what could be done to solve the problem. The problem would be solved "not officially" but privately.

It took several more weeks of back and forth and waiting to receive a response from Salman. Judy Rouse from the State Department called and said, "The Arabs won't give the ambassador the satisfaction of a response without making him go through the waiting game." It was amusing for them to play with people like that; they got a great deal of sadistic pleasure from watching someone on a string. I was the mouse and they were the cat. Salman and Hejailan took such delight in participating in these matches. The problem was, the playing field was never level. Now I had Ray Mabus, an honest man. Since he was a political appointee from the president and not a foreign service diplomat from the State Department, he had more freedom in dealing with the Saudis. I wondered how that would affect this tournament with Salman and Hejailan.

At last, I received word that Khalid was called into Salman's office and forced to sign a document granting permission for me to visit my daughters. He was under orders from Salman, who met with him personally. He was very hostile and Bleihed told the embassy it took much persuading by Salman for him to sign the statement. Hejailan came up with one of his plans. He wanted me to write a letter of apology to Khalid to soften his heart. I refused.

It was April 1995. David and I had been together for five years. He was still living with his father and I had rented a large house about three miles away. My daughter Daina was engaged to be married on May 14, 1995—Mother's Day. The trip to Saudi Arabia was coming up and I was beside myself. I couldn't relax. I had panic attacks whenever I thought about getting off the plane and seeing my daughters in Khalid's clutches. They were sixteen and thirteen. I hadn't seen them since they were seven and three. ABC television was interested in covering my story and Barbara Walters wanted to interview me for *20/20*.

Death of An Angel

It was during that time that I received a strange letter from the mother of Sarah Anderson Noman. She had apparently tried to rescue her two children from Yemen and had disappeared. On Christmas Eve 1994 she and a companion were in Eritrea on the African coast near the Red Sea. They were loading supplies onto an old Arab dhow—a fishing boat. Some of the locals saw them as they shoved off the dock during the night. They were never seen again. Since Sarah's family had no knowledge of this plan and thought she was merely on a holiday, as she had told them, it was weeks before anyone reported the incident.

I knew that the previous year Sarah had been on another failed rescue mission in Yemen with a detective from Los Angeles. Sarah, the detective, and his crew departed in a zodiac boat from Dbouti on the African coast above Sudan and went across the Gulf of Aden into Yemen. They had a navigator with them and still got off course. Once in Yemen they found out that her children were being guarded by a group of men with AK-47 rifles. There was no way to get them out. The detective speedily left Yemen but Sarah refused to leave without her children. While in hiding, she was almost raped, then developed a severe pain in her abdomen. She was forced to flee to the American embassy for help. They sent her to Dubai in the United Arab Emirates where surgery was performed. A tumor had burst in her colon. Her mother, an oncology nurse, couldn't believe the pathology report—cancer.

After recovering from surgery in Dubai, Sarah was flown back to Tacoma and treated with chemotherapy and radiation, but as soon as she could get her strength back she started preparing for another trip to Yemen, unknown to her mother and family.

She had appeared on a television program, and a man who had watched the show started to write her letters and asked for her phone number. Sarah began a dialogue with this man, who called himself Derek Smith. He told her he was a former Navy SEAL and wanted to help her rescue her children from Yemen. That was all Sarah had to hear. She thought he was going to be her savior.

Sarah's family found out too late that he had never been a Navy SEAL but was dishonorably discharged from the navy because of psychiatric problems. He led her to her death in the black waters. No one knows if she drowned or ran into foul play. Neither of the bodies was found. She once told her mother, "If this cancer is going to kill me, I don't want to be in this country. I want to die near my children."

If Sarah had been able to secure the return of her children with the help of the U.S. State Department and the government of Yemen, she would have never lost her life under those harrowing circumstances.

Again and Again and Again

After the unimaginable ordeal of the last ten years, I'd ended up right where I began—in the middle of Hejailan and Salman. Hejailan kept Salman officially not involved with my case but still able to "pull the strings and tighten the screws." He grandstanded before the American embassy and told them he would sponsor me into the kingdom and pay for lodging and meals at the hotel. He kept bragging about how he was doing so much for me because he was a great humanitarian. He drenched himself in the embassy culture and was now the embassy's "legal counsel." Diplomats like Gretchen Welch valued his opinion and advice. It was impossible for me to avoid his manipulation and of course, I ended up signing another one of his "letters of gratitude" that he dictated and faxed to me.

Finally it was time to leave. Bandar himself had signed my two-month visa. I was told that I would be able to visit my children each day while I was in Riyadh. That was the arrangement made with Prince Salman. I had obtained permission to stay at the Sheraton Hotel in Riyadh as a single woman. The American embassy had to vouch for me with an official letter, and I had to carry a card with me at all times so if I was stopped by the religious police, I would not be arrested. Everything was in place. I was scared.

Daina's Gift

May 14, 1995: My daughter Daina was married to the son of a longtime family friend from Chicago who had grown up with my former husband, Jerry. It was a marriage made in heaven and the wedding festivities were delightful. David arranged all the music and played for both the ceremony and the reception. Daina's cousin, Tanya, sang "Sunrise, Sunset," and we all laughed, danced, and toasted the newlyweds for hours at the Brazil Room in Tilton Park in Berkeley, California. Jerry gave them his Porsche to drive away into the sunset and the next day they were off to Hawaii for their honeymoon.

Barbara Walters insisted that I come to New York for the taping of *20/20* the very next day after the wedding. My sister and her children were in town and I didn't want to leave so soon, but that was the only date she could do the show. On May 16 I met Ms. Walters and her crew at the Pierre Hotel near Central Park. They had rented an entire suite for the day. The interview went very well and she promised that the segment would be run when the fall season started in September.

I still had security issues concerning my trip to Saudi Arabia and felt better about having taped a program with a celebrity like Barbara Walters in case something went wrong. Of course, people were "accidented" all the time, and I had a lot of enemies between the Saud princes, Hejailan, and Gheshayan. I requested security from Hejailan and the American embassy. It was refused and dismissed as "nonsense."

I hadn't slept for many nights and my flight was leaving the next morning for London and then Riyadh. Everything was finally arranged. My daughter Daina called, from her honeymoon in Hawaii—"Hello, Mom, I'm so worried about you. Are you sure you're going to be safe over there? What if he tries to kill you? Oh, Mom, I just want you to know how much I love you and I admire you for what you are doing for the girls. Remember, Mom, they are your little girls, he has no right to them. Tell the girls I love them. Be careful. Love you . . ."

My poor mother was in very fragile health and was staying with my sister Bobbie in Chicago. She called me three times the day before I left. Her frail heart could hardly take this excitement.

Finally my dear friend Peter Aragon called: "Pat, I think you might need this. Let me read it to you:

Finally, grow strong in the Lord, with the strength of his power. Put on the full armour of God so as to be able to resist the devil's tactics. For it is not against human enemies that we have to struggle, but against the principalities and the ruling forces who are masters of the darkness in this world, the spirits of evil in the heavens. That is why you must take up all God's armour, or you will not be able to put up any resistance on the evil day, or stand your ground even though you exert yourselves to the full.

So stand your ground, with truth a belt round your waist, and uprightness a breastplate, wearing for shoes on your feet the eagerness to spread the gospel of peace and always carrying the shield of faith so that you can use it to quench the burning arrows of the Evil One. And then you must take salvation as your helmet and the sword of the Spirit, that is, the word of God.

In all your prayer and entreaty keep praying in the Spirit on every possible occasion.

"That's Ephesians 6:10–18. I know you can't take a Bible into Saudi Arabia but take this passage. It will protect you. God bless you."

I was sitting on the runway at Heathrow Airport in London—Saudia Flight 100 to Riyadh. I scanned everyone on the plane to see if I recognized Gheshayan or his relatives. All the men seemed to look like Khalid. They were returning from vacations in England and the States. There were many young Saudi families with little children. I remembered that smell . . . Aramis—he used to wear that. I could smell the spices in the food being served—definitely Saudi. This was my first contact with that world since the girls and I had been able to leave Saudi Arabia in 1985. It took me ten years to get back to the prison that held my Flowers. I knew I would have to take that journey moment by moment or I would not be able to emotionally survive. Who knew what tricks Hejailan, Salman, and Gheshayan had cooked up for me?

Checkpoint Charlie

We finally landed in Riyadh late in the evening of June 8, 1995. I had an uneasy feeling in my stomach. The guards were dressed in uniform. I thought to myself, *They could arrest me, and no one would be able to find me again.* I knew the power of the Saudi government, and the lack of concern by the embassy for Americans worried me. The intensity in the room could be cut with a knife— that heightened alertness that comes with the presence of armed men.

I approached Saudi immigration and showed the uniformed guard my passport and visa. Would he press a hidden bell and have his comrades come and take me away? For the longest moment on earth I stood at that window as he punched my name into the computer. The guard asked who was picking me up. Myles Webber, vice consul from the American embassy, was supposed to meet me at the airport. I could not leave without that escort and he was not there. I died inside. The guard motioned for another guard to take me into a small room where other women also were waiting for some male to pick them up. No women would be allowed to leave the airport without a male. After about an hour of looking out through the open door, I saw a tall, gangly, American-looking guy coming my way. I yelled out, "Myles?"

He came forward to where I was standing and I whispered, "Get me out of here." He had documentation from Hejailan that allowed me to leave the airport. Waiting outside was an official car from the embassy and a driver to take me to the Sheraton Hotel. When we were seated in the backseat, Myles turned to me and said, "You're not going to like this, but Gheshayan flipped out in the governor's office yesterday and said you are not allowed to see your daughters. He found out that Hejailan was sponsoring you and he went crazy. He said, 'What do you mean she is coming without my approval? That is not possible.'" Khalid had hated Hejailan since that taping at his father's villa in 1986 and had gotten into a fistfight with Hejailan's driver when they came for the second taping. "He said he will definitely not allow Alia to see you. I guess he got a lecture from Bleihed and was told that in a Muslim court you had a right to see your daughters. Gheshayan said to Bleihed, 'Don't quote Muslim law to me!' They all got totally disgusted with him and told him to go home and think about it."

"Well, we'll see about all that," I said. "I know the ambassador will help me."

Myles signed me in at the desk of the Sheraton and gave them the document from the embassy vouching for me to stay alone as a single woman in the hotel. I was exhausted but knew I wouldn't sleep. I got to the room and double-locked the door. This room with two twin beds would be my cage for the next twenty-one days.

Dream Walking

For the next twelve hours I slept on and off. I felt like I was in one of my dreams about the kids where I was fighting Khalid off but all of a sudden the dream became reality. Would this be the battle of battles? The American embassy was my only lifeline.

Gretchen Welch had been transferred back to Washington, and the incoming consul general was not expected to arrive until the end of summer. A man named Glen Cary was temporary consul general. I was so afraid that Khalid would try to kill me, possibly show up at the meeting with a gun under his robes. I called the embassy and spoke with Cary. "Is there any word about when I can see my daughters? Is Khalid still refusing to allow me to see them? Is it possible for me to see my daughters in the embassy for protection?"

"The meetings will be anywhere Mr. Gheshayan feels comfortable. We don't want to upset him."

That would be it. We couldn't upset Khalid. I wondered if I was just going to be able to view my daughters, note the damages done to them after living with Khalid under a totalitarian regime, and then board a plane and leave.

I looked out the window of the hotel room and could see a mosque with a minaret. At times the athan (prayer call) would drift over the microphone: "Allaaaaaaaaaaaah, Akbar."

The haunting refrain reminded me of when I lived on the road to Mecca with Khalid and the night he almost killed me—the girls crying and the pain in my chest. The memory of that fear still overwhelmed me. The desert hadn't changed much. I looked out at the sand and beige-colored buildings with no sign of anything green. The heat of the desert beat against the glass—44 degrees centigrade. I closed the curtains. It was just me and the walls and the telephone line to the embassy.

Several days went by, and I was still not able to see my daughters. Gheshayan wouldn't budge. It was my birthday—June 11. My only diversion was going to the restaurant near the lobby three times per day. With an abaya in place I would walk through the lobby filled only with men and go into the restaurant, sit behind a screened wall for women only and eat my meals. I tried to stretch the mealtimes as much as possible to avoid going back to my room. There was nowhere for me to go and nothing for me to do. I couldn't bring my Bible and had already read the books I'd brought with me. The television had a station in English and I was so out of my mind that I would sit there and watch reruns of *M*A*S*H* for hours. Finally the phone rang. I sprang up to answer it—it was my mother. "Pat, are you all right? I'm so worried about you. Did you see the girls?"

"Don't worry, Mom. I'm okay. I haven't seen the kids yet. He won't cooperate. The ambassador might have to get involved again."

"If anything happens to you, I don't know what I'll do. Daina called. Pat, Daina is going to have a baby."

"What? Oh, that's wonderful news, Mom. Daina and Tony are going to have a baby? What a birthday present for me! God is blessing us. I'll call her from here. Thanks, Mom. It's going to be all right. I'll call you as soon as I see the kids."

After the call from my mother, Hejailan called. He said Gheshayan would be summoned to Salman's office the next day. He instructed me to do him a favor and "neutralize" Gheshayan by being nice and not in any way emotional. He repeated that under Sharia law I should be able to see my daughters every day. I must build a rapport with the girls—that was the key. It would be very possible for me to take the girls home with me. It depended on me, the girls, and our chemistry. The girls had a "high lifestyle" in the kingdom; would I be able to offer them that in the States? He suggested that Ambassador Mabus and I request a personal meeting with Prince Salman.

He was the master of lies, but I wanted to believe him so much. I put on the abaya and went to the lobby. It is unsafe for a single woman to take a Saudi taxi so I hired a driver from the desk to take me to the American embassy. The hotel had a car service with drivers from Pakistan, India, and

Bangladesh. Since they worked for the hotel and were not Saudi, I was told I would be safe.

Driving Back a Decade

I met everyone at the embassy including Ambassador Mabus. He invited me into his office and we sat down and had an informal talk. He lovingly showed me a photograph of his two redheaded young daughters. "I don't know how you can live without your children. But I can tell you one thing, I'm gonna do everything I can to help you get them back, and this embassy is here to assist you. Call me anytime."

I told him about Hejailan's suggestion that he and I meet with Salman, and he orderd the embassy to send a "Diplomatic Note" to Prince Salman's office requesting that meeting on June 13.

Mazen and I had a long talk in his office. He said he didn't know where Khalid worked and could contact him only through his brother Omar. He had seen the girls with Khalid a few years ago at the market near Headchopper's Square. Khalid had two other children with him besides Alia and Aisha. "Alia looked so pretty. I didn't realize how much the girls really do look like you."

Khalid would still not allow me to see the girls and told Salman's office he would "take it to the king" if necessary. Mazen said he would either be put in jail or get an order from Salman's office. Even Ali Al-Otaibi, the vice-governor in Salman's office, agreed Khalid was crazy and "getting worse and worse." Everyone acknowledged that he was capable of killing. I wanted him to be searched before the meeting—if the meeting ever happened.

When I met with Ray Mabus, he told me that just a few months before, he had gotten four children out of Saudi Arabia with their American mother. The Saudi father had molested all four of them. I worried about Gheshayan sexually molesting my daughters. He was sick enough to do anything.

I slept fitfully, finally got up and made tea, wrote in my diary, and practiced using the Hi-8 video camera ABC *20/20* had given to me to film the girls. I'd brought a relaxation cassette, *The Peaceful Pond*, with sounds of a summer night to help me cope with stress. I put the headphones on and played it over and over again—it didn't help. I heard the athan and knew dawn was near so I just stayed up. Another day spent in the room with the heat beating against the window. There was still no word about the meeting with my daughters.

After dinner I decided to try to find the place where Khalid and I had lived on the road to Mecca. I went to the lobby and found the same driver, a young man from Bangladesh who spoke English. He had taken me on several short trips before and I felt comfortable enough in the car with him.

I simply told him, "Drive." Riyadh had changed a lot in ten years. The infrastructure was in place, roads had been built, and large buildings had been constructed. The telephone system was much easier to use and there were more supermarkets—*"supermarche."* Saudis were also using them now instead of only expatriates. Foods from all over the world were imported. And the livestock souk was gone (part of the old Arab site for picking out lambs, camels, and goats).

We passed downtown Riyadh with the old market, the gold market, and the palace of the governor—Prince Salman. The parking lot of the palace was still the site of public executions each Friday. I asked the driver to take me for *shawerma*, or shish kebab. He pulled off the road alongside a small stand and got out to get the food and drinks. We ate in the car and then continued on our way to the "Hamad Al-Gheshayan Establishment" on Dirab Road, the road to Mecca.

By the time we got there, it was dark. I could see all the old and familiar structures as well as some new ones. The two Coachman prefab houses were gone and in their place were two new villas. Ed had told me about that before. It was all deserted; I saw no one on the property. Mazen said Khalid lived there until 1990 and since then had moved three times. All those years the State Department never gave me any information about where my daughters lived. I didn't even know the girls did not live with Khalid until several years after his marriage to a Saudi wife.

I found no clues there for me, and I got a chill just looking at the place.

As the driver continued on the road to find a turnaround point, I caught a glimpse of Al-Ali Hospital where Khalid took me after that beating. The road was now a freeway. When I lived there it was on the outskirts of Riyadh, but like Los Angeles, Riyadh had spread and the entire area was built up.

Through the Looking Glass

When I returned to the hotel there were three messages. One was from Robert Thoms in Hejailan's office. I called him back. He said Gheshayan had been in Salman's office and was now cooperating. Salman spoke to Mabus and canceled our meeting for the thirteenth. Gheshayan wanted the American embassy to choose the place for the visit. Supposedly my daughters didn't want to meet with me, but Prince Salman spoke with them and they agreed to the visit. If there were going to be any more meetings, it would be up to the children. (Hejailan was so predictable.)

I said it was unfair to expect me to undo ten years of child abuse in a few hours. I had rights as an American citizen and my daughters had rights as American citizens. They had started the game . . . to ultimately remove any sanity I had left.

A few minutes later Hejailan himself called me. He wanted to allay my anxieties. "Ms. Roush, I spoke with Mr. Gheshayan myself today in the office of Prince Salman. There was an Islamic judge there and Gheshayan was told that I am not conspiring against him but am only a third party trying to solve this problem. Mr. Gheshayan only wants to make peace with you now but doesn't want to be humiliated by you in front of his Saudi wife. You have to understand that he is a poor, uneducated man who is simple, and we should feel sorry for him. You'll see your children without Gheshayan present in the room and the meeting will be at the Equestrian Club or my villa with my wife serving as hostess. She is perfectly capable of handling this. Everyone is on your side. Prince Salman is on your side, the embassy is on your side—kind of—and I am on your side. All I want you to do is relax. You must get out of that room more. I don't know why the embassy doesn't entertain you more and lets you stay alone in that room. We will see you tomorrow." (I later found out that there was no Islamic judge present and Salman had never spoken to my daughters.)

It was the Mad Hatter's Tea Party and I was Alice trying to make sense of it, but different characters kept coming onstage with lines of gibberish. It was as if we were all in the same play but the scripts didn't match.

June 13 was my fifth day in Saudi Arabia and I still had not seen my daughters. At 11:00 A.M. the phone rang in the hotel room. It was Mazen: "It's tonight at 7:00 P.M. at the Equestrian Club. Khalid is coming with one of his brothers. A woman from the Dhahran consulate is coming to help with Khalid. She is a grandmother type and the Saudis like her. Her purpose is to make it go smoothly. If there are no problems with Gheshayan we will have access to the children . . . Don't bring your camera or you will not be allowed to see your daughters again. Those are strict rules from Khalid. If you take a picture, he will use it as an excuse not to allow another visit. Maybe next time. An embassy car will pick you up at five o'clock."

I didn't know what to do. They promised me I could see them every day and it had taken a week to get one visit arranged. What if this was my only chance, and I didn't take a picture? I started to pack the gifts I'd brought for my daughters into a large black bag. I'd brought the blue jeans Aisha requested and Alia's Cabbage Patch and Care Bear dolls.

It was just as Sarah Pang said, "Pat, I had a dream that you were going to see your kids and you were entering a room carrying dolls." The night before I left San Francisco I went to the boxes in the basement where I had stored all the girls' toys. I picked up those two dolls because they were the girls' favorites. They were much too old for dolls but I thought it would bring back happy memories of us together.

Hejailan sent one of the American traitors that works for him to pick me up at the hotel. Myles Webber was with him. The Equestrian Club was closed on Tuesdays so we went to the Intercontinental Hotel. Hejailan had reserved a VIP room off the lobby for the visit with my daughters. Bridget Burkhart from the Dhahran consulate, Mazen, and Glen Carey came in an embassy car shortly after we arrived. I was ushered into the room carrying my black bag. At the last minute I had stuffed one of my cameras into the lining—just in case. The room had an overstuffed sofa, chairs, bed, and small kitchen area with table and chairs. I arranged my gifts for the girls on the bed and began to pace back and forth in the room. The embassy personnel and Hejailan's man were seated in the lobby.

American Daughters

Thirty minutes passed and Glen Carey came into the room. "Khalid is here with his brother Younis. The girls are in the car. He will not allow you to see them alone. He must be in the room or he will leave."

"Glen, go back and tell him that he has an order from Prince Salman allowing me to see the girls alone. I haven't seen my daughters for ten years, and I'm not going to allow them to be frightened and coerced by his presence. Not this time. We deserve that much."

He went back into the lobby. After a few minutes Khalid's brother Younis entered the room. "Hello, Pat. How are you?"

"Hello, Younis. How do you think I am? He took my children."

"I know, Pat, but how are you doing?"

"How are the girls?"

"They are very fine. This is a moment the girls will remember all their lives, and it is important that you don't say anything that will disturb them."

"I'm their mother, and they are my children. You have a mother, don't you? Well, I'm their mother, and I love them. We have a right to be together."

He then searched the room and left.

A few more minutes passed by and Khalid came into the room. I stopped pacing and froze. Our eyes met. "Hello, Patricia."

"Hello, Khalid."

He also searched the room and left.

I hadn't seen him in ten years. He was wearing a Saudi white thobe and headdress and was very overweight, wearing glasses. I paced harder and harder and all of a sudden, Glen Carey walked into the room and said, "Patricia, your daughters are here."

I turned around and saw two young girls wearing black abayas standing near the door. They took the black head scarves and face covers off and draped them around their shoulders. I caught the taller one's eyes. "Is that Alia?"

"Yes."

I ran to them and encircled them both with my arms, kissing their faces all over. "I love you. I love you. I love you."

They stood motionless like tin soldiers, with eyes downcast and empty—tears glistened down their cheeks. Mazen entered the room. I needed him to translate for Aisha. I put one arm around each girl's waist and we walked to the sofa together. I sat in the middle with Alia to my left and Aisha to my right. Mazen sat on one of the overstuffed chairs near Alia. "Mazen, translate everything I say."

I wanted to smell my children, feel their hair and touch their skin. I took their hands in my hands and gently caressed each finger. "I can't tell you how long I have waited for this moment. I have loved you all these years and I will never stop loving you."

Aisha started to cry again. I wiped her tears with my hand. "Don't cry, Aisha, we will be together." Alia said, "My Father told us we would never see you again after tonight."

"No, Alia. That is not true. I am working with the American ambassador and the emir. I am going to get you out of here. I will never stop until you are home with me again."

"My father will never let us leave. How can I leave? I don't have a passport."

"Don't worry about that now. If I get permission for you to leave, that will be arranged."

Then I got up and walked to the bed where I had placed the gifts for the girls. "Aisha, look. I brought you the blue jeans you wanted."

"Helwa" (pretty).

"And a photo album for each of you with pictures of us together when you were my babies. You are still my babies—I don't care how old you are. Nobody can take that away from us." Then I walked up to Aisha and placed a silver and garnet Navajo bracelet on her wrist. "Wear this and remember me."

I tried to dispel some of the lies Khalid had told them about me and what happened. They were confused at first but when I told them the truth, Alia confessed that she did remember. She was forced to obey her father and go along with whatever he ordered her to do. I asked her: "Did he ever touch you anywhere or do anything to you?"

They both denied it. "He won't let me do anything and won't allow anyone except family to come to the villa," said Alia.

Just then the door opened—it was Younis. Alia flashed her black eyes at him and the muscles in her shoulders tensed. Her spine straightened—she was "at attention." I put my arm around her and held her close to me. I placated the brother with small talk and after fifteen minutes, he left. He and Khalid were sitting in the lobby right outside the door with the embassy staff and the lawyer from Hejailan's office.

I asked Aisha, "What do you do all day?"

"Nothing. I stay in my room and listen to my tapes. How old am I?"

"How old do you think you are?"

"Fourteen."

"No. He didn't even tell you how old you are. You are twelve and will be thirteen in a few weeks. Your birthday is July 2, 1982. Alia how old are you?"

"I was born 5 January 1979?"

In Saudi culture birthdays are not celebrated. Alia was sixteen and I gave her a "Sweet Sixteen" birthday card. She didn't understand the significance. Her strong Arab accent was understandable, and she answered readily even though she didn't have opportunities to speak English. Aisha neither spoke nor understood any English words but paid attention to everything I was saying.

The girls were getting tired and it was getting late. I'd only seen them for two hours but the evening had gone quickly because of the conflict created by Khalid. It was eleven o'clock and I didn't want the girls to be overwhelmed. They began to show signs of fatigue and I wanted to be sure we would see each other the next day as I had been promised. So I began to pack up their things as the girls stood by watching me with sad, downcast eyes like dogs that had been kicked and punished and forced into submission.

I said, "I'll see you tomorrow. Remember that song, Alia: 'Tomorrow, tomorrow, I love you, tomorrow. It's only a day away'? Remember that? That was one of your favorites. From *Annie*? You remember—here, I brought you the song on cassette."

She nodded yes. Aisha had been quietly standing near me almost in tears. Unexpectedly, she lunged toward me and threw her arms around my waist and said in English, "I love you. I love you. I love." She wouldn't let me go and tightened her grip. As Aisha and I were in an embrace I turned my head to Alia, "Do you love me, Alia?"

"Yes, I love you, but we will never be able to see you again. My father told us. Please, please don't leave us here, Mama. Take us with you to America."

II

❧

The Princes and the President

June 1995–June 1996

You can't win the election unless your name is on the ballot.
—Ray Mabus

Establish the Work of Our Hands

As they placed the black veils over their faces, my daughters slowly slipped into the dimly lit lobby of the hotel where their father and uncle were waiting to swiftly transport them back into the ninth-century Arab world that had been their prison for the last ten years.

I stood at the doorway and blew kisses to these two shadowy figures in black. Aisha walked a few steps and then turned to face me, waving her hand "good-bye" as she used to do when I would drop her off at preschool. I couldn't see her smile under the veil but our hearts were joined in love. Alia was trying to be brave and kept walking; it was too painful for her to look at the mother she was told she would never see again. Then suddenly she stopped and turned to catch one more look before they disappeared into the night.

My heart and gut ached. I sat on the edge of the bed in the room and stared. The embassy staff walked in. Bridget Burkhart shook my hand. "You were great! You handled that all by yourself. You didn't need us here."

They took me back to the hotel. I couldn't sleep and stayed up all night. I called my mother to tell her about the girls. She started to cry. "Pat, are you going to be able to take them out of there? What if you can't?"

I took a car to the American embassy as soon as they opened. I was sitting in the consul general's office with Mazen and Glen Carey when Khalid called. Mazen spoke to him. Khalid told him I would not be able to see my daughters again because I brainwashed them and made them too confused. He said I told the girls that life in the United States is free. He did his duty and allowed me to see them once, and now it was over.

I asked Mazen to call Prince Salman's office. They said they'd done their part—I got to see my daughters. That's all they ever promised, nothing more. Ray Mabus was traveling and unavailable. I would have to wait for him. Mazen and I talked about the girls. We both agreed that Aisha was very neglected and withdrawn. She was thin and pale and unsure of herself—a little broken bird. Alia appeared a little more robust but looked so unhappy and confused. Mazen said that he was friendly with a Gheshayan relative who told him that Khalid had made Alia his special project and indoctrinated her against me, the United States, and anything of the West. It was not working.

I called my old friend Sarah Pang, who was now working for Mayor Daley in Chicago. She had a friend in the White House and said she would call him.

The next day Ray Mabus called me at the hotel. I filled him in on the meeting with the children and told him I wanted them to come home with me. I asked him to go to the princes and let them know how much this meant to the American government. I would go to the press, and ABC *20/20* would be airing the interview with Barbara Walters in the fall. He said, "I will do everything I can to help, Pat. I'll call Hejailan in the morning."

I was cooped up in the hotel room and got a call from the lobby. I had received a fax. It was from David:

Dearest Pat:

I'm thinking about you. It's 7:30 P.M. and I'm wondering where you are and what you're feeling. I sat in silence trying to hold you in my thoughts. My message is I love you so much and I am very worried about you. I pray for your safe return.

It took a few days for the reality of this to hit me. I had to be strong before you left. I think about you every day but today I felt it important to write my feelings down and send them rather than call.

I realize how much danger you are in and can't imagine the anxiety you must feel at this time. I know the Holy Spirit is with you and that's reassuring. I feel hopeless because I can't protect you from this one.

It remains to be seen whether or not you will return with your children, but I can say that you are in my prayers. There are a lot of people praying and hoping for the best for you.

I love you and pray for your safe return.

David

His words and love sustained me in that cell. In the long days and hours I spent alone in the hotel room, my thoughts would drift to David and our love. He was the love of my life. I was sure that God had sent him to me and that we would be together into the next life. I had never felt that way about any man.

I strategized all day and all night—wrote copious notes on plans of attack and kept my diary full. I had such bad insomnia, sleeping like a cat on guard every minute. The days and nights blurred together: playing *The Peaceful Pond,* watching *M*A*S*H* reruns, Saudi TV, making tea in the room and eating dates from the souk, *Saudi* men in the lobby smoking cigarettes and sifting me with their eyes whenever I would slip into my abaya to get a meal behind the screen.

Court of Death

I asked the embassy to request a personal meeting for me with Prince Salman in his office at the governor's palace in Headchopper's Square. It was granted.

An official government car picked me up and took me to the American embassy. Mazen and Myles Webber were waiting for me and we were driven to the palace. I was dressed in a long black abaya and black headscarf and wore no makeup. As my feet touched the stones of the parking area in front of the gigantic, wooden doors of the medieval castle, I remembered the documentary *Death of a Princess*. Was this the spot where she died? How much human suffering did these stones hold?

A guard opened the castle doors, and I walked in with Mazen and Myles on each side of me. I knew they would not be able to help me and had no authority with the Saudi government. They were just escorts and couldn't speak for the U.S. government. I was on my own. We were taken down long, dark, narrow hallways that turned and twisted into many other passages. It looked like a scene from *Arabian Nights*.

Then we were led into a small room where the chief of protocol for Prince Salman, Bandar Al-Yousef, sat. A small desk lamp provided the only source of light. Smoke billowed from an electric incense burner on the table. Mazen spoke to the man in Arabic. We were told by Hejailan that we had an appointment with Prince Salman. The man left the room to do some inquiring. When he returned we were told that we had no such appointment. Prince Salman was not available. He said I could go to the "women's room" and write a letter to the governor about what I wanted. Mazen said it would do me no good.

Mazen spoke to Al-Yousef again. Bleihed was called and the three of us were escorted down another long hall to a huge receiving room, the majlis, with overstuffed chairs all along the walls. Myles and Mazen sat on my right. Then Deputy Governor Bleihed and Assistant Deputy Governor Ali Al-Otaibi came in and sat on my left. I thanked them for everything Prince Salman had done and then told them, "As you know, this has been going on for a long time. I saw my daughters for two hours after ten years of separation and they told me they loved me. I want to be allowed to take my daughters home with me for the summer. I am grateful for any assistance your office can give to me. Girls need their mother, and I am willing to suspend all the warrants for the arrest of Khalid Al-Gheshayan. He can travel, and we can work this out amicably. There is no need for things to go on like this. I am asking you for this favor."

Bleihed spoke in English: "I'm sorry, but we cannot do that. You must go to court to decide such matters. It is not for this office to get involved with this matter."

"But they are my children. Girls need their mother. Mr. Gheshayan has had them for ten years. I want them to know me, and I want to know them. Please, as a mother, I ask you."

The response was unchanged. I returned to the hotel and called Hejailan. I told him what had happened. He didn't flinch. "Ms. Roush, your ambassador is good friends with President Clinton. Why don't you ask him to call the president. I think if the American president calls King Fahad, things could go well for you."

Ambassador Mabus called and I explained the course of events of the day and what Hejailan said about the president calling the king. He said he could easily get through to the White House—he always got through to the president. The problem was that any presidential call to a head of state goes through two channels: (1)the national security adviser and (2) the State Department. It takes a long time through protocol to get that kind of call approved. He said he would call Bleihed in the morning and try to see what it would take to get the girls out. He repeated, "I'm totally committed to getting those two girls out of this country."

Careful, Careful

Finally I was able to sleep for eight hours straight. I got myself under control and put my faith in Ray Mabus. After breakfast I went to the desk and requested my Bangladesh driver. I asked him to take me to Al-Badia, the neighborhood where the girls supposedly lived. I took my camera. We drove up and down the streets and passed a school for children. I wondered if that was the school my daughters attended. It was a weekend and no one was there. We pulled off to the side of the road. I did not have my face covered and almost immediately a Saudi man pulled up alongside our car. "Can I help you? Are you lost?"

"No, I'm just drinking some water. Thank you."

No wonder Ed couldn't do surveillance—they knew every move a stranger made. No one was on the street and yet eyes were everywhere.

The driver told me a story: He was driving two English women who worked at one of the local hospitals from a party. It was about one in the morning. A Saudi with a utility vehicle pulled in front of the car and would not allow them to pass. When the driver got out of the car, the Saudi beat him. He then ordered the two women out of the car and told them to strip to the waist. He started to fondle them and was going to rape them when another Saudi pulled up. He told the women to get dressed and told the first Saudi to leave. There was no recourse. If the driver went to the police, they wouldn't do anything because he was not a Saudi—the women had no rights at all. Case closed.

Mabus Takes Over

Ray Mabus met with Bleihed and outlined a plan—the girls would leave with me and all warrants against Gheshayan would be dropped. The girls could go back and forth and visit Saudi Arabia and the U.S. Bleihed said he would talk to Gheshayan about letting me see the girls again. He would speak to Salman about Mabus's plan.

I called Mazen to tell him the news. He asked, "Did Khalid ever finish the university in the States?"

"No. He basically just drank. He was a big-time alcoholic."

"He still is."

"How do you know?"

"Because he has asked me in the past if I knew anyplace where he could buy alcohol."

Mazen didn't think Khalid made much money. If he was still drinking, where did he get the money to buy black-market alcohol? He had all those children and a Saudi wife and still drank. Why couldn't I just take my daughters out of this mess?

I lost ten pounds in four days. I was feeling dizzy when I stood up and almost fainted in the shower. The whole thing was too much for me. Mom called and said she went to the cemetery and prayed for the girls on the grave of Bella Papa. I never dared to tell her what was happening to me.

Ambassador Mabus had an appointment to meet Khalid in Governor Salman's office. He brought the deputy chief of the mission and the political officer of the embassy with him. Bleihed was there. Khalid kept them all waiting for over an hour.

Mabus offered him a release of all warrants and a visa to the United States in addition to free air tickets for his entire family. "Why should I trust you or the United States?" Khalid asked. Bleihed leaned on him heavily: "Take it. It's a good offer. Take it."

"I'm not interested in this. I don't want to travel."

Mabus prodded, "These warrants will stay forever. You will never travel outside of this country. I'm offering you a good deal. You're still young. You might want to travel."

It ended with Khalid standing up, calling the U.S. ambassador a liar, and walking out. Mabus called me after the meeting. "Pat, this is the meanest man in the whole world. He blamed you for everything in his life that has gone wrong. He said, 'It is all her fault.'"

I said, "What's my fault?"

"Apparently everything."

"You know, I'm not going to be able to stay here any longer. I almost fainted this morning and I feel so sick. I don't know what to do."

"Pat, just go on home. I'll get your kids out of here. You need to rest. We can do this from here. Once I get the girls released, we'll have someone from the embassy fly home with them."

I started crying. "Don't worry," said Mabus. "Just remember, there's a lot of people at this embassy who love you and we won't give up."

Glen Carey took me to the airport in an embassy car. We went through security and were sitting at the departure gate. There was a little Saudi girl about four years old dancing in front of me. She held her mother's burqa to her face as she twirled in circles to her own music. I was numb and stared in silence. I wondered how long it would take for this child's spirit to be broken, and her joy turned into a life of sadness.

The final boarding call was made, and as I stood up to walk down the ramp and enter the aircraft, I took my abaya off and threw it on the seat of the boarding area. Carey said, "Don't you want that?"

"No, I won't be needing it anymore."

Almost comatose, I landed in New York. As I was leaving the customs area I heard my name over the loud speaker. Then I saw the producer from *20/20*, Gwen Gowan. She was there with a camera crew and a car. After a brief interview they took me to Brooklyn where I would stay for a few days with my longtime friend Jeanette. I couldn't make it to San Francisco. I was almost near collapse. My friend said, "They got what they wanted; they wanted you to leave."

When I returned to San Francisco, Ray Mabus called. He had been trying to call Bandar for several days. He left messages for him and the calls were never returned.

Mabus said Bandar was in Aspen at his palace. He knew what Mabus was calling about and didn't want to talk to him. This went on for a week and then an article came out about me in *Jewish Week*. I tried to enlist the help of two U.S. senators from California, Barbara Boxer and Dianne Feinstein, but their assistants would hardly speak to me.

At least I had *20/20* lined up for the fall television season. I thought the interview with Barbara Walters would force the Saudis to make the final arrangements. I had been able to make some home videos in the hotel room in Riyadh chronicling the ordeal. We had tapes at the airport before and after I left and the interview with Barbara Walters at the Pierre Hotel. The producer told me, "We are very happy with the films we have."

It was August 1995. I had been home for six weeks and was so needy. I felt so alone. Visions of the girls standing in that hotel lobby with those black robes and veils haunted me. The image of their sad eyes cast down in submission and fear, devoid of hope, remained etched in my heart.

No Help at Home

Coping with all the high-stakes politics for my daughters, the stress of a nursing job, and living alone was finally becoming too much for me to bear. My relationship with David was not the way I wanted it to be. I hardly saw him. His two jobs kept him busy seven days a week, and he never had any time for me. I was alone and in tears.

There were a number of issues with David that bothered me but I didn't want to leave him. I wanted to work on these matters together with him. He smoked and liked to drink. Some evenings he would buy a bottle of wine and drink the whole bottle throughout the evening. On the musical gigs he drank Scotch and bourbon throughout the night. Sometimes I would find a half pint of tequila in the garbage. He didn't act drunk, and I never noticed any overt changes in his personality, but I thought his lifestyle patterns were not healthy. He had gained thirty pounds since I met him. He was full of indulgences and excesses. That, coupled with his seven-day-a-week work schedule, put him on a treadmill. As a nurse I saw a time bomb ticking. I said, "Dave, I have patients in the hospital your age who have heart attacks. Can't you cut some of this stuff out?"

He avoided answering me. He always said he would stop smoking when he was ready. He told me he liked to drink and denied there was a problem. "Have you ever seen me drunk?" He had two grandfathers who died from alcoholism. I wanted to keep the good qualities about him and get rid of the bad.

David and I had planned to take a few days off and rented a cabin on a lake, just north of San Francisco. I wanted to talk to him about the future and what we wanted as a couple together—our goals. We had known each other for five years, and I certainly loved him and wanted us to be committed to each other.

So I thought once we were alone at the lake it would be a good time to bring up our relationship and bring everything out in the open. He loved the water. He loved to swim and I just loved to watch him. His strong, broad shoulders moving through the water were poetry in motion. We had spent so many wonderful moments around the water. The first night we met, we went to the beach. I loved him and I wanted him. But I didn't like what was happening to him.

While we were achored in a cove at Lake Almanor, north of San Francisco, I was sitting on the side of the boat, watching David swim a few feet away. Suddenly, he threw his bathing suit on the deck. "Dave, are you crazy? You can't skinny-dip here."

He just laughed and smiled at me with his dancing green-hazel eyes. "Who's here?"

He was always up for mischief. He had an exuberant spirit that was infectious. At first, I'd found it refreshing, but after five years I found it frustrating. He was like a child that wouldn't grow up—an overindulgent child. His Latin mother made him the center of her life and even read all his college textbooks to him because he couldn't see the print. His former German wife "waited on him," according to his father and friends. He rewarded her by cheating on her, and she became very bitter. Of course, he didn't tell me this. I found out many years later. His two daughters were given the honor of taking up where the wife left off. I refused to either wait on him or indulge him. I was trying to change him.

"Dave, why don't you come up here . . . I need to talk to you."

"Can I ask you a question, Pat? Why do you want to ruin my vacation? Whenever I'm having a good time, you want to ruin it. Why?"

He refused to discuss anything meaningful and honest while continuing with his self destructive lifestyle. I would grow weary of all of it and ultimately a great division would occur.

On the Trail

In the meantime, Ray Mabus made a trip to Washington and while at the State Department met with Assistant Secretary of State for Near Eastern Affairs Robert Pelletreau. They talked extensively about my case, and Pelletreau brought the matter up with Bandar personally. According to Mabus, Pelletreau told Bandar it meant a great deal to the U.S. government to have my case closed and settled. Mabus pressured the number two man at the Saudi embassy, Adel Jubeir, and spoke with him for one hour about how to settle it all. Jubeir asked that Gheshayan be given a chance and Mabus answered, "Given a chance! This guy's a criminal here and defied our courts. You're talking about assurances! First, he illegally took those children and broke our laws. Then he kept them away from their mother for ten years, and now you want guarantees that if those children come to the States for a visit, we will send them right back to this guy?"

Mabus said he was still waiting for Bandar and had his aide call Bandar's office in Riyadh twice per day, just to get their attention. He said he had a dinner meeting scheduled with Bandar in Jeddah but "I wouldn't bet my paycheck on it." He wanted to meet with Salman, but he was in the United States with one of his wives getting medical attention.

Eventually, Mabus did corner Bandar in Jeddah. "I told him about the deal I promised Gheshayan and Bandar said, 'Why won't this guy do it? This is a good deal. I promise you, Fred Dutton or Adel Jubeir will put something together on this.'"

Mabus told Bandar about Barbara Walters. "I said, 'You know, Barbara Walters is going to do this thing, and it's not going to look good.'"

I asked him what Bandar's response was.

"He said, 'Yeah, I know. I met Barbara Walters at a party and she told me about it. I will make this thing happen.'"

My attorney placed a conference call to the Washington attorney for the Saudi embassy, Fred Dutton. He asked about the conversation between Ray Mabus and Bandar. Dutton responded, "That's the biggest con game out. No Christian or Jewish judge in the U.S. would send kids back to Saudi

Arabia. This is an impossible situation that would take the 'wisdom of Solomon' to figure out. I know a very wealthy Saudi who can't even get visitation with his kids in the U.S. I could quote you horror stories about the Saudis losing their children to American mothers. Besides, Israel has more of these cases than Saudi Arabia—no deal."

Dutton was asked if he represented Khalid Al-Gheshayan and he responded, "No, I represent the best interests of the Saudi Arabian government."

My attorney then called Adel Jubeir at the Saudi embassy—no response.

Two weeks after Mabus spoke with Bandar in Jeddah and mentioned the Barbara Walters show, the executive producer from *20/20*, Victor Neufeld, would no longer accept the calls from my attorney, and Barbara Walters's interview with me was canceled with no explanation. The segment never aired.

Ray Mabus went to Washington in September 1995 for the signing of the Mideast Peace Process. I telephoned him at the Four Seasons Hotel on September 28, 1995. He'd been to the White House a few days before, seeing people who could help. "I spoke to Harold Ickes the other day. You know him? His father was the secretary of state under FDR. He's known here as a mover and shaker and definitely in the loop. I also spoke to Mac McClarty, former chief of staff and now deputy chief of staff. He's a good guy from Arkansas—kinda next to the president's heart." He also spoke with staff from the Senate Foreign Relations Committee.

"Prince Sultan, Bandar's father, is coming to the U.S. sometime in late October, and I will be meeting with him several times before his trip to Washington," he told me. "I'll be with him while he's here. I'll tell Sultan that it would be a nice gesture if he brings the girls with him on his trip."

I told Mabus about the conversation with Fred Dutton. "I'll call Dutton myself," he said. "He's nothing but a hired hand, anyway. Pat, you know, I tell people . . . anyone who wants to marry a Saudi ought to go talk to Pat Roush before they do anything."

I asked him who had the power in the Saudi government to make the decision for the girls to come home. "Can any of the princes just order Gheshayan to sign the paper and put them on a plane? I know in 1986

Salman was going to bring him in and 'persuade' him to cooperate. They have their methods of influence—they can pretty much do anything they want. It's not a democracy, and their Sharia law is ambiguous; totally up to the interpretation of the individual . . . I was wondering if one prince gives his okay and another tries to stop it, what happens? Salman might resist, but Sultan might say yes. What is the order of power in that family?"

Mabus responded, "We don't know for sure. This is a problem with that government."

Another month went by and Prince Sultan did come for his visit. He was accompanied by his son Prince Bandar, Saudi ambassador to the United States. Their visit to the White House was televised and they made a deal with Boeing—$6 billion for passenger planes for the Saudi-owned national airlines (Saudia). But no deal for my daughters. Ray Mabus was not able to be alone with Sultan or Bandar during the trip.

Pins and Knives

At the White House after almost everyone had left, Mabus and Pelletreau met with Saudi Deputy Chief of the Mission Rehab Mahsoud. He had been present at Senator Dixon's office in April 1987 when Dixon requested a meeting with Bandar regarding the return of Alia and Aisha.

I'm sure Mahsoud remembered my name when Ray Mabus brought up the matter some nine years later. They spoke to him for about twenty minutes about the plan Mabus had outlined, and Mahsoud agreed the plan sounded good. Mabus asked him to call me or my attorney and work on the details together. They shook hands and Mahsoud said he would cooperate. Mabus was excited to tell me about this. He finally thought he had someone on the other side we could work things out with.

A few days later I called Mahsoud at the Saudi embassy. He took the call.

"Mr. Mahsoud, this is Patricia Roush. I'm calling about the conversation you had at the White House a few days ago with Ambassador Mabus and Ambassador Pellatreau."

"Who? Who? I never heard of you or anything about you. I never spoke to Mabus. I will refer you to Consular Affairs."

"Do you have a problem with your memory? Have you heard of Alan Dixon?"

"I don't know who you are and none of what you are saying ever happened. Did you hear me? It never happened! *Never happened!*"

I started crying so hard, I couldn't stop. I was hysterical. He treated me as Hejailan had, like something to be discarded—"How dare you bother me." They got just what they wanted—their airplanes. They thought they could buy anything and anyone, and they did. I had to deal with people like Hejailan and the Saudi hierarchy—all men—to get back what they stole from me, while my innocent girls languished with their madman father in a fiery inferno.

I called Ray Mabus at home and told him what had happened with Mahsoud. I was still crying. He was shocked. He told me not to worry; he would come up with another plan.

November 14, 1995: A car bomb exploded in Riyadh, killing at least five Americans and injuring thirty-five others near King Fahad Hospital where Khalid worked. Located remotely outside the city, the hospital was built for the Saudi National Guard, which is composed of mostly bedouin. The building that was bombed was used by the American military to train Saudi personnel for the National Guard. Similar to the Oklahoma City bombing, a van was filled with explosives and then detonated. Ray Mabus was overwhelmed, and I couldn't get through to him. I spoke to his wife, Julie, and she said she was just trying to "stay out of his way." He was interviewed on CNN.

Things had quieted down a little by Thanksgiving and I called him at home for an update. He said he had gone back to Prince Bandar, who said he thought the matter was solved. Mabus told him about Dutton and Mahsoud, but Bandar danced around it again. Because of the bombing, Mabus was seeing the princes almost daily. During a meeting with Prince Saud Bin Faisal, minister of foreign affairs and powerful son of the late King Faisal, he told him the story. Prince Saud said, "I hate people who kidnap children. This is an awful story." The prince was British-educated and even-tempered. Mabus said he was the most reasonable of them all.

"Your Highness, this woman hasn't seen her children but once in ten years and girls need to be with their mother," Mabus told him.

The prince agreed that girls needed to be with their mother. He asked if this was an official request from the U.S. government or just an informal matter. Mabus said it was official. Saud then requested that it be in writing on an official diplomatic note. Mabus said he would send it by the end of the day. The conversation happened about noon and the note was on Prince Saud's desk by 5:00 P.M.

Since the bombing Mabus had been under extreme stress and was quite upset about the loss of American lives in Saudi Arabia. "I want the girls out, but I don't know about these guys. I just don't trust them," he said. "I'll see Prince Saud once a week for the next few months because of the bombing and will be able to follow up about the kids."

The Royals

In December of 1995 the Saudi king had a severe stroke and the entire Saudi government shut down. Prince Salman became the host for visiting family members at the King Faisal Hospital Royal Wing. Ray Mabus was not able to follow through with Prince Saud Bin Faisal. The king was expected to recover, but his physical and mental capacities would be greatly diminished. Crown Prince Abdullah became the de facto ruler.

Before the king's stroke, Ambassador Mabus was able to meet with Prince Salman and gave him an official diplomatic note from the U.S. government. Salman said, "If this is official, then you shall have an official answer." Mabus told Salman that Gheshayan was rude to him and called him a liar and that he had taken it to the foreign minister, Prince Saud. "Pat, I told him, 'This is personal now.'"

The holiday season was upon me, and I was slipping into the deep blues again. On Christmas Eve I was most depressed. I called Mabus at his home in Jackson, Mississippi. He said he saw Prince Saud before he left Saudi Arabia for Christmas and Saud said, "I'm trying to give Mr. Gheshayan a big headache. I'm going to try to solve this."

"This is the one I really want to solve," Mabus told Saud, adding, "The only way is for you guys to solve it. We've done everything we can from this side." Saud responded, "If a government can't be human, they don't deserve to be a government. We don't have enough joy. You're better at joy than we are."

The Saudis might have been the only ones who could really bring the case to resolution, but Mabus told me of his plan to pressure them. "I've put everyone in that family on the Watch List. If any of them want to come to the United States, they have to come in and see me. Nobody gets in."

When I told him about Khalid and his father coming to the Cleveland Clinic with diplomatic passports, he answered, "Well, I hope his mama wants to come to the Cleveland Clinic, too. Because she's not coming! The new consul general, Dick Herman, said, 'What's the justification for holding up these visas?' and I said, 'Because the ambassador says so, that's why!'"

In early January 1996, Mabus met with Prince Saud Bin Faisal and he said the prince was ready for him. He told Ray Mabus that he was talking to Minister of the Interior Prince Naif about the situation and Prince Naif would call Gheshayan into his office and force him to sign the papers giving the girls the freedom we sought for them. Mabus sent a diplomatic note to Prince Naif when he returned to the embassy.

On February 5, 1996, Consul General Dick Herman called me in response to the diplomatic note they'd received from the Saudi Foreign Ministry. It stated that if all charges against Gheshayan were overturned, the girls could come back to the United States for the summer of 1996. My first reaction was that this was just another stall mechanism or trick, but Ray Mabus confirmed that it was real and this was the first time in ten years that we had something in writing—something official from the Saudi government allowing the girls to leave.

"I Could Get a Pistol"

An irate Khalid began calling the American embassy two and three times a day to scream at Mazen or Dick Herman and then hang up on them. The princes were calling him in and he didn't like it. He blamed Dick and Mazen for "this problem with my family." He told them there was unbelievable pressure from his family and he was being "backed into a corner." Dick offered to meet him at the embassy and promised him no harm would come to him. Khalid adamantly refused and threatened Mazen and Dick, "I could get a pistol and kill both of you."

Then Khalid's brother Younis called the embassy. He said Khalid was very angry and had hung up on him, also. Younis was upset with Khalid because he needed the visa censorship to be lifted for their mother, but we didn't know that until later. Every prince was after Khalid and he was out of control. He told Mazen that they were singling him out and this visa censorship had never been done before; this was discrimination against his family. "You are ruining my reputation with my family." For a Saudi, it is very humiliating to be embarrassed in this way in front of your family. The family is everything, and they were all mad at Khalid.

Mazen told me, "Pat, you should come here. There is so much action going on now. This is the first time anything like this has happened."

Another family member wanted to obtain a visa, the Royal Air Force pilot, Lt. Colonel Magik Al-Gheshayan, who had met me at the Dhahran Airport in 1985. He was ordered to lead a training mission into the United States. When he went to the American embassy for his visa, he was told he had to meet with the American ambassador. He proudly refused.

Shortly after that I called Ray Mabus—he was having a dinner party at his residence that night. He was jubilant: "The general of the American army called me tonight and said, 'What should I tell this Lieutenant Colonel Gheshayan? He was supposed to lead a training group into the U.S.' I said go tell him to talk to Khalid."

Mabus continued, "All the guys at the embassy are loving this so much right now. They can finally fight back. They are empowered and are now encouraging me to hold the visas. This has never been done before. They just had to take all this stuff from these guys and couldn't do anything. Now they can use the visas. It works. And it has the blessings of the State Department."

I told Ray Mabus that Khalid was threatening to kill Dick Herman and

Mazen and asked if they shouldn't report this to the Saudi authorities. He said, yes, that was a good idea, especially with the security problems and bombing. I also asked him if he would put all the members of Khalid's wife's family on the Watch List and he said that also was a great idea—he would get right on it.

Dick and Mazen were trying to see the girls again and take a photograph for me. Khalid refused to let them see Alia and instead brought Aisha and his youngest daughter by his Saudi wife. It was too dangerous for Alia to be able to talk to the Americans—she understood English and wanted to leave. Mazen noticed that Aisha was wearing the silver bracelet I had given her during the visit. She could not speak to them and Khalid kept her under his total control. He said he would never allow them to come to the States but wanted the visa censorship removed. No photographs of Aisha were allowed.

The Oval Office

Dick Herman then informed me that he was sorry but some of the Gheshayan family members—Fatima, and Khalid's brother Younis—had gotten through the Watch List and been issued visas to the States. I couldn't believe it. "When did they come in?"

"Last September. They came for medical treatment for the mother, who has been sick."

"The brother told me she was not well last summer when I saw my children. They had the nerve to refuse to allow me to visit my daughters and then come into my country for medical treatment to save their mother—the queen herself, who wouldn't even let me speak to my little girls when I would call her house, the woman who would hang up the phone on me while my children wept in the background, came into my country to have my countrymen save her life?"

"I'm really sorry, Pat. It was a mistake, and it will never happen again."

"Does the ambassador know about this?"

"Yes, he is very upset."

"How could this happen? The ambassador gave the order. After all they did to me last summer and now she gets to come into my country so American doctors and nurses can save her? I wonder if they knew they were treating a criminal who is harboring American children held hostage? This is more than unfair."

"Pat, this was an oversight. I know it's hard for you."

Ray Mabus called to apologize and said, "Pat, I told everyone down at consular services, 'If this happens again, someone's gonna get fired.' I'm sorry. It will not happen again." He went on to say, "But I have some good news for you. I did go to Washington last week and saw the president."

"Were you able to talk about the girls?"

"Yes, I did. I only had a moment but I said, 'Mr. President, there is a matter of great concern here that I think you should know about. It is a tragedy that involves an American woman who hasn't been able to see her children but two hours in ten years. He asked what I was doing about it and I told him about the visa situation."

"What did he say, Ray?"

"He said, 'You're doin' the right thing. Keep on holding up the visas and let me know what happens.'"

Quid Pro Quo

Within the next week one of Khalid's relatives, General Shakir Al-Gheshayan from the Crown Prince's National Guard, tried to get a visa to the United States. He was told he had to go to the American ambassador—no visa would be issued. Herman was told by the consular section at the embassy that there was a very irate Saudi general who wanted to speak to him. He told the general that the problem was because of Khalid. The general stated, "I hate this man. No one in the family likes him. I'll take this to the crown prince."

Then Mabus and the deputy chief of the mission were summoned to the crown prince's office two days later and General Gheshayan was present. He told Mabus if he didn't go to Houston for cancer treatment, he would die. The ambassador stated, "I don't want to kill you; I just want this done."

The general said, "What do you want me to do with him? I'll kill him and put him in a box!"

Mabus said, "No. I don't want you to kill him, and I don't want you to die. I'll give you the visa, but no one else will get in until this is settled. I want this straightened out with Khalid and these children returned to their mother." He told the crown prince about his meeting with Khalid and how he was insulted. The crown prince apologized to the ambassador and told him if Khalid was rude, then Mabus did the right thing in holding up the visas to family members.

Then Mabus told the crown prince that he was leaving; he had to go back to Mississippi for family matters. He would resign as U.S. ambassador to Saudi Arabia. The crown prince said that Mabus had been the best ambassador and wanted to grant him one last favor. He thanked him for saving the life of his general and asked what Mabus wanted personally from him. Ray Mabus said, "Your Highness, I don't want your medals, thank you. I just want these two little girls to be able to go home to California and be with their mother. That's all I want."

The crown prince said he would do it and appointed his assistant, Abdul Mohsen Al-Tuagery, to work with the embassy to make the final arrangements for the girls to leave.

Mabus called me to tell me the news. "Pat, I'm sorry, but I have to go back to Mississippi. I miss my girls. My wife didn't come back here after Christmas—she's had just about as much fun as she can handle here. I can't live without my daughters. So I'm leaving in two weeks."

"Oh, no. Then the girls are lost. Once you leave, the State Department will drop the whole thing again."

"No. That's not going to happen. Pat, I've made believers out of these guys. Dick Herman and Ted Katouf—they're empowered now. They can finally fight back. You see, before they had no ammunition to use. This visa stuff works. They feel good about it."

"Who's taking your place?"

"He's another political appointee—Wyche Fowler, former senator from Georgia. I've already briefed him about your case."

"Have you ever met him? What kind of person is he?"

"I met him once briefly. Don't know much about him. Only know that he lobbied really hard for this job. Really wanted it."

"I'm afraid. I don't trust the State Department. They've double-crossed me and lied to me so many times. You're the only one I trust, and now you're leaving. What are we going to do without you?"

12

❧

DARK NIGHT OF THE SOUL

JUNE 1996–DECEMBER 1997

*God takes what we give Him; but He doesn't give
Himself completely until we give ourselves completely.*
—St. Teresa of Avila

Two Paths

Ray Mabus resigned just a few weeks before another tragic loss of American lives occurred in Saudi Arabia. In late June 1996 a powerful truck bomb exploded outside a high-rise apartment building housing U.S. Air Force personnel near Dhahran, Saudi Arabia. Nineteen American airmen were dead and 345 others injured. The two-path strategy used by the Saud princes was backfiring. Repression of the Saudi population by the use of censorship, strict Wahhabi Islamic rules, quick, severe punishment for any dissidence, and use of the secret police, military police, and religious police kept a lid on a cauldron that was ready to burst.

Saudis could switch on Saudi state television on any Friday and see a panoply of preachers—officially approved and even paid by the Saudi government—routinely referring to Christians and Jews as "infidels," "atheists," and "usurpers of Muslims."

Speaking to millions of Saudis, the preachers inveighed against traveling to the West and called upon believers to shun satellite dishes and all contact with foreigners. The same messages were heard almost daily on radio and in thousands of mosques around the country, even as the Saudi government maintained close strategic, military, and political ties to these same "infidels" in the United States and Europe.

The Saudi royal family had maintained this approach by declaring its diplomatic and economic friendship with the outside powers whose support was vital to its survival, while allowing a totally different view of the West to be promoted by the country's vast religious establishment, which provided a much-needed connection between the ruling family and the country's fifteen to eighteen million people.

For decades that two-path approach served the ruling family well. The Saudi royal family was able to sell huge amounts of oil to the West, which was eager to provide them with enormous wealth and protection from hostile neighbors like Iraq and Iran.

Tens of thousands of foreigners worked in Saudi Arabia and had been confined to compounds isolated along the Red Sea and the oil-producing area around Dhahran.

But the poorly educated Saudis had been insulated from the modern trends sweeping much of the Middle East and were instead hearing the increasingly intense messages of the mullahs. The high unemployment, a youthful population with no outlets, and increasing religious fervor of these disenfranchised Saudis created a breakdown in this system that had worked so well for the Saudi ruling family. Since the Persian Gulf War of 1991, it had been harder and harder for the royal family to keep their contradictory approaches to the West on separate planes.

The Soviet invasion of Afghanistan provided an outlet for the hundreds of Saudis who believed in fighting for Islam against the atheistic Soviets. At the end of the Soviet occupation these men returned home to Saudi Arabia to continue the struggle. The four men executed for the November 1995 bombing in Riyadh that killed five Americans and two Indians had all served in Afghanistan.

A hard-core group of religious scholars founded the Committee for the Defense of Legitimate Rights, demanding more rigorous enforcement of Islamic law and an end to government corruption. They hated the regime, and Americans became a symbol of everything they loathed: corruption, joblessness, exclusion from decision making, and anything alien. The American air base was a convenient target. The militants became heroes and the regime had a hard time cracking down on them because they fought for Islam against atheism and the Soviets, and the religious establishment admired them. If the regime started rounding them up, they would lose more religious clerics, which would widen the ideological base of the militants. The process seemed unstoppable and the Saud family had no solutions.

One of the young airmen killed at the Khobar Tower bombing was Mike Heiser. He was thirty-five years old and "married to the air force." June 25, 1996, the day of the bombing, was the seventeenth anniversary of Mike's enlistment. It was also the day he died. He was an only child of an only-child mom who looked forward to planning a wedding and spoiling grandchildren. His father was a retired military man, and Mike had spent part of his childhood traveling with his parents. He enjoyed his job as a radio operator on the Gulfstream jets that were part of a fleet that transports dignitaries around the world. Assigned to General Norman Schwarzkopf during the Gulf War, Mike loved his job and wasn't afraid to live in Saudi Arabia.

Mike Heiser was so dedicated to the U.S. Air Force that he became one of the most decorated enlisted men—the top 5 percent. According to his mom, Fran, "Mike was just a regular guy who came home on leave whenever he could, slept late, didn't clean his room, wore jeans, drank beer, drove a new BMW, and played the stock market when it was worth doing. He was a great shopper and would always send boxes from strange places regularly with something special for us." The epitaph on his headstone at Arlington National Cemetery reads, "Everyone's Best Friend." His grieving parents wonder why their son's life was senselessly taken in Saudi Arabia—their government has neither given them an answer nor provided any redress.

Judas's Kiss

Ray Mabus was back in Mississippi where he was working on the Clinton Re-election Committee. Deputy Chief of the Mission Ted Katouf became the chargé d'affaires of the American embassy in Riyadh. The new ambassador had not arrived yet. I waited until the excitement of the Khobar bombing subsided to call the American embassy in Riyadh. The deputy chief of the mission and acting consul general would never take my calls, and when Consul General Dick Herman came back from his leave one month later, he was very evasive. We no longer shared an open trust and communication as we did when Ray Mabus was ambassador. Herman was guarded.

It had been three months since Ray Mabus resigned. I found out that the visa to the United States for Majik Al-Gheshayan, the lieutenant colonel in the Saudi Royal Air Force, had gone through. I called Mazen. "Pat, you can't believe the pressure Dick was under from both governments. The American Air Force, the Saudi Air Force, the Ministry of Defense—it was too much for him to handle. He had no choice but to issue that visa for Majik. He said he had nothing to do with the kidnapping and shouldn't be a part of this. He called Khalid and had a fight with him on the phone. Then Khalid hung up on him. You know how Khalid is, Pat."

"The visa hold policy was so effective because we finally had something they wanted—and the family pressure was working to get Khalid to sign the kids out. Now," I said, "we have nothing."

Herman tried to reassure me that he and the embassy would continue to try to get the girls out, but they would not go to the crown prince or any of the other princes. I had to work it out with Khalid and his family. I said, "What are you doing? You know what happened with Ray Mabus. For the last year this has been on the level of the Saudi royal family and now you want me to work it out with Khalid and his family? The crown prince gave his okay to the whole thing. It was a quid pro quo—the life of the general for the release of the girls. He even appointed his assistant to help the embassy with the details. Today you let the pilot in and tomorrow it will be the whole family. It's back to where it was ten years ago . . . Do you know what it is taking for me to control myself? Instead of Khalid being put in a box, I'll be the one in the box."

"Well, Pat, we think that maybe if you write a letter of apology to Khalid's brother Younis, maybe he will help persuade Khalid to allow you to see the girls again."

"You've got to be kidding. These people have terrorized me and my daughters for over ten years and you've just given them back everything they wanted and sacrificed the lives of my children, and now you want me to apologize to them?"

I called Ray Mabus in Mississippi and he said he would call Katouf but couldn't offer much else now that he was no longer ambassador.

In August there was a message from Dick Herman—Khalid's mother was dead. My mother became ill at the same time they were seeking medical treatment in the U.S. for Fatima. I had made a request to the Gheshayan family that the girls be allowed to come home to see my mother. She was scheduled to have a very serious heart operation that summer and might not live after the surgery. They refused my request but insisted that the American embassy give a visa to their mother to enter the United States so the American doctors could save her life. She had come into the States right after I saw the girls in June 1995, but Mabus would not allow her to enter again unless the girls were returned to me. Gheshayan's brother Younis told Consul General Dick Herman that they would take the mother elsewhere and would not return my daughters, no matter what the cost. My mother almost didn't make it when the back wall of her heart broke open during the surgery. She was not lost, however; a miracle happened, and God worked through the hands of the surgeon to save her. She lived and Gheshayan's mother died.

It was almost like Moses when he was struggling with Pharaoh to free his people and during the Passover the plague came and killed the firstborn of Pharaoh and passed over the firstborn of Israel. Despite all their trickery, their mother died and my mother lived.

Khalid took the event of his mother's death as an opportunity to run me down in the eyes of my daughters. He informed the embassy that he told the girls I was responsible for the death of their grandmother because I wouldn't allow her into the United States for medical treatment.

Medal from Heaven

I could hardly keep on working and fought off depression constantly. My daughter Daina had given birth to a beautiful baby boy, which countered some of the sadness and grief in my life. I was with her for the birth of Ryan and helped her after she came home from the hospital. David and I were on our way to see Daina and her family one afternoon. He got into the car and while I was driving he handed me a small, plastic baggie with a tiny object in the bottom. I looked and then looked again—it was my St. Jude medal!

I pulled the car over and asked him where he got it. He explained that a few days before, on the anniversary of the day Joyce had given the medal to me, he was cleaning out his carpeted walk-in closet and was on the floor on his hands and knees. Since his vision is limited he had to get close to the floor to make sure all the objects were removed before he vacuumed the carpet. Suddenly, the medal just dropped from the ceiling and made a clinking sound like metal on metal right in front of him so he wouldn't miss it. It had fallen on a carpeted floor and there was no reasonable explanation why it should have made any sound at all.

The medal had been gone for three years. It had mysteriously disappeared, even though it had been placed in a small, plastic box that was secured tightly with a rubber band around it and placed in the bottom drawer of my jewelry box. Now it had mysteriously appeared again, dropping from the ceiling. Soon after, I put it back on a chain and around my neck where it belonged.

Undoer of Good

Wyche Fowler arrived in Riyadh in August 1996. He was sent to the post during a congressional recess so he wasn't officially confirmed through the Senate Foreign Relations Committee. Ray Mabus told me that he had fully briefed him about my case before he resigned. After waiting about one month for the new U.S. ambassador to Saudi Arabia to acclimate himself to the job, I sent a detailed fax and followed up with a telephone call to the ambassador's office in Riyadh.

The secretary answered. "Debbie, this is Pat Roush. I'm wondering if Ambassador Fowler is in his office and if I could speak with him. Do you know if he got my faxes?"

"Hi, Pat. Yes, I made sure I put them right on his desk. He's not in Riyadh today, but I know he's in the consulate in Jeddah. I can put you straight through to him if you like."

Everyone in the ambassador's office knew me from the frequent phone conversations I had with Ray Mabus. They were friendly to me and anxious to help as much as they could.

Wyche Fowler had never returned my calls and I was relieved that his secretary was now putting the call directly through to his office in the consulate. Fowler answered the phone.

"Ambassador Fowler, this is Pat Roush."

"Who?"

"Pat Roush. Ambassador Mabus spoke to you about my daughters. We are trying to get them out of Saudi Arabia. Did you get my faxes?"

"Oh, no, I never received anything from you."

"That's strange . . . Ray Mabus spoke to you about my daughters. We need your help. He got a promise from Crown Prince Abdullah that they could leave. He saved the life of one of the prince's generals in exchange for the girls. He said he told you. I sent you a ten-page letter—"

"Look, Ms. Roush. You're not doing your case one bit of good by interrogating me. I'm in the middle of an Iraqi war right now. Your daughters are Saudi citizens and under Saudi law, their father decides if they can leave. I'm sorry, but I don't see how I can help you."

"What do you mean? Ray Mabus was holding up the visas to the family and got promises from the princes. You must go back and collect on those debts. He saved the life of the general. He got a diplomatic note from the Saudi foreign minister. Please . . ."

"Ms. Roush, I don't have time right now. I'm sorry."

Fowler dismissed me like I was an impertinent school girl. I hung up the phone and started shaking. My gut hurt, and I couldn't speak. After a few hours I called Ray Mabus in Mississippi. "I spoke to Fowler. He took the visa hold off the family and told me there is nothing he can do to help us. The entire embassy has changed toward me. Dick told me they won't go to any princes, and he wants me to apologize to Khalid's brother. We're back to begging Khalid after eleven years of constant fighting for the girls. I don't know what to do. I can't take this anymore."

"Pat, I'm sorry. I don't know what I would do if I were in your situation. I would have probably gone crazy and started shooting people from some tower by now. I love my daughters and couldn't live without them. You know I would do anything I could to get those girls out of that place for you and bring them back to California."

"Why is Fowler doing this?"

"I don't know. I do know that he lobbied real hard for that job. Not like me; I didn't really want to go there . . . But don't be so hard on the others in the embassy. They really don't have a choice. If the ambassador gives an order, they must obey. They have no power or authority and have to do what he says, or they'll lose their jobs."

Several months went by and I could hardly sleep or eat. I looked ten years older. It was now December 1996, and Mabus said he would take a letter from me to the Clinton White House. I had a dream about Alia. We were walking outside in the cold on a winter day. There was snow on the ground. It was a prairie with small hills and an ice pond was on our left side. She wanted to walk on the ice and I yelled to her, "Don't go there—it will break." It was too late and just as I yelled to warn her, she fell down into the ice. I ran to grab her and I saw her head go under the water. I grabbed for her hand in the ice hole but couldn't get it. Just as I was going to jump in to get her, I woke up screaming.

Friend or Foe

It was about that time I began talking to Mohammad Khilewi, a former Saudi diplomat—second secretary of the Saudi mission to the United Nations. He had defected and asked for political asylum. I called him after seeing him with Barbara Walters on a *20/20* interview. Since he also had a problem with the Saudi regime, I thought he might be able to help me. We started kicking around ideas. Khilewi came up with an idea that he thought might work. He told me there was a Saudi businessman worth about $500 million from the opposition movement who was living in Afghanistan undercover, working with the mujahideen. He would go to this man and ask him to help me finance another rescue mission. Khilewi said the man was difficult to find because he was living underground, but he was sure he would find him. It didn't occur to me who this man was until I was writing this book and found a note in my diary—*Osama Bin Laden!* Khilewi never called back.

No Exit

My letter to President Clinton was hand-delivered by Ray Mabus on December 19, 1996. I called Mabus in Mississippi a few days later for a readout.

"Did he get the letter, Governor? What did he say?"

"Well, Pat, I just had a few minutes and I told him about the kids and gave him your letter. He said he knew these countries are pretty bad on children's issues and would appoint someone to investigate the case."

Clinton asked Mabus if he was interested in a cabinet position and the governor declined. I asked him why. He said he was a Southern white boy and didn't fit the Washington profile.

It was Alia's eighteenth birthday, ten days after Christmas. She still couldn't leave Saudi Arabia and was not free to make any choices about her life. The pain of the last eleven years culminated for me when she reached the age of maturity. It was a rite of passage: She was no longer a child. Her childhood had been lost to me, and things didn't look promising for her womanhood. Was she doomed for a life sentence in Saudi Arabia?

I was so depressed and almost suicidal. David and I went to Mission Dolores and to Mass at St. Dominic's Cathedral in San Francisco, then for a walk on the beach. I didn't know what to do next. The pain of living with this constant gnawing at my heart was like having terminal cancer for eternity. I was dying, but I didn't have the relief of death. I didn't believe in suicide—I loved the life that was given to me, but now I was suspended in a perpetual state of helplessness and hopelessness. The human creature cannot live without hope, but everything I did to save my daughters failed. Why did God give me the signs, if I was never to get them back? Was this just a cruel trick by some spirit of the darkness or was my God trying to tell me, "Not yet"?

I was so unhappy. I was living alone, working a nursing job with so much negativity all day long, making phone calls during work and on my lunch hour to try to get the girls, and then coming back to an empty house with just me and the cats. David and I had known each other for six years and were growing apart. I resented him because he had no time for me. Occasionally, we would be able to slip away for a few days to Big Sur or up the coast. He remained aloof, and I remained resentful. I felt so alone. So removed from everyone and everything and driven by the goal of freeing my daughters—no matter what the price.

I would go to the beach and walk and walk in the surf. I thought about leaving David and then would change my mind. He was all I had, and I just couldn't give up whatever little crumb of happiness I had with him. I had deeply loved him, but he was refusing to compromise or listen to reason. He just became more belligerent and stubborn and continued to drink and smoke and overeat. He rarely spent time with me and seldom gave me affection. Still, I couldn't make the break. I was praying for a miracle that would keep us together and bring us close again as we had been in the beginning.

It was the spring of 1997, and the Associated Press reported that Wyche Fowler was having an affair with a Scottish woman half his age and telling her all about how he sat around at night telling jokes with the Saudis: "We trade tales and laughs." He'd met her on an airliner the summer he came into the post after Mabus. He was too busy to go back to the crown prince to make the final arrangements for my daughters to leave but not too busy for a secret affair. Apparently, the twenty-four-year-old physical therapist had given the story to the *Glasgow Evening Times*.

One night I was so depressed and desperate I called Mazen at the embassy and asked if he could just tell me where Khalid lived. He knew the Arab street well and always seemed to know just how to find Khalid. "Please, Mazen, I just want to know where they live. What part of Riyadh is it? I have a right to know. My God . . ."

He wouldn't tell me, and about a week later I received a call from Steve Senna from the Office of Children's Issues: "It was reported that you called the embassy in Riyadh and asked Mazen Shahan to reveal to you the whereabouts of your children. Ms. Roush, you cannot call and ask for that type of information. We don't want any incidents with the Saudi government over some commando raid you may be planning." I couldn't trust Mazen. All I wanted was the place where they lived. I had no more money for mercenaries, but apparently the location of my children was top secret information that the Department of State was not going to disclose to their mother. I didn't know at that time that Mazen had written a memo to the State Department where he "embellished" what I had actually said in my telephone call to him. I had only asked for the address of where my girls were being held. He stated that I had told him I had "lined up some type of commando assistance to come to Riyadh to take the girls back to the U.S." I only found out about this memo after it was made public by the House of Representatives Committee for Government Reform in June 2002. It would be one of several "created" documents from the pen of Mr. Shahan.

In April the *San Francisco Examiner* magazine retold my story with drama and suspense: ten pages full of color pictures caught the media's attention. ABC television wanted to pick up the story and sent a camera crew to my home. I held a press conference in Washington at the bottom of the steps of the Capitol, and the cameras followed me to the senatorial offices of Dianne Feinstein and Barbara Boxer.

Dead Deal

Due to this flurry of press, Wyche Fowler and Hejailan surfaced again and offered me another whirlwind visit to the kingdom. When my attorney questioned Fowler about the arrangement Mabus had made with the crown prince, Fowler responded, "The deal is dead. Pat Roush can either come here and see her daughters another time or she can let the chips fall where they will."

My attorney replied, "That means the girls are forgotten, then. Why not do what Ray Mabus did?"

"Why not get Ray Mabus then? You seem to get my name in the papers. The ball is in your court. The Saudis trust me. Take it or leave it."

Another Hejailan "letter of gratitude" was faxed to me, ready for me to sign and supplicate myself to Hejailan for his great humanitarian work. I was to ingratiate myself to him once again for permitting me to view my stolen children. They were willing to "allow" me another chance to see all the damage they'd done to my Flowers and then get on a plane and quietly go back to America. I marked the sickening letter "Garbage. Give this to the Sheik" and faxed it back to Hejailan.

I called Ray Mabus and told him about the situation. "Fowler refuses to help the people he was appointed to help and is too busy playing ambassador and putting his commercial interests ahead of the people," he said. "It's gonna kill him. It's gonna kill him."

"Et Tu, Brute?"

I was a guest on *Good Morning America* and called David from the ABC studio in Washington. He was even more distant and acted very strange. I was hurting so bad and needed him to give me a word of encouragement or tell me he loved me, but he didn't offer.

I took a flight home and David and his father met me at the airport. They pulled up to my house and David, cold and distant, took my bag up the stairs for me and left. This man that I'd loved so deeply for seven years was slipping away. It was the anatomy of a breakup and there was nothing I could do to stop it. As the door closed behind him a bleak hollowness resonated throughout my being.

After I changed my clothes the phone rang. It was the girls from the eighth-floor nursing station at the hospital. "Pat, we saw you on television the other day in Washington. You were great. And that article in the San Francisco paper—wow! We want you to know we're thinking about you, girl. Hey Pat, Ellen wants to say something."

The Filipina nurse's aide got on the phone. "You know, Pat, I have this roommate and she is a very good psychic in the Philippines. She was reading the paper on Sunday and saw that picture of you—the one with the Arab black veil and robe. She said to tell you she saw the Blessed Mother on top of that picture. Then she said, 'I don't know why she is worried. Her daughters are coming back.' Pat, she is always right. She has told me many things that came true. Anyway, I just wanted to tell you."

David wasn't answering my calls. I couldn't understand what was happening. It was a sunny Saturday morning in early June 1997 and I decided to go to his father's house to see what was up. David was home and opened the door to his small apartment. I walked in and confronted him. He was vague and uncomfortable. Then he suggested we take a ride to the beach.

While I was driving I asked him if he was seeing someone else. I could hardly bring myself to say the words but they just came out. This was my love, my heart—the only man with whom I was ever one. And now with a heavy loaded pause I held my breath for his answer.

"I met a woman, and I want to see how things go with her. Maybe in six months after the smoke blows over, we'll reevaluate our relationship."

What was he talking about? Smoke blowing over . . . I pulled the car to the side of the road. I stared at him in disbelief. It couldn't be true. After seven years of trying to help him, begging him to change and loving him and being patient with him and his time schedule and his daughters and going through his divorce and a million other hurts and joys and tears and laughter. I couldn't stand it.

We got to the beach and walked to the sand. I was wearing a green sun dress with white polka dots: David sat down near the water and told me how pretty I looked. I cried. "Why are you doing this? Don't do this to us. David, you're going to regret this. It's like a death."

Tearfully he said, "Pat, I'm looking for someone to take care of me. I've been looking for quite a while now. This woman is not very pretty or very smart. But she talks nicely to me. You always want me to change. She doesn't ask anything from me. I've hurt a lot of women. If they don't do what I want, I wait and at the right moment, I hurt them. I guess that's what I'm doing with you. I'm going to see this thing through with her."

By this time the pain was overwhelming: I started to vomit in the sand then fell into the surf and was completely wet. The seizurelike trembling throughout my body was frightening. I was choking on my tears and coughing up blood. This couldn't be happening.

He had been having an affair with this woman for the past two months and while I was in Washington fighting for my children, he finalized the arrangement. There was nothing I could do to take away this pain, this hurt. My birthday was just a few days away and we had reservations at the Wawona Hotel in Yosemite. But we wouldn't be going.

Unable to sleep in my room, I tried sleeping on the floor in the living room in my sleeping bag, or on the sofa—nothing brought rest to my body. I had never taken any medications or over-the-counter preparations throughout all my trials and wouldn't do it then. I tried hypnosis and meditation tapes, yoga, massage, and running on the beach. Nothing brought relief. I went to my daughter Daina and in her wisdom she said, "What did you love about him? He was never there for you, Mom. He was preventing you from going on with the rest of your life."

Was I just not seeing him for what he was? In the end his icy green-hazel eyes riveted toward me as he said, "My friends say I've become hard and cold. They say I've changed." The others were confirming what I had been feeling but couldn't do anything about. He was on a path of self-destruction and God had mercifully taken him away from me. (He apparently hurt the new woman also and she left him after one year.)

My anxiety attacks and depression continued. I couldn't eat or sleep or concentrate and was barely able to get through the day at work. I'd been the victim of eleven years of constant betrayal, lies and deception by the State Department and the Saudi government, and now the person closest to me had deceived me. It was pushing me over the edge. I had nowhere to go.

Purgation

I called my old friend Peter Aragon. I needed to talk to someone, and the solace of his monklike cell provided the backdrop for the healing that I needed. For months I would return to the quiet and peace of that simply furnished kitchen and seek the counsel and spiritual direction that I so needed from this holy man. These moments allowed me to return to the depths of my soul and search for all the hurts and pains and curses that were inflicted on me from the beginning. Peter always had the right word or advice to give me and the appropriate scripture or spiritual passages for me to digest after I'd gone home.

It was like I was being burned into ashes. Ground into dust. So that just like the Phoenix that returns to Arabia every five hundred years to be burned on the altar only to rise again from the ashes, I could undergo this transformation. The death of my ego—of all I had to hold on to—was going, going, gone and I had to go back to the time when I was a child, to where it all began, to find out what really happened.

Who was I? I didn't know anymore. Did I ever know? Or was who I thought I was just an illusion? Just as who I thought David was turned out to be an illusion? I wanted the truth this time.

I was fifty-one years old and had spent the last eleven years in a heartbreaking struggle for the lives of my children, but before then I was Esther's daughter, a teenager in the sixties, a middle-class housewife, a college student, a single mom, and a battered wife. My life was in turmoil almost from the beginning. I was always somehow able to cope externally with whatever I had to deal with, whether it was my emotionally complicated mother or the hunger for my father's love or the abusive men or even the wrenching loss of my beloved daughters. I could pull it all off and still get up in the morning and go to work. I didn't drink or smoke or take drugs of any kind. I had confidence in myself, and God gave me the abilities to survive quickly on my feet. But this time I hit a wall and couldn't pull myself over it. My very being was taken out by the roots and laid on the earth.

Peter's simple, ascetic words of wisdom and truth were all I had to place my hopes on. I had searched for my God since I was a little girl kneeling in the pew at Mary Queen of Heaven Church at the side of my Italian family. As I grew up and turned to priests for spiritual guidance in my teen years I discovered they had little to offer. I had an inquisitive mind with more questions than they had answers. I kept searching through various modalities and churches and ideologies from an ashram in San Francisco to Zen Buddhism to philosophy and theology classes in universities. Where was the truth, and who was I?

I had an identity problem as a child. Did I belong to my mother's passionate, exuberant Italian family from Chicago or to my father's soft-spoken, country people from Indiana? Was I the unwanted, illegitimate daughter of a woman who had severe labile personality changes or was I the beloved little princess of Bella Papa and the aunties?

I grew up in emotional disarray and then found myself in an early marriage and motherhood that I was not prepared for. I had to adjust quickly to these changes and to the incredible times of social unrest and change that were taking place when I was a young woman. Then there was Khalid.

My rebellious and experimental nature worked against me. With my quick wits and overly confident self, I had a powerhouse personality that relied on me and me alone to solve just about anything—until the moment I lost David. For some reason God worked through that experience to bring me back to Him, the ultimate Power.

I saw my entire life on a timeline. I was not afraid of my death. Nursing had given me a front-row seat and I overcame any fears I had about the physical demise of my body. I wanted to be free of the pain from the loss of my children and I wanted whatever time I had left on earth to be lived anew. I wanted to be clean. I wanted to wash it all away and become a new person— the real person that was always inside me just waiting to be free. What was

I searching for? Perfection? Maybe that's what I looked for in a man and in myself and in my God. But who was this God?

Purification

Peter was a Catholic contemplative. He enticed me to read the mystics and the Holy Scriptures. As a cradle Catholic I was not encouraged to read the Bible and found the Old Testament boring and difficult to read. Now I hungered for the Word and began to read the Bible in its entirety along with St. John of the Cross, St. Teresa of Avila, the fourteenth-century English mystics, the lives of the saints, C. S. Lewis, and books written about the search for God and meaning.

My vulnerability was exposed, and I stood naked before God. I revealed the truth about myself and my past to Peter and to God, and this was freeing me. I began to feel light and slowly came back to life—the real life—not the persona that I had created. I had a dream that I was blindfolded and led up a spiral staircase holding the Lord's hand. As I ascended each stair another blindfold would come off my eyes until I got to the top where I was spun around and then all the blindfolds flew off and I could see clearly. My sackcloth dress turned into a dress made of fresh flowers and a beautiful orange sun appeared on the horizon.

I had been given many signs from God, experienced raptures and witnessed miracles, but I had still not made the changes necessary to progress to the next spiritual level. But God, being wiser than me, made the changes for me. One of the changes was the removal of David from my life. I had tried to change him as I tried to change Khalid and as I had tried to change my patients from noncompliant lifestyles to a medical regimen that could save their lives.

I picked up a book on codependency for a dollar at a book sale at St. Dominic's Church: It shocked me that I fit the profile. I thought codependency was something related to alcoholics. But it is much more than that. I couldn't save anyone and couldn't save the world and couldn't "make it nice."

I had to stop this impulse I had—this tendency to remake the situation and the person—to make them something they didn't even want to become. I needed boundaries and separateness from them and me. I had to totally empty myself from pride and ego and false confidence. The total reliance on my God called for a "new me" with no illusions or fantasies. "Just the facts, ma'am."

I learned more deeply about humility and was "baptized in the Holy Spirit" at a Charismatic Mass. The power of the Holy Spirit was made known to me and guided me. I wrote letters to my mother in love and honesty, forgiving her for the past. The process was freeing me, and I longed to go further into the mystery.

Message at the Last Supper

I started visiting the Saint Jude Shrine at Saint Dominic's Cathedral in San Francisco. I would stop in to pray in the quiet chapel near the statue of Saint Jude. Although still attending the Orthodox liturgy on Sundays, I was becoming more and more drawn to the homilies of the eloquent Dominican friars. It was Holy Thursday, the night of the Lord's Last Supper, and I decided to go to the services at Saint Dominic's.

While I was getting dressed I checked to make sure my Saint Jude medal was intact on the chain on my neck. I always made sure it was with me. The service was beautiful; the Gothic architecture, the exquisite choir, soft candles and the flow of incense rising, the procession with the exposure of the Blessed Sacrament. I felt as I had the night I first saw the Theotokos weeping—surrounded by a powerful presence of peace.

This holy of holy nights hushed me into a gentle sleep. When I awoke in the morning, Good Friday, the St. Jude medal was gone. The chain on my neck was intact and the medal had disappeared—again. I am awaiting its return.

Peter and I continued our discussions and took frequent retreats to the Camaldolese Hermitage in Big Sur, California. I became involved with contemplative prayer and turned further inward. I'd never known the joys of the

DARK NIGHT OF THE SOUL

internal life. My life had always been "other-oriented." My motherhood and my desire for a spouse or mate were driving forces in my life. Then I discovered the Holy Spirit and the experience of God that is ineffable. I was finally inching toward the person I wanted to be; not in bondage to anyone or any desire. The peace I so longed for all my life was gestating inside me.

The Healing of Forgiveness

My search for God and a spiritual community led me down many paths, and the sorrow and grief I experienced with the loss of my children only brought me deeper into the mystery and deeper into the longing. Almost since the day they were taken away I began to be touched by God in a special way. At first, I couldn't comprehend what was happening to me: the slap on the shoulder, the presence on the tennis court, the weeping icons, the St. Jude medal, the raptures and feeling of a "presence" with me at all times, all the messages sent by other people, and so much more that I could never explain.

I was trying to balance my need for God and my desire for my daughters. My anger toward Khalid for destroying the girls was difficult for me to let go of. I had fantasized about murdering him. I had reveries concerning how I would torture him, if given the chance. Then David—a pain on top of pain. And my "dark night" when the culmination of my life's hurts, pains, curses, betrayals, deceptions, and trials came to an apex.

I knew through reading the Holy Scriptures, the mystics, and my own conscience that I would never be able to advance spiritually unless I let go of my past memories and my fermenting anger.

It happened at the Feast of St. Jude at St. Dominic's Church, October 28, 1998. I had attended the evening Mass and found myself praying for Khalid and David and everyone else who had harmed me. I started crying and felt light and unburdened. After Mass I went to Our Lady's Chapel where I often received messages. The peace surrounded me—the darkness was gone. Maybe that was the message of the medal.

13

❧

CHRONICLES

JANUARY 1998–DECEMBER 1999

Start by doing what's necessary, then what's possible,
and suddenly you are doing the impossible.
—St. Francis of Assisi

Collapsible Barriers in Cow Pastures

Shortly after the New Year 1998 someone sent me a fax about a proposed Islamic academy in Loudoun County, Virginia. It sounded innocent enough: Followers of the religion of Islam in the United States wanted to build a K–12 school in northern Virginia. But this particular school was to be built and subsidized by the Saudi Arabian government. Some of the students would be the children of the Saudi diplomats and businessmen who were moving into Loudoun County, a suburban area near Washington, D.C. Their campus in

Fairfax was too small, and they wanted to build this expansive institution that would grace the rolling hills of the Virginia horse country.

I couldn't understand why my daughters had to languish in Saudi Arabia without any education except the Koran and cooking and sewing classes while the children of the wealthy Saudis who were now colonizing my country—many who worked for the government of Saudi Arabia—would attend a modern, posh academy equipped with the latest learning modalities. This was another injustice, an affront to my American daughters. I was propelled to protest this academy and tell my story to the good people of Loudoun County in hopes that the Saudi school would not be built until my girls had a chance to come home and claim their education.

The Saudis had hired attorney Robert Gordon of Leesburg, Virginia, the man who represented the plaintiff in the Sam Bamieh lawsuit in 1986. Apparently, Gordon had done quite a bit of work for the Saudis, and so they hired him again for the project in Virginia.

The proposed $50 million center would be located on one hundred acres of former cow pasture. The campus, which would accommodate thirty-five-hundred students, was to feature a sixty-five-foot mosque dome, an eighty-five-foot minaret, and collapsible pop-up security barriers like those designed to prevent truck bombs. It was unlike any private school the residents of Virginia had ever seen before.

County residents opposed the academy on a variety of grounds, notably the loss of tax revenue on land that was otherwise zoned for business uses, and the security threat posed by the school, either from Muslims that would be attracted to the county or from the possibility that anti-Saudi Islamic groups might see the academy as a tempting target.

But the central issue was the character of the Saudi regime, which, according to the school's bylaws (specifying even that the Saudi ambassador is ex officio chairman), would exercise total control, to the extent that the school would be part of the structure of the Saudi Ministry of Education—an establishment of a foreign sovereign on American soil.

The Loudoun County Planning Commission hearing was the first attempt to win approval for building the one-million-square-foot facility. I decided to attend this hearing and flew from San Francisco to Virginia to speak before the commission.

The *Loudoun Times Mirror* interviewed me and ran the headline, "Mother Wants Academy Held Hostage":

> A spokesman at the Saudi American embassy has said that Roush first abducted the children from Saudi Arabia, brought them to the United States, and divorced her husband. An American court awarded her custody. The ex-husband subsequently abducted his daughters. At the 1995 meeting, said the Saudi spokesman, the children told their mother they did not want to return with her. The State Department source elaborated, "Since 1986, when the ex-husband abducted his daughters, the issue has been raised by every ambassador, and the embassy in Riyadh has forwarded appeals to the king."

The State Department and the Saudi embassy's misrepresentations of the truth were even more elaborate than usual this time.

More than three hundred citizens packed into the Leesburg hearing room—it was already standing room only half an hour before the proceedings started. Another large room with closed-circuit-television coverage of the hearing accommodated the overflow. Media from all over covered the event—the BBC, the Arab News; camera crews from the United Arab Emirates and Bahrain also set up their tripods.

As the time for the hearing approached, the atmosphere thickened with blue-collar workers, suited men, Arab women in black headscarfs, Loudoun housewives, Middle Eastern–looking males, and a battery of Saudi-hired attorneys and point men. I was fourth on the list to address the commission.

As I approached the podium, I asked one of the Saudi hirees to put my signature picture of the girls in their white dresses with puff sleeves on the overhead for everyone to see. The entire room was filled with the image of my Flowers on the giant screen in front of the audience. I began, "These are my children . . ." At the end of my allotted three-minute speech, the sound of the entire room clapping brought the wrath of the commission chairman, who threatened to expel anyone who created a disturbance in the room.

Following my speech, a Saudi man asked for the approval of the academy. Although the citizens were warned not to address any other issues except those specifically involving zoning ordinances, people could not help but raise the subject of the human rights record of the Saudi Arabian government, including abuses by the Saudis through their treatment of women and possible terrorist activity in and around the "academy."

Poolesville Housewives Defeat Bandar

A few years before, Prince Bandar had tried to obtain the approval for the academy in Poolesville, Virginia, but was defeated by a campaign organized by the local Farm Group housewives. His efforts were thwarted even though he sent a videotape of Saudi propaganda to each household. The people of Poolesville couldn't be fooled. But Bandar had learned his lessons well and was determined that the same scenario wouldn't be repeated in Loudoun County.

As soon as Saudi Arabia and Islam became the issues, the only response from progressive opinion had to be that rejection of the school would be intolerance of "diversity." A case in point was one county resident who symbolically displayed a crescent and star in the window of her home to show that "Islam is welcome here." The *Washington Post* editorial blasted the opposition to the school as "religious intolerance" and "the worst kind of bigotry." The *Post* continued, "Ugly statements that have been made in public meetings on the issue have run the range of mean-spiritedness with some residents asserting that the school should be rejected because 'the Saudis execute their own people who convert from Islam.'"

Pastor James Ahlemann of the Christian Fellowship Church in Ashburn, a nearby town in Loudoun County, protested the building of the Saudi academy on the basis of human rights abuses of the Saudi government. "Saudi Arabia . . . is a nation that has a background of killing and imprisoning those who do not share the faith of Islam," he told his congregation. "They are proposing a school. It would be the largest [Saudi school] in our country. It is being built by a government. I am against their right to do this when they are killing Christians." His courage to speak out against the Saudis was met with death threats to him and his family, and as a result his voice was silenced.

Chairman Bandar

The Planning Commission approved the Saudi Islamic academy despite strong objection by Loudoun residents. The next step was the Board of Supervisors hearing in February 1998. I had joined with some dedicated people of Loudoun County who were steadfastly against the Saudi Academy, but there was less of a crowd at this hearing and the local organization, Concerned Citizens for Loudoun's Future, seemed to be losing members as the hours passed. We voiced our opinions and appeared on the media, but I could see then that the Saudi group was getting the support of the board members. Chairman of the Board Dale Meyers was extremely friendly with the Saudi retainers and referred to me as "that woman from California."

The fawning by county authorities extended to a blatant disregard of the county's own laws, which state a private school can neither be funded nor controlled by any government, on both of which counts the planned Loudoun Islamic Academy failed. Yet the county board even rejected testimony to that effect by a former board member, who himself was the author of the relevant ordinance, that the academy was not a private institution. It didn't matter. Neither Loudoun County, nor the Commonwealth of Virginia, nor the United States would be able to create and run an educational institution based on any religious doctrine, but a foreign government—a government that was every bit as bigoted, intolerant, and ugly as the *Post* that wrongly tagged the school's critics—not only could do so but was seen as having a positive right to do so.

A few of the concerned citizens appealed the decision of the Board of Supervisors to the Board of Zoning Appeals in May 1998. Just a few of us were present and tried to convince the already-made-up-our-minds members to do the right and just thing. But the power of Saudi money won in the end. It was as though we were at a funeral—the buying and selling of America. The Saudis wanted it and the Saudis got it. The politicians of Loudoun County gave it to them and the people surrendered without a fight. The whole population should have been at that hearing and spoken up for their rights—but they chose to stay home. There was a lawyer in Leesburg who said he could bust the case wide open, but his business would be ruined by the Saudis. They gave their land up to a foreign country with hardly more than a whimper.

One of the attorneys for the Saudis actually said, "The people of Loudoun County have nothing to say about whether this school is built." Washington, Jefferson, and Lincoln must have rolled over in their graves.

The *Arab News* and *Saudi Gazette* reported on the victory and tried to marginalize and discredit the Loudoun residents by referring to those who objected to the academy as bigots, xenophobes, and racists.

Elixir of Death for Vietnam Vet

One of the people I met during the Loudoun campaign was Herb Mallard, a former prominent business executive turned human rights crusader from Boston. As an operations manager for the Saudi Industrial Supply and Construction Corporation, part of Mallard's job was to hire workers for projects in Saudi Arabia. He sent two men, John Keene and Jim Maes, both Vietnam vets, to the kingdom in 1979. The two men thought the new construction jobs would bring them financial security. But, like hundreds of other Americans who worked in Saudi Arabia, Keene and Maes returned with tales of torture and virtual enslavement by their employers.

Immediately after arriving, Keene stated their passports were confiscated by the employers and they were prohibited from leaving the country. Mail and phone calls were stopped and paychecks never came. Their employers began making threats to their safety and lives, sometimes leaving them in the desert for days at a time without any food.

They feared for their lives and wanted to leave the country, but their Saudi employer, Mohammed Al-Zahid, owner of the company and a close business partner of King Fahad, refused to give them passports and exit visas. The two men escaped the watchful eye of their employers one day during work and went to the U.S. consulate in Dhahran to complain about their situation, but a marine at the door would not let them in to speak to an American official. The State Department later denied the incident.

A few days after they returned from the consulate, they asked to speak to Mr. Al-Zahid himself about returning to the United States. He offered the men tea—only Jim Maes accepted. Immediately after drinking the tea, Keene said that Maes became violently ill.

A few days later Keene and Maes were arrested by the Saudi religious police and put on an airplane with no explanation concerning the charges. Maes's condition got progressively worse. He suffered from weight loss, vomiting, swelling, and headaches until he finally succumbed. The autopsy revealed the cause of death to be isocyanate poisoning.

Mallard was outraged when the men told him their story. He said, "At first I didn't believe them, but then I started getting calls from people who didn't know each other, complaining of the same thing." He was later told by one, Essam Al-Zahid (a relative), that they meant to get Maes very sick so they could use him as an example to keep other foreign workers in line. According to Mallard, once—while Keene and Maes were literally begging for food and water in front of Mohammed Al-Zahid—the one-time business partner of King Fahad addressed hundreds of guest workers from other countries: "If we can do this to American Vietnam soldiers, we can do it to you. What chance do you think you have? We have power. We have connections in Washington."

When Jim Maes died, his wife was pregnant with their fifth child and had no other means of support. Jim believed in the freedoms our country stands for and was willing to put his life on the line for our Constitution and Bill of Rights when he served his country in Vietnam. He was a Native American of Apache ancestry. Jim Maes believed he could better support his family by leaving the then-depressed Southwest and going to Saudi Arabia.

He was a cautious man, checking things out with the State and Commerce Departments through Senator Harrison Schmitt before he took the position in Saudi Arabia. It did him no good.

Not long after Keene and Maes returned home, according to a report in the *Harvard Crimson*, Al-Zahid closed the company, clearing out of the Boston office in the middle of the night and leaving about $6 million in unpaid bills. Mallard then began his battle to help Keene's and Maes's families in their search for compensation and redress.

He pursued the matter with then Vice President George Bush, who, he stated, slighted the workers' complaints in order to maintain good relations with the Saudi Arabian government and business interests. Bush's response was that the State Department did not have a responsibility to assist Keene and Maes, referring to the matter as "a private contractual arrangement" that fell under the jurisdiction of the legal system of the kingdom of Saudi Arabia.

Mallard rejected the idea after being assured by the Saudis and Americans that Americans have no legal rights at all in Saudi Arabia. The State Department's failure to acknowledge this, according to Mallard, is an abandonment of American citizens who have been mistreated abroad.

Though no redress ever occurred for the families of John Keene and Jim Maes, Herb Mallard continued his endeavors to expose the evils of the U.S.-Saudi special relationship. The name of his Web site says it all: www.Sauduction.com.

Beliefs and Beheadings

My search for God led me onto many paths, but I always raised my children in the Catholic faith. When they were kidnapped and taken to Saudi Arabia, their father forced them to convert to Islam. Unclassified cables I obtained through the Freedom of Information Act revealed that my girls were forced to recite the Koran from memory, pray as Muslims, and go on pilgrimages to the Kaaba in Mecca.

When I heard about preparations in Congress for legislation that would address the long-neglected but widespread problem of religious persecution in a number of countries, notably persecution of Christians, I wanted to be sure a section of the bill specified the forced conversion of minor children abducted abroad. Through working with the Republican Policy Committee, such a provision for these children was included in the International Religious Freedom Act of 1998.

The primary purpose of the bill was to address the rampant persecution in many foreign countries by the governments of those countries against their own people. It mandated that an International Religious Freedom Report be submitted to the Congress by the Department of State each year. This Annual Report on International Religious Freedom would supplement the most recent Human Rights Reports by providing additional detailed information with respect to matters involving religious freedom.

It required the Department of State to assess and describe in the report the nature and extent of violations of religious freedom in each foreign country, to describe U.S. actions and policies in support of religious freedom, and to provide specified information on a variety of topics related to religious freedom. It also prescribed an Executive Summary that highlights the status of the issue in certain countries, including those countries designated by the president as countries of particular concern. This Annual Report would include 192 country chapters on the status of religious freedom worldwide.

Saudi Arabia does not allow religious freedom, and there are swift reprisals for apostasy in Saudi Arabia. In fact, to convert to Christianity is an offense punishable by immediate public execution.

"It is even illegal to wear a cross necklace, read a Bible, or utter a Christian prayer in the privacy of your own home," according to Catholic human rights advocate Nina Shea, head of the U.S.-based Freedom House.

While researching the issue of persecution of Christians in Saudi Arabia, I read about a case involving a Filipino pastor who was arrested for conducting Christian services in his home in Riyadh. He was sentenced to death by beheading on Christmas Eve for this crime. Intercession after intercession by religious leaders from around the world did not soften the hearts of the

Saudi government. Finally, only hours before Pastor Wally's execution was to be carried out, he was blindfolded, taken to the airport, and flown home with no explanation. I invited Pastor Wally and his wife to my home for dinner and extended an invitation to him to speak at my conference at the National Press Club about his abuses. He declined because he feared that the Saudis would harm his family, especially his children.

A few months after the enactment of the International Religious Freedom Act, I was once again in Washington lobbying members of Congress on Capitol Hill for the release of my daughters. I heard about the International Religious Freedom Act of 1998 Conference II at George Washington Law School. I thought I could make a personal appeal to the commissioners at this conference to apply pressure on the Saudi Arabian government to return my daughters on the basis of their forced religious conversion, which amounts to persecution, so I "crashed" the conference.

Many of the commissioners were at the conference. I stood up to briefly mention the plight of my young daughters. Among about thirty intellectuals and religious leaders that were supposedly advocating religious freedom all over the world, I dared to speak up about real-life people who needed their help. I was sitting next to Commissioner Michael Young, and surrounding me were leaders from a wide variety of belief systems—from the Church of Scientology to Baha'i to Southern Baptist. As soon as I began and mentioned my name, the chairman of the commission, Rabbi David Sapperstein—who had refused to meet with me personally the day before the conference—frowned, looked at me with disgust, and then turned his body away from me. Not one of those paradigms of advocacy for religious freedom approached me or offered me a single word of sympathy. An older black minister was the only one in the room who gave me any acknowledgment. The moderator of the conference, noted author Paul Marshall, did manage to say to me, "They needed that wake-up call."

The commission was supposed to look at this report, write their own report, and then make recommendations to the State Department concerning countries that should be designated as "a country of particular concern." Recommendations to the president concerning various sanctions against the offending countries that continued to persecute individuals for their religious beliefs were then to be made. The International Religious Freedom Commission has twice included Saudi Arabia on its annual report as a country that persecutes and murders Christians, but the State Department has steadfastly refused to list them as a "country of particular concern," which would, according to the law, warrant the appropriate sanctions.

I wrote letters to the commissioners and gave them handouts at the conference encouraging them to do the following:

Insist that the State Department take firm action to secure the release of victimized American children in Saudi Arabia.

Hold hearings on the issue of forced religious conversion of my children and others.

Require that Saudi Arabia be designated as a country of particular concern for its violation of religious freedom and forced conversion of American Christian children.

The State Department was aware of the forced conversion of my daughters well before the bill was written, as evidenced by unclassified cables from the U.S. Embassy to the State Department in December 1986 and March 1990, noting Khalid Gheshayan's bragging that my daughters were practicing Islam. They refused to bring the matter up with the Saudis but later admitted at a congressional briefing before the House Committee for Government Reform staff that my daughters were, in fact, victims of forced religious conversion.

The Commission for International Religious Freedom has recently been reporting on the forced conversion of abducted children, as stated in the annual report of October 26, 2001:

Under the law, children of Saudi fathers are considered Muslim, regardless of the country or the religious tradition in which they may have been raised. In some cases, children raised in other countries and in other religious traditions who came to Saudi Arabia or who were taken by their Saudi fathers to Saudi Arabia reportedly were coerced to conform to Islamic norms and practices, although forcible conversion is prohibited. There were no reports of the forced religious conversion of minor U.S. citizens who had been abducted or illegally removed from the United States during the period covered by this report, or of the Government's refusal to allow such citizens to be returned to the United States. However, there was a report that prior to the period covered by this report, at least one U.S. citizen child in the country was subjected to pressure—and at times force—by her Saudi relatives to renounce Christianity and conform to Islamic norms and practices. The child has since returned to the United States.

The child they are referring to is the former Yasmine Shaloub (Dria Davis), daughter of Miriam Hernandez-Davis. She was a devout Catholic who was kidnapped from her mother in Miami when she was eleven and beaten when she refused to forsake her Christianity and convert to Islam. Her family arranged for her to escape from Saudi Arabia when she was thirteen.

The State Department's obsession about protecting the Saudi government from any mention of their abuse/murder of Christians and religious intolerance was indicative of their whole approach to the U.S.-Saudi relationship. The Saudis, of course, were quick to dictate to other countries about religious "rules" inside their kingdom. The logo on the tail wing of Swiss Air is a cross. The Saudi government informed Swiss Air that it was offensive to have their planes, with the symbol of the cross emblemized on the aircraft, land in the kingdom that protects the two holy shrines. The Swiss told them that they would not repaint their aircraft and supplicate themselves to the Saudis' demands. Faced with their steadfast refusal, the Saudis stood down and Swiss Air continues to land its planes in the kingdom.

Many Faces with the Same Pain

After twelve years of carrying the banner alone through my Joan of Arc battles with the State Department and Saudi government, I met a spirited woman who was involved in her own gallant crusade to free her young daughter who had been abducted to Syria.

When I first spoke to Maureen Dabbagh, she was organizing a conference in Washington for parents of internationally abducted children. There were only fifty of us at that first conference in May 1998. We exchanged stories and laughed and cried and walked to the White House in procession with our candles glowing. "Who Hears the Cries of the Little Children?" a song composed by one of the fathers, became our mantra. As we stood in the cool Washington evening, singing in front of the White House, visitors who were passing by joined our protest and songs. We bonded into a beautiful medley as only people who are united for a just cause against a great monolith can do. I will never forget the pain and sorrow of my fellow sufferers: The loss of a child through abduction is something no one but another victim can understand.

I joined Maureen's group, PARENT, and we had many plans to fight for justice for America's stolen children. We organized demonstrations in front of foreign embassies, went to outlandish, rural regions to testify as expert witnesses to thwart possible future abductions, and personally confronted the lobbyists/retainers of the Saudi Arabian government.

Herb Mallard popped up and offered to sponsor a press conference at the National Press Club if we provided the speakers. I spent the summer of 1998 organizing and had a lineup of witnesses for the September conference. We were also planning a huge march on the Saudi embassy to coincide with Saudi National Day—September 22. I had met a man during the Loudoun campaign who wanted to organize the march for me, so I left the details to him while I concentrated on the press club conference. Maureen, Margaret McClain (whose daughter had recently been kidnapped and taken to Saudi Arabia), and I began receiving emails from Hill & Knowlton, a well-known international public relations and public affairs consulting firm.

Jim Jennings, the director of National Practices, stated:

I have seen recent email traffic about your concerns over meetings at the National Press Club next week . . . you are mistaken if you believe in any way, shape or form that our company is involved with this matter or representing any aspect of the government of Saudi Arabia on any matter. I have been with this firm for 25 years and do not remember a time when we have ever represented the Saudis—yet you state boldly in your email that we do.

Although Mr. Jennings denied that his firm ever represented the Saudi government in "any way, shape or form," Hill & Knowlton is mentioned in a book, *Agents of Influence* by Pat Choate, copyright 1990, as being retained by the Royal Embassy of Saudi Arabia. The role of powerful lobbyists such as Hill & Knowlton is further explained in the December 15, 1992, *Houston Post:*

HUMAN RIGHTS ABUSERS PAY LOBBYISTS MILLIONS

Nations that abuse human rights pay millions every year to Washington insiders—Republicans and Democrats alike—seeking foreign aid and special treatment from the U.S. government says a report due out today.

"U.S. taxpayers are indirectly supporting the activities of lobbyists, lawyers and public relations firms who were paid more than $24 million in 1991–92 to represent foreign interests that are persistent abusers of human rights," concludes a report by the Center for Public Integrity. The center, a nonprofit group that examines public policy issues, calls its "torturers" lobby report the "first comprehensive, thorough analysis of who does the bidding in Washington for these controversial governments."

Leading the list of lobbyists for nations that abuse human rights was Hill & Knowlton, a well-connected firm with a reputation for handling tough assignments.

Lockout at the Watergate

The march on the Saudi embassy was not coordinated well, and we were left to continue the protest with only a handful of demonstrators. All of us had exhausted every possible avenue to get our children back, and this effort to draw attention to our sorrow and loss was a way for us to vent our frustrations in public. My daughters had been gone the longest, and it saddened me to hear of cases like those of Maureen and Margaret, whose little girls were just starting their journey of tears.

It was Saudi National Day and our small group had assembled in front of the Saudi embassy across from the Watergate complex near the Kennedy Center. At first, we tried to speak to someone at the embassy. I walked into the reception area and asked to speak with Adel Jubeir who handled everything for Prince Bandar. He had been involved in my case from early on—creating problems and obstacles for me. The receptionist made a call and then told us to go to the other entrance around the block. We walked quietly around the city-block-sized embassy and when we got to the other entrance, they told us to go back to the front. When I put my hand on the door of the front entrance, a "click" was heard and the guards, obeying orders, locked us out of the embassy.

My friends and I stood at the huge door of the Saudi embassy in amazement. What were they afraid of? Why couldn't they let us in? We were mothers who lost their children to the Saudi men who were cowardly hiding out as criminals. Many of the children were not wanted by these men, but taken away from us, their mothers, to be abused and given to family members or maids. And now these officials were nervously hiding inside their marble structure with security guards, weapons, and steel barriers.

Feeling further rejection and frustration, we began to walk in front of the embassy on the sidewalk with our placards: "Free America's Children." It was the lunch hour and many people at the Watergate complex across the street were sitting eating sandwiches or taking a leisurely stroll. As our voices rose and the momentum quickened the Watergate crowd began to take an interest: Cars honked in sympathy and peace signs were flashed. I was crying and chanting at the top of my voice, "Let my children go." A member of our group stood on the sidewalk and began taking pictures. One of the Saudi guards came running out and pointed a finger at the photographer. "No pictures," he said. I yelled, "This is America. We can take photographs in this country."

After the crowd subsided, I beckoned Maureen and Margaret to follow me to the office of Hill & Knowlton at the Watergate across the street. I was the first to cross into the traffic. As I stood at the curb looking toward the embassy with my placard in one hand and the Saudi flag in the other, a plainclothes Saudi security guard approached me. Holding a steaming cup of coffee as he waited to cross the street back to the embassy, our eyes met. The brown-suited Saudi read my placard and shot a look of contempt at me.

"What are you looking at?" I said, and, though I probably shouldn't have, I tagged on an insult. Hearing that, he lunged toward me.

Right then, Margaret seemed to appear out of nowhere and placed her body between me and the guard then said, "Don't touch her." Maureen was on my other side. Seeing the skirmish, the applause from onlookers at the Watergate was encouraging. The guard sheepishly went back to his den and I then threw the Saudi flag on the ground and stepped on it. I was going to burn it, but I thought I would be arrested. Those women and I had suffered so much pain at the hands of the Saudi authorities; the slight satisfaction from this small victory was symbolic. For a brief moment we were empowered.

Torture Lobbyist Territory

Then we continued to the offices of Hill & Knowlton in the Watergate. At first the guard had reservations about allowing us in, but I told him we wouldn't cause any disturbance. He sympathetically directed us to their suite. At the reception I asked to speak with Tom Buckmaster, the general manager of the Washington office. Maureen and Margaret and I, hot, tired, and perspiring from the protest and confrontation, were escorted into a chic, glass-doored conference room with a full bar. We sank down into the luxuriously padded chairs with our posters at our sides. I said, "Let me do the talking." We were kept waiting for about twenty minutes and just as we were readying ourselves to walk out, Buckmaster came into the room, accompanied by a nervous, bespectacled companion carrying our "file."

He asked if we wanted something to drink. Remembering Jim Maes, I told the women to refuse. Buckmaster again denied that they worked for the Saudi embassy. I told them we wanted all of our children released and that all their deception couldn't and wouldn't stop us. I told them to give their boss, Prince Bandar, that message.

Three days after that meeting I received the following certified letter:

September 25, 1998

Dear Ms. Roush:

We are legal counsel to Hill and Knowlton. You have been repeatedly advised that Hill and Knowlton does not now, nor has it ever, represented the government of Saudi Arabia, its embassy in Washington, DC, or any of its individuals in diplomatic or community matters.

You have persisted in disseminating information about Hill and Knowlton in connection with your allegations of the company's involvement on issues relating to human rights abuses. All of what you have published is false and obviously disseminated with malicious intent, since you have previously been advised of the true facts.

We request that you immediately cease any public statements about Hill and Knowlton that do not reflect the true facts with respect to this issue. If you do not immediately cease this improper, untruthful and intentionally malicious attack on Hill and Knowlton, we will take whatever steps are necessary to properly protect our clients' interests.

> Davis & Gilbert
> cc: Doug Burton
> Associate Editor, *Insight* Magazine

I then sent the following letter to Davis & Gilbert:

December 28, 1998

Dear Mr. Davis and Mr. Gilbert:

In your letter addressed to me dated September 25, 1998, you stated that you are legal counsel to Hill & Knowlton, the public relations firm and large international lobbyist group. You emphatically and most aggressively affirmed that your client, Hill & Knowlton, "does not now, nor has it ever, represented the government of Saudi Arabia, its embassy in Washington, DC, or any of its individuals in diplomatic or community matters."

. . . It is obvious to me that you are quite misinformed about who your clients are and who your clients were in the past. It is stated quite factually in the national bestseller *Agents of Influence* by Pat Choate, published by Touchstone Books in 1990, that Hill & Knowlton have represented the Royal Embassy of Saudi Arabia (pg 246) and His Royal Highness Prince Talal (pg 236 and pg 256). I have included faxed photocopies of these pages from the book to you in this correspondence. The book also states that Hill & Knowlton have represented the Saudi arms dealer, Adnan Khashoggi (pg 242). I suggest that next time before you send any threatening letters to me or any other victims of Saudi torture, you check things out a bit more thoroughly.

Patricia Roush

cc: Doug Burton
Insight Magazine

I never heard from Davis & Gilbert or Hill & Knowlton again, but I did call Doug Burton, associate editor of *Insight* magazine. He had no idea why Davis & Gilbert had copied him on their letter to me. I told him the story and he was excited to cover the whole issue. Thus began the four-year coverage by *Insight* of the international child abduction issue.

Interestingly enough, according to the *New York Post*, the post-9/11 list of spin doctors hired by the Saudis to create a better image includes Hill & Knowlton with a one year contract at $77,000 per month.

Marriage to Saudis and the AMC

After Wyche Fowler Jr. betrayed my children to his Saudi friends in 1996 when Ray Mabus resigned as U.S. ambassador to the kingdom, the State

Department decided to post on its Web site an eight-page article as a warning to U.S. women who might be thinking of marrying Saudi men.

This very frank, honest portrayal of what life would really be like for an American woman who marries a Saudi man spelled out in no uncertain terms. Compiled by the American embassy in Saudi Arabia from hundreds of interviews with American women living in Saudi Arabia with their Saudi husbands, it profiled the Saudi male in the United States before the marriage and then examined the "myth of the Westernized Saudi."

The site offered helpful information concerning real-life questions such as: With whom will you live? What freedom of movement will you have? Will you be able to travel separately from your husband? How do you feel about a second wife? What happens when the marriage fails? Who will get custody of the children? Can an American flee the kingdom with her dual-national children? Can an American woman be denied visitation rights with her children?

The American Muslim Council, outraged by this warning by the State Department to American women pondering whether to marry a Saudi or not, applied intense lobbying pressure to have the document removed from the Internet. The "courtesy culture" of the State Department, of course, complied with those wishes and the warning was removed in 1999.

GAO Meltdown

In the autumn of 1999 a pair of congressional hearings were held concerning international child abduction. Both the State and Justice Departments went in to explain why they did little or nothing to recover children or bring them home. Insufficient resources were cited as one of the reasons so little is done. That's why parents were told to rely on the Hague Treaty. But the Hague Treaty is routinely broken and violators are allowed to do so with impunity; most of the Middle Eastern countries have not signed.

The Justice Department confessed it rarely pursued prosecution under the 1993 International Parental Kidnapping Crime Act, or IPKA, the bill that

Sarah Pang and I worked so hard on. In five years, only sixty-two indictments and thirteen convictions resulted from the thousands of cases of abductions.

It's true. The law is rarely used. Alan Dixon, at my insistence, first introduced the bill in 1987, one year after my daughters were kidnapped. It was hung up in the Senate Judiciary Committee and kicked around for five years before it finally passed—on Alia's fourteenth birthday—January 5, 1993. Apparently, children kidnapped by a parent are not a high priority for the U.S.C. Congress, State Department or Justice Department.

Mary Ryan, assistant secretary of state for consular affairs, defended this lack of concern by saying that these cases are merely "child-custody disputes." The Saudis picked up that line from the State Department. Now it's used by everyone in government to quickly end all responsibility for the children.

After these hearings, Representative Benjamin Gilman of New York called for an investigation by the General Accounting Office, or GAO, into the handling of international child abduction cases by the State and Justice Departments. We were heartened and hoped this would force changes to be made.

An interested GAO investigator began interviewing me and other parents concerning wrongdoing by the State and Justice Departments. He was thorough and objective and open to suggestions made by the parents. He attended our conference in Washington in 1999 and told us he was writing his report truthfully. It was later revealed by *Insight* that this investigator was grilled by his boss, GAO supervisor Boris Kachura, and forced to "tone down" the report.

Suddenly, that investigator was pulled off the investigation and replaced. None of his findings were used in the new investigation. When the report finally came out, it was a whitewash. It glossed over the dismal Justice Department record and made no mention of the pattern of abuse of parents by the State Department. This ranged from calling parents "mentally unbalanced" as per a memo about a Texas father: His "name is Bubba—that should tell you something about him." This information was obtained from the State Department by Freedom of Information requests by the parents and was reported by *Insight*.

Despite the overwhelming evidence of State and Justice dereliction, the GAO claimed the failure to pursue these cases was due to lack of resources.

It's not about money. Change can happen without money. It's about heart and caring about our most valuable resource, America's children. My goal in pioneering this issue has always been for America to show the world that it cares about its own littlest citizens. I was naive enough to believe that I could convince our elected officials, have laws changed, and bring my daughters home. I played a self-taught game of high-stakes politics for the lives of my daughters and never believed what I would uncover—a Pandora's box filled with deception, betrayal, trickery, and greed. I couldn't believe the lengths my government would go to in order not to help me and to turn everything I did upside down for the sake of a foreign power. And it seemed there was no way to hold the government of the United States accountable for its actions.

Her Name Was Esther

A few weeks before Christmas in 1999 I received a message from my sister, Bobbie. They had found my mother barely alive. She had spent three days on the floor of her house, trying to crawl to the phone and later slipped into unconsciousness. Her frail heart failed, but the paramedics were able to resuscitate her and get her to the hospital. She was admitted to the Intensive Care Unit and was not expected to live.

But she rallied. She awoke a few days later, and I was able to speak to her. I told her I was on my way and not to worry. All she could say behind her oxygen mask was, "I'll call you." I thought it was strange that she would say that. How could she call me?

Two days before Christmas the doctor phoned me to say she'd had a stroke and slipped into a comatose state. I asked the nurse to hold the phone near her ear: "Mom, it's okay to let go. Just go toward the light. Go to the other side. Bella Papa and the others are waiting for you, Mom. I'll see you in a couple of years. And Mom, ring me twice when you get to heaven." The nurse told me that while I was talking to her, her eyelids were moving.

That was Christmas Eve and at Midnight Mass I prayed, "Jesus, just take her on Your birthday, please." I knew He would.

On Christmas morning I called the hospital. The nurse answered, "Pat, her blood pressure is 70/30. She won't make it much longer."

"Yes, I know. Can you do me a favor? Don't leave her alone—stay with her and call me when she passes over."

One hour later I got the call. "She's gone, Pat. She was so peaceful. Not like before. Don't worry, another nurse and I were on each side of her holding her hands when she stopped breathing."

The day after she died was a Sunday. At 8:30 A.M. the phone rang—twice. I picked it up: "Hello . . . Hello." No one answered. "Hello . . . Hello, Mom?"

I started to cry. I knew it was her. Not only was she able to send me that message, but she died on the first day of a Jubilee Year. On Christmas Eve, the night before she died, the pope had opened the Holy Door to Saint Peter's Basilica in Rome, which happens only once in fifty years on the eve of the new Jubilee. The significance of the door being opened lies in its message—God's mercy bending over man's misery. The sixteen panels of the door are like the verses of a hymn, which sing of God's infinite mercy. They start from the reality of sin, which degrades man, and move to penance, which rehabilitates him. They enlighten every moment of any situation with the certainty of divine forgiveness.

After Mass that day, I went to the Our Lady Chapel of St. Dominic's to pray. My mother appeared on my left high above the altar. She was young and beautiful—transparent and transfigured. I could almost see through her. She spoke to me: "Don't cry for me, Pat. I can breathe now. I am at peace."

She never appeared or spoke to me again. I had gotten the message. A few days before she died my silver rosaries from Medugorje turned golden.

14

❦

BURTON'S LIST

SEPTEMBER 2001–OCTOBER 2002

The bravest are surely those who have the
clearest vision of what is before them, glory and danger alike,
and yet notwithstanding go out to meet it.
—Thucydides

A New Campaign Begins

It was five days before the terrorist attacks of September 11, 2001, and I was about to make a call to my daughter Aisha. We had not been able to speak to each other for more than seven years and had only seen each other once in sixteen years. She was nineteen years old and living with her father, his Saudi wife, and their five children somewhere in Riyadh, Saudi Arabia.

Three months prior to this Khalid Gheshayan had successfully arranged for a marriage to take place between my daughter Alia and a Saudi man. I was informed about this marriage by a call from the United States State Department, who would give me no further information or details regarding the man's identity, the whereabouts of Alia, or how I could contact her.

At that time I again begged the American embassy in Riyadh and the State Department to allow me to go to Saudi Arabia to meet with my daughters and the man that married Alia. They refused. Instead they gave me the cell phone number of Gheshayan. I contacted him and he told me I could speak to Aisha if I called back the following week.

"Hello, Khalid. How are the girls?"

"They are fine. Alia is very happy with her new husband. I asked her if she wanted to talk to you, and she said not at this time. She doesn't want it to cause problems in her marriage."

"May I speak to Aisha?"

"She is in her room. Don't worry. I know exactly where she is all the time. She quit the school and spends most of her time in her room, alone. I screamed at her and told her to go back to school, but she doesn't want to do anything and stays in that room all day and night." With Alia gone, Aisha was losing all motivation for living. What did Khalid expect?

As I waited, I wondered if he would let me speak to her on a regular basis or if this would be the only time I would hear her voice. I tried to think of any Arabic words I could. I wondered if she spoke any English and if she had been able to study English in the Saudi schools.

Then suddenly, "Here's Aisha."

Her English was clear, "Hello, Mom. I love you, Mom. I love you. I love you. I love you."

"Aisha? Is that you? I love you. I love you so much. Can you hear me?"

"Yes. I love you."

She knew no other words in English, and I knew little Arabic. "How—is—Alia?"

There was a long pause. I am sure she didn't know that I knew about her sister's marriage and wouldn't dare tell me any information that might upset her father. So she answered, *"Qaes"* (fine).

I started to cry and kept telling her that I loved her and wanted to see her so much. She knew what I was saying, but couldn't speak except to tell me in Arabic, *"T'alla hena, Riyadh"* (Come to Riyadh). And then in English, "Help, Mom."

Khalid took the phone away from her and ended the conversation. I called every week after that for one month, and he never allowed us to speak again. Gheshayan told me that Aisha was "very sad" after that single, short conversation. I begged him to allow me to talk to her again, and then he hung up on me. My desperate pleas to the State Department and the American ambassador's office got me nowhere. Assistant Secretary of State for Near Eastern Affairs William Burns would never take my calls or reply to my letters, and Karen Sasahara from the Saudi Desk actually yelled at me: "Your daughter doesn't speak enough English to tell you she loves you!"

I couldn't believe that after sixteen years without my children, the torture and torment we had suffered, the recent marriage of my daughter Alia, and the cry for help from Aisha, the State Department was still turning its back on us.

Then fifteen Saudi nationals blew up two high-rise office buildings in Manhattan, killing almost three thousand Americans on their way to work one morning. Not being a television watcher, the morning of the tragedy I had merely turned on the set to make a duplicate tape of some interviews I had done for the media. When I saw with disbelief that the World Trade Center's Twin Towers were crumbling before my eyes and that the planes had been manned by Saudi nationals, I wondered how this would affect the possibilities of getting my daughters released.

As America got more deeply involved in the post-9/11 time period—with the anthrax scare and chaos on Capitol Hill and then the war in Afghanistan—I couldn't get near the topic of Alia and Aisha's plight in Saudi Arabia until several months later.

I had scheduled a trip to Europe for October 2001 and was gone for almost one month. When I returned, I began trying to get media attention for my daughters in view of the fact that the plight of the Afghan women had overwhelmed the American public. The president had even appointed a special liaison in the White House to advocate on behalf of this issue. (I called her, but she didn't return my call.) I wondered why they weren't concerned with American women's rights when they were held hostage in Saudi Arabia

While on a cable talk show, I met a young Washington attorney, Jack Burkman, who was eager to help me. I was quite skeptical about getting involved again in Washington politics but Jack was willing to set up some meetings with congressmen he knew personally in the hope that they would be able to bring some pressure upon the Saudi government to release my daughters.

Congressman Dan Burton was one of the members of Congress that I met through Jack Burkman on a cool December evening in Washington. I came to the meeting armed with one of my many huge, white binders filled with documents and photographs that I had collected for almost two decades. Burton listened compassionately and his staff took notes. I left wondering if the trip would bear any fruit.

A few months later we were in the planning stages of a congressional hearing before the Committee for Government Reform, where Burton held the position as chairman. Burton and his staff were understanding, savvy, and willing to help. Not since Dixon and Mabus had I seen such integrity from anyone in government. I gave them the names and histories of other egregious cases involving Saudi Arabia. Documents were subpoenaed from the State Department and the American embassy in Saudi Arabia.

The further the staff delved into the investigation, the more disturbing the facts became about State Department cover-ups, bumbling, abuse, false documents, misinformation, obfuseation, damage control, abandonment, endangerment by the American embassy of American women and children in dire need of help in Saudi Arabia, and the continued refusal of the State Department to protect the lives of American citizens, be they child or adult, when in jeopardy in a dangerous foreign country.

Trail of Deception

Interest in the hearing was heightened because all but four of the nineteen 9/11 hijackers were from Saudi Arabia, and the press and U.S. policy makers were increasingly talking about the U.S.-Saudi special relationship. The American public was questioning just how "special" this relationship really was.

The committee asked for prehearing briefings from the State Department about my case. Eight people from State attended that meeting. They all came fully armed with documents and sixteen-year-old standard State Department statements about why they didn't help me. Represented were the Saudi Desk, Human Rights, Consular Affairs, Religious Freedom, Children's Issues, Overseas Citizens Services, The Legal Department, and American Citizens Services.

The committee confessed that the State Department had so much paperwork on my case that much of it didn't even arrive before the hearing took place. The State Department admitted that no one from the American embassy had even seen my daughters for years and my children were, indeed, victims of religious persecution: Alia and Aisha would have better access to the American embassy if they were convicted of a crime in Saudi Arabia and locked up in jail.

The Mazen Ingredient

An interesting document from the American embassy in Riyadh surfaced after the committee had subpoenaed all records concerning my case. It was written by Mazen Shahan, the foreign service national who had been working in consular services at the American embassy in Riyadh for more than twenty years. He had been present during the original Hejeilan taping of my daughters in 1986 and had sat in on the meeting with my daughters and me in 1995, acting as a translator for Aisha only; Alia spoke English perfectly.

The four-page memo was entitled, "My Recollections of the Meeting Between Patricia Roush and Her Daughters on 6/13/95." It was dated May 24, 1997—two years after the event happened. In this document Mr. Shahan describes how my daughters made fun of me, berated me in Arabic to Shahan behind my back and were disgusted and embarrassed by me. He goes on to say, "At one point when Patricia kept pressuring the girls to say yes about coming to the U.S., the older daughter said in Arabic that, 'We do not want to go to the U.S. with you; we do not want to be prostitutes there . . . We are Muslims and we do not want to end up being girlfriends who have illegal relationships.' . . . At one point, the older daughter directly called her mother a prostitute . . . The girls kept saying that they like it here and that their father treats them well. They did not seem to have missed the mother that much after nine years of separation."

The entire document was created by Mazen Shahan two years after the fact and a sister document that explains why this document needed to be fabricated also came to light in the form of an unclassified cable written in May 1997 by Wyche Fowler from the American embassy in Riyadh to the State Department in Washington. He and Prince Bandar and, of course, Hejailan were offering me another visit with my daughters in Riyadh. All of a sudden Gheshayan became very cooperative and Bandar got involved. It just happened to coincide with the *San Francisco Examiner* magazine's ten-page color cover-story article about me and the involvement of ABC television, which was following me around Capitol Hill with a camera crew while I held a press conference at the steps of the Capital and visited various senatorial and congressional offices.

In the cable Fowler nervously refers to the interest of Congress and the media:

But at a minimum, it is crucial to brief these three key senators and their staffs. [Who these three are is not known.]

We also urge that the Department put someone on camera to defend our position if any news program requests the appearance of a Department official to discuss the case. It would be a mistake to refuse to comment on the case, especially since we now have a deal by which Pat can visit her daughters . . . It is crucial the senators and their staffs understand that if the case had been solvable, it would have been resolved in its first few years . . . There is no legal remedy under the Saudi and U.S. systems which would compel the return of the girls to their mother . . . Both girls are happy with their lives in Saudi Arabia and have expressed no interest in leaving their father and returning to the U.S. . . . . We would appreciate receiving a quick read-out if the case does indeed come up at noon briefing on 5/9 [He is referring to the daily State Department Press Briefing—it did come up, twice] . . . We would also appreciate receiving confirmation that Dept. will brief the three key senators or their staffs, as well as any other interested members of the Foreign Relations Committee on this case prior to Ms. Roush's May 13 Press Conference.

The intense interest Fowler took in covering himself so well with the visit, the Mazen memo, and the cable was fairly obvious. He was appointed to the post in Riyadh in August 1996 during a congressional recess and had never been confirmed through the Senate Foreign Relations Committee. He knew he was responsible for losing my daughters when he refused to continue making the final arrangements with the Saudi crown prince after Mabus resigned. He took the visa hold off and allowed all the Gheshayans into the United States—releasing any pressure that had been put on the family.

Ten months after these actions, I was in the spotlight on Capital Hill talking to the very same senators on the Senate Foreign Relations Committee that could block his confirmation as ambassador and cause him to lose the position for which he lobbied so very hard and that the Saudis so frantically wanted him to keep—U.S. ambassador to Saudi Arabia. Bandar wanted him there; he was exactly the kind of ambassador the Saudis liked. He played ball with them and wanted so desperately all that they could give him. My daughters were expendable.

Wyche Fowler's allegiance to his Saudi masters seems to come out even more clearly in a recent book, *The Two Faces of Islam* by Stephen Schwartz:

Ambassador Wyche Fowler brought no discernible expertise or wisdom to the job of representing American interests to our most important Arab ally. But once ensconced at MEI [Middle East Institute], he showed a remarkable capacity for rage and invective when faced with criticisms of the Saudi kingdom. Calling on Aramco's retired professional personnel for support, he railed at those whose disregard for American strategic commitments led them to express concern for the difficulties encountered by U.S. citizens in conflict with Saudi authority. Fowler had played an especially questionable role in the case of two girls kidnapped by their Saudi father from their American mother, Patricia Roush . . . Although Fowler's predecessor as U.S. ambassador to the Saudi kingdom, Ray Mabus, blocked issuance of visas to Al–Gheshayan's family, Fowler refused to assist Ms. Roush and lifted the visa ban on the abductor's relatives. Confronted with these facts at a seminar in Washington, Fowler replied by calling his accusers—including a distinguished Middle East scholar—liars . . . Fowler has also loudly condemned those whose cultural insensitivity, according to him, made them think it acceptable to criticize Wahhabism. On the same occasion when he labeled defenders of Ms. Roush as prevaricators, he angrily defended the Wahhabi clerics and accused their critics of prejudice.

When the committee called Fowler for a prehearing briefing, he lied about his role in sacrificing my daughters for political and financial gain. He told staff members that my daughters didn't want to come home. Even though he never met my girls and had never spoken with them, he insisted that they didn't want to be with their mother or come to the United States. He said I ruined things for myself when I visited them and was totally out of line with the girls. Fowler adamantly repeated that my daughters hated me and told me never to come back again. Then he bragged that he had offered me many chances to visit Alia and Aisha in Saudi Arabia and I refused. The Committee staff was not impressed with his statements.

She Only Wanted Her Mom

At 12:01 A.M. on June 11, 2002, my fifty-sixth birthday, I was tiredly walking to baggage claim at National Airport in Washington, D.C. I had been traveling all day, and in additional to the long cross-country flight had spent four hours on the tarmac in an airplane at O'Hare Airport due to foul weather. Scheduled to testify before Burton's Committee for Government Reform the next day, I was exhausted from media calls, writing, briefings, and the emotional stress always involved in the pain of once again going to the nation's capital and pleading for help for my daughters.

While standing at the baggage carousel I turned on my cell phone to listen to my voice-mail messages: "Hello, Ms. Roush, this is Kim Richter from the Department of State. Your youngest daughter was recently married. We have no further information."

I was numb. And now it was Aisha's turn. This is what they were planning. Khalid knew about the hearing and had a trump card—Aisha. I warned the embassy and the State Department that he would sell her as he had Alia. They just laughed at me. Khalid retaliated for the hearing by punishing Aisha. And by hurting her, he knew he would hurt me. The State Department seemed to take great delight in giving me this information and waited until the eve of my testimony before Congress to unleash it on me, hoping that I would be further emotionally shattered.

Aisha, my baby. She was almost twenty and had spent sixteen years of her life locked up inside a dungeon with her deranged father as her keeper. And now she, too, would be forced to bear some strange man's children without ever knowing the mother who loved her.

I stood alone in the Washington airport and I couldn't cry. The pain was so deep and so compounded with the sixteen years of continual heartache and disappointment after letdown after betrayal. I couldn't let this destroy me. I had to prepare myself for a presentation before Congress and the media. But why did the State Department have to leave that message on my cell phone voice mail? It was so impersonal and coldhearted. How long had this information been kept from me? And then to drop it in my lap the day before the hearing? If I thought the Saudis were sadistic, what did I think of my own government?

The next morning, with only two hours of sleep, God's grace pulled me up and out of my depression. Before I left the hotel to attend the hearing, I opened my Bible for a word from the Lord; it fell open to Job 4:2–9:

CONFIDENCE IN GOD

If we say something to you, will you bear with us?
Who in any case could refrain from speaking now?
You have schooled many others,
giving strength to feeble hands;
your words supported any who wavered
and strengthened every failing knee.
And now your turn has come, and you lose patience,
at the first touch on yourself you are overwhelmed!
Does not your piety give you confidence,
and your integrity of life give you hope?
Can you recall anyone guiltless that perished?
Where then have the honest been wiped out?
I speak from experience: those who plough iniquity
and sow disaster, reap just that.

Hearing No. 1: Burton Begins

The hearing entitled, "Should the United States Do More to Help U.S. Citizens Held Against Their Will in Saudi Arabia?" was held on June 12, 2002, in the Rayburn Building before the Committee for Government Reform with Chairman Dan Burton.

After the opening statements from members of the Committee, I began my testimony:

Saudi Arabia has violated my human rights and the human rights and constitutional rights afforded to my daughters as American citizens. The U.S. State Department is an accessory and active conspirator in the denial of these rights. The U.S. government receives benefits from the Saudi Arabian government in various forms which induce it to violate these rights . . . We have been separated by two systems of evil that have broken the moral law that governs all human beings. My daughters have been taken hostage by a medieval, totalitarian system and the Central Authority of our government, the U.S. State Department, has done everything to enable that evil system to destroy the lives of my beloved daughters and shatter my family . . . Contrary to the statements appearing in the Saudi-owned press, Asharq Al - Awsat, listed on the official Web site of the Saudi embassy, which recently published a very biased, slanderous article about me concocted by the Saudi government and Gheshayan, these are American women, not "Saudi daughters" . . . I found out by reading this Saudi-owned newspaper that I will be a grandmother . . . What a way to find out about such a sacred event . . . It's like I have been erased from their lives. And now it is extending to the next generation . . . Why not an exchange—the Saudi Al-Qaida killers in Guantanamo for the lives of my innocent daughters? . . . This is a moral decision of conscience. As Moses pleaded with the obdurate heart of Pharoah for his people, I am beseeching you, let my family go.

To my surprise, the room filled with applause. I started to cry. Burton's staff later told me that they had never heard an ovation at a hearing before.

Monica Stowers was still inside Saudi Arabia with her nineteen-year-old daughter, who was unable to leave. She had made a videotape at the American embassy in Riyadh and sent it to the Committee in a diplomatic pouch. The State Department did not deliver the tape until twenty-five minutes prior to the hearing. After I spoke, Monica's image appeared on the two screens in the hearing room.

I hadn't seen her for approximately nine years. Although her age is near forty-seven, she now looks like a woman of sixty-five. Her emotional pleas and stark appearance with frequent, uncontrolled crying caused a sacred silence throughout the room:

When I married my husband all Saudi students were given diplomatic visas. I thought this was a little strange. I didn't know that he had another wife in Saudi Arabia. When I went to Saudi Arabia I didn't know that I couldn't leave and my children couldn't leave without my husband's permission. For almost twenty years my children and I have had a degrading existence with no help from the American embassy. These people were arrogant and cruel. I've been to Washington and to the Missing Children's Center and no one helped us. The agencies all asked why I married a Saudi? I went to the Saudi court and as a U.S. citizen, non Muslim, I couldn't even see my own children. Their father totally controlled them.

I was separated from my children for five years from 1985 to 1990 when I was able to get back into the country on a one-month visa. My son was nine and he ran away from his father and met me at the airport. He was like a skeleton and had a horror story to tell me. His stepbrother had forced him to have sex with him and beaten him. When he told his father, he was taken to the police station and stripped, then lashed. Then when his father took him home, he was beaten again. I had my son's friend drive me to my daughter's school and we went to the American embassy for help. When we entered the embassy, I thought, *This is it. Now we will be going home.* They didn't want us to be there and told us we would have to leave. The consul general, Karla Reed, told us, "The American Embassy is not a hotel. You have to leave."

She called my ex-husband and told him we were at the embassy. Then he really started to make trouble for us, calling all his friends in the government. We waited and refused to leave at five o'clock when the embassy closed. Then things really started to get worse. It was like a horror picture. Two marines showed up and one of them picked up my daughter and we had to follow as he carried her out. He said, "Ma'am, I'm sorry, but we're only doing our job."

They put us outside the gate and then locked it behind us. We had nowhere to go and my ex-husband was looking for us. He found us the next day and took my daughter away. I didn't see her for several months. Then my son and I had to go into hiding because the police were looking for us.

My ex-husband then said I could see my daughter on her birthday. We met them at Pizza Hut and the manager told me that someone was looking for me. I walked outside and the *mutawwa*, religious police, were ready for me and put me in a paddy wagon. My son threw himself on the ground and screamed, "Mom, save me." I told him to take a note to Princess Noora, whom I was tutoring.

After a few days the consul general from the American embassy came to see me at the jail. She had no solution for me and only stayed a few minutes. She said she had to go visit some American who was in jail for drug smuggling. They put an innocent mother who just wanted to be with her children in the same category as a drug smuggler.

Princess Noora's mother sent a car for me and I was finally freed within a few days. She arranged it so that I could see my daughter twice a month in a lobby of a hotel.

Several years passed and I had to go home to Houston. I called my daughter and she said, "Mom, I'm married." Her father waited until I was gone to marry her off at age twelve to a Saudi religious policeman. When I got back, I got her away from the man and went into hiding with her. My son was able to escape and went to Houston with my mother. He had two nervous breakdowns while he was in Saudi Arabia. When he got to Houston, he couldn't cope and got mixed up in drugs to stop his pain. I was still in hiding with my daughter. It was one crazy scene after the other for several years and finally I got uterine cancer and had to come back to the States for surgery. My son had to return to Saudi Arabia to take care of my daughter while I had my operation. I didn't think I was going to make it and worried that my children would never be able to come home.

My children were degraded, neglected, and abused. They should be awarded the Purple Heart for what they have been going through.

It's not safe to be here if you are not a Muslim. These people at the embassy go to their parties and don't know what it's like to live in the neighborhoods with the people and the law.

That's a shame these Saudis can go to the United States, buy property, and the people you go to for help just laugh at you. It's a shame on our country. My children's lives are destroyed and you just can't forget them. It's time for the American government to step in. It's a shame on our country and on the White House. No country needs a special relationship like that.

It's dishonorable. How much more do I have to take—and live in fear for all of our lives?

The State Department needs to take more care. These are dangerous countries. No special relationship is worth sacrificing U.S. citizens for. Not even one. Where did it get us?

They feel that what happened in New York was great. To see Americans on their knees. There is no loyalty here. Please help us. That's all I have to say.

Monica's seventy-three-year-old mother sat next to me and cried when she saw her daughter's prematurely aged and anguished face filled with tears. Ethel Stowers had a prepared statement but was unable to deliver it due to uncontrolled, sweeping emotion when Monica came on the screen. In between tears she whispered to me, "My God, she looks so terrible. Look what they've done to her. I am afraid she's going to die there."

The only thing Ethel could say between her sobs was, "Can you tell me why no one will help us? Can you tell me why this government won't help our children?"

Sixteen-year-old Dria Davis (Yasmine Shaloub), who escaped from Saudi Arabia when she was thirteen, and her mother, Miriam Hernandez-Davis, gave compelling testimony.

Ray Mabus was disappointed that he would not be able to attend the hearing. He had made prior vacation travel arrangements with his daughters. A two-page statement to the committee was submitted for the record:

While a case like this may not seem to be a big policy issue, it is everything to the people involved. I believe that one of the main jobs of the American government is to protect American citizens and to uphold American law. I have read that an unclassified cable sent from the State Department to our embassy in Riyadh instructed our embassy to remain "impartial." How can our government remain impartial when two American citizens were taken and are being held in violation of our laws? Is this not exactly the type of situation where our government should be active and involved in trying to get them returned to their legal custodian, their mother?

I believe that this case and others like it should be raised by the very highest levels of our government to the very highest levels of the Saudi government.

The next panel consisted of former U.S. Ambassador to Saudi Arabia, Hume Horan; Mideast expert Daniel Pipes; senior fellow of the Washington think tank, the CATO Institute, Doug Bandow; and two members of the State Department, Deputy Assistant Secretary of State for Near Eastern Affairs Ryan Crocker, and Deputy Assistant Secretary of State for Overseas Citizen Services Diane Andruch.

Ambassador Horan began by saying that he was briefed by U.S. Senator Alan Dixon about my case before he left for Saudi Arabia in 1988 and when he made the initial request for an audience with Prince Salman after arriving at the post in Riyadh, he was told by Salman's assistant that he was not to bring up my case or the appointment would not be granted. He still brought the matter up at the end of the meeting with Salman.

Horan was the only U.S. ambassador to Saudi Arabia who was ever expelled persona non grata. He was the best Arab speaker at the Department of State and an Arab scholar who translated for former U.S. presidents. Yet the Saudis didn't like him.

Said Daniel Pipes, "An answer can be found in a statement of the Saudi ambassador to the United States, Prince Bandar Bin Sultan. He boasts of his success cultivating powerful Americans who deal with Saudi Arabia. 'If the reputation then builds that the Saudis take care of friends when they leave office,' Bandar once observed, 'you'd be surprised how much better friends you have who are just coming into office.' This effective admission of bribery goes far to explain why the usual laws, regulations, and rights do not apply when Saudi Arabia is involved. The heart of the problem is a very human one: Americans in positions of authority bend the rules and break with standard policy out of personal greed."

Ryan Crocker confessed that the testimony of the witnesses was "wrenching" and that he was "shaken." He then responded that U.S. policy is to "work with the legal structure of the country in which the child is located" but admitted that American children often never are returned home. Diane

Andruch had little to say except that this was a "crisis" and did not even prepare a statement.

Crocker and Andruch remained silent when Burton pressed them on the State Department's plan of action. "There is no plan," Burton stated. He vowed, "If I have to hold ten hearings and use the remainder of my time, then we're going to do it."

Pipes, when further questioned by committee members, added, "If you please the Saudi government, then they will reward you afterward. It is a syndrome present in domestic affairs called the revolving door. The people who oversee the insurance company then go to work for the insurance company. It can take many different guises, but in the ultimate analysis, it's all money. And the striking thing is to contrast the Saudi case with the other oil-rich countries of the region, say, Qatar, Kuwait, and UAE. They do not engage in this kind of policy and we have a much more normal relationship."

Refusing Involvement

At a press briefing the day before the hearing, State Department spokesman Richard Boucher stated that my daughters were adults now and could decide for themselves if they wanted to come home. It's laughable that an official spokesperson for the State Department would come right out and make such a statement. The next day when White House Press Secretary Ari Fleischer was questioned by several correspondents about my story, he replied, "It's a heartbreaking, difficult issue that the State Department works very hard on in a very individual way to do what's best for the interests of the child. It's just as complicated and just as sad as any domestic case here where you have parents who are fighting for the custody of a child, and it's compounded and made more difficult by the fact that it involves laws of a sovereign nation that the United States cannot control, whether it's Saudi Arabia or any other nation."

Mr. Fleischer evidently forgot to mention that my daughters were not children and "child custody" was not the issue (there's the 'catch wording' again.) The continual reference to what happened to my daughters as a child-custody issue was meant to deflect from the fact that the U.S. government—from the White House to the State Department—refused to acknowledge that my adult, American daughters were not free to leave the kingdom of Saudi Arabia and were kept as prisoners of Saudi men, be it their father or, now, strange Saudi men who paid their father for their bodies.

The *Wall Street Journal* continued to pummel the issue with editorials and articles about my case: "Saudi Christmas," "Saudi Arabia's American Captives," "Daughters of America," "All the President's Women," "Civis Americanus Sum." The paper also pointed out that when the shoe is on the other foot, the Saudis don't like it very much. Saudi Interior Minister Prince Naif told the Arab News that the United States should send back the captured Saudi nationals being held in Guantanamo, Cuba. "We'll demand that the Saudi detainees be handed over, because they are subject to the kingdom's rules," Prince Naif stated.

Visa Express

A program offered by the U.S. State Department that allowed Saudis to apply for nonimmigrant visas to enter the United States at travel agencies inside Saudi Arabia instead of at the U.S. Embassy/consulates was initiated just three months before the 9/11 terrorist bombings. In fact, three Saudis, who were among the last of the hijackers to enter the U.S., used the Visa Express program—only submitting a short two-page form and photo.

This whole concept was the brainchild of Mary Ryan, assistant secretary of state for consular affairs. This "courtesy culture" had been intentionally sown by Ryan in her nine years as the head of consular affairs. She had continually stressed the importance of "fundamental fairness"—for foreigners.

Even after 9/11 the Visa Express program was still being used and no changes were made. In October 2001, just one month after the terror attacks involving fifteen Saudi nationals, the U.S. consulate in Jeddah interviewed only 2 of 104 applicants, rejecting none, according to Joel Mowbray, a young investigative reporter for *National Review*.

It was clearly business as usual with the Saudis until Mowbray was able to unveil Visa Express for the open invitation to terrorism that it was. Mowbray was able to testify before Burton's Committee for Government Reform concerning the Visa Express program one week after the June 12 hearing. The issue of whether to remove the power to issue visas from the State Department and give it to the new Department of Homeland Security was at stake. During this hearing Undersecretary of State for Political Affairs Marc Grossman declared:

> In creating the new Department, with its proper emphasis on homeland defense and law enforcement, it is important to recognize that visa policy plays a vital role in foreign policy concerns of the United States. For example, the U.S. uses visa policy to advance our goals of promoting religious freedom, opposing forced abortion and sterilization, enforcing the reciprocal treatment of diplomats, and in punishing the enemies of democracy around the world. These priorities will continue to inform our policy and the Secretary of State would support the Homeland Security Department to advance them.

What they are saying is that the State Department doesn't want the control of the visa issuance taken away from them because they use that power to pressure foreign governments for various reasons. But in my case, when Ray Mabus was using the power of the visa to pressure the Saudis to return my daughters—the only effective tool we had—it was taken away by Wyche Fowler because he didn't want to offend the Saudis. He did this for personal gain and as Daniel Pipes explained, the Saudis reward their friends very well. Hume Horan expounded even further by saying this visa "weapon" is used all the time by the State Department. But not for two innocent children who were sacrificed for Saudi money.

Colin Powell was forced to get involved. He certainly did not want State to lose the visa power and fired Mary Ryan just to prove that there was a change in how things were being done at the Department. Ryan's nine-year reign as "queen of mean" at consular affairs had ended. Visa Express was stopped on July 20, 2002, but only after congressional hearings, a media blitz, and public outcry.

As assistant secretary of state for consular affairs, Ryan had continually blocked any progress in my case and wrote derogatory remarks in my file on a regular basis. (I've seen some of my files obtained through Freedom of Information Act requests.) In January 2001 Edward S. Walker Jr. (or better known as Ned Walker)—assistant secretary of state for the Near East who was deputy chief of the mission at the American embassy in Riyadh in 1986 when my daughters were kidnapped—and I had a very heartening conversation regarding possible interventions to get the girls released after an article came out in the *Washington Post.*

Several weeks later, however, Walker was no longer returning my calls, and I was getting the same old runaround from the underlings at the Near Eastern Bureau of State. I couldn't understand the abrupt change and "cold shoulder" after receiving this very personal call from Walker, who seemed to be making a strong commitment just a few months before he was to retire from the State Department.

I didn't find out the answers until the Committee for Government Reform prehearing subpoenaed documents revealed that deliberate efforts were made to stop Walker. It was Mary Ryan again who intervened with a memo to Secretary Powell: "Ms. Roush, who has pressed for U.S. government action to have her two daughters returned to the United States since their father abducted them to Saudi Arabia in 1986, occasionally publicly criticizes the Department . . . There is no action for you to take at this time . . . We simply wanted to ensure that you were aware of the case in the event that it garnered further media attention."

Then after a June 7, 2001, letter to Powell was signed by twenty-three U.S. senators asking that the issue concerning my daughters be brought up with the Saudis on a state-to-state level, Ryan quickly responded by urging Powell not to get involved. "This is unlikely to produce the desired result and could inhibit our access to the Gheshayans, undermining our efforts to resolve the case . . . We expect her [Pat Roush] to continue her efforts in as public a manner as possible."

The List

Dan Burton kept his promise to try to bring American citizens home from Saudi Arabia. His dedicated staff worked tirelessly to bring about a resolution to my family's tragedy and in this process they unearthed a plethora of similar cases.

American women who were abused by their Saudi husbands, sometimes with five and six children each, had gone to the American embassy for help. After they were told that the embassy would not get involved, these women were sent back into the streets of Saudi Arabia—and often never heard from again. The State Department did not know the whereabouts of many of these women and their children and never questioned the Saudi authorities about them. They could be dead, locked up by their husbands, made into household slaves, or used as sex slaves. Their fate and the fate of their children were totally unknown to the U.S. government, who had basically written these people off.

The names of these women were released to the Burton committee only after the records from the State Department and the American embassy were subpoenaed. These numbers were not complete; we knew there were more women but had no information about them. The State Department had closed many of the cases and continued to be uncooperative.

Then there was the group of adult American women with Saudi fathers who could not leave Saudi Arabia, which included my daughters and many others. The American-Saudi children under eighteen who were kidnapped from their mothers in the United States were a separate group.

Burton and his staff organized a bipartisan congressional delegation for the trip to Saudi Arabia during the last week in August 2002. It included four Republicans, one Democrat, and one Independent: Dan Burton (R-Ind.), William Delahunt (D-Mass.), Bernard Sanders (I-Vt.), Benjamin Gilman (R-N.Y.), Mike Rogers (R-Mich.), and Brian Kerns (R-Ind.).

The staff spent weeks preparing for the trip and had put together a list of all American women, American-Saudi women, and American-Saudi children in the kingdom and proceeded to try to contact as many as they could before leaving the U.S.—asking them if they wanted to leave and telling them they were coming to fight for their freedom.

It was decided that no attempt would be made to contact my daughters while the congressional delegation, known as a "CODEL," was inside Saudi Arabia because they would certainly be coerced into making a statement that they didn't want to leave. We knew this would happen because Adel Jubeir, the now "special liaison to the crown prince," had been trying to arrange for such a Stalinist show trial ever since the June 12 hearing.

In July 2002 Jubeir made his first attempt. This was done at the State Department with Assistant Secretary of State for Near Eastern Affairs William Burns. Jubeir told Burns that my daughters would be available to give a statement to the American embassy consular officers in Riyadh concerning where they wanted to live but this statement had to be made known publicly. The State Department called me shortly after this request was made by Jubeir and asked for my permission to allow the American embassy personnel in Riyadh to meet with my daughters. I rejected it and was shocked that the State Department would even consider the request.

I asked them what Mr. Burns told Jubeir when the request was made. Randy Carlino from American Citizens Services said, "He told Mr. Jubeir that it would appear to be staged." I then asked Carlino if Burns had asked Jubeir to return the girls to the United States. He replied that Burns had not asked.

I requested that the delegation make appointments with the most powerful Saud princes—Crown Prince Abdullah, Foreign Minister Saud Bin Faisal, Defense Minister Sultan Bin Abdul-Azziz, Interior Minister Naif Bin Abdul-Azziz, and Prince Salman—and tell them we wanted all of our American citizens to be returned to the United States and for my daughters to leave the kingdom and come to their mother in the United States.

I asked them to go into these meetings with ammunition that could really make a difference in negotiating for the freedom of our people: visa restrictions for the diplomatic corps, revocation of landing rights for Saudi Arabian Airlines, reduction in military assistance, and future investigations on Capitol Hill concerning the "special relationship" with Washington.

The Factor of O'Reilly

A few weeks before the Committee left for Saudi Arabia I received a call from Kristine Kotta, a producer for the FOX television show *The O'Reilly Factor*. I had been on the program earlier in the year and we had spoken several times since then. She was very excited and wanted to let me know that Adel Jubeir had been a guest on the program a few days before. Bill O'Reilly had asked Jubeir if my daughters were being held against their will in Saudi Arabia, and, of course, Jubeir denied it. Then O'Reilly asked Jubeir if he could interview my daughters. Jubeir said that would be fine. He said the Saudi government didn't get involved in these matters and told O'Reilly that he could call the girls directly and set it up. (Jubeir knew he had found the right contact to carry out his dastardly plans for my daughters.)

Ms. Kotta said that O'Reilly really wanted to do this. I told her this was not a good idea and it would sabotage everything we were working for. She said she would call me back. She didn't. O'Reilly called me the next day after I had asked a media friend to intervene. I plainly told him that I did not want him to go near my daughters. I explained that Jubeir had been salivating to pull something like this off and had previously gone to the State Department to get them to be their lackeys and that Rod Dreher had written about the request from Jubeir in *National Review*. It was common knowledge that Jubeir wanted this to happen.

O'Reilly then told me I had twenty-four hours to think it over. I told him there was nothing to think over and asked him to please stay out of it. He spoke to Dan Burton the next day and I assumed the matter was dropped.

The Home Team

Burton's staff worked tirelessly in the weeks preceding the departure of the CODEL to Saudi Arabia. They met with one obstacle after the other. The dedicated, honest men and women that surrounded Dan Burton became frustrated with the lack of cooperation from our own government and the continuous lying and posturing by the Saudis and their representatives, namely, the Washington law firm of Patton-Boggs and the large public relations firm Qorvis Communications.

Burton's team was basically hamstrung by the State Department, who refused to provide anything but the bare minimum of information about the cases and whereabouts of the Americans in Saudi Arabia. The Department of Defense proceeded to make matters more difficult by refusing to allow certain requested personnel to board the military plane to be used by the delegation for the trip. It was later discovered that the Saudi government had paid lobbyists to meet with both the State Department and Defense Department at the same time that these details were being sorted out, according to the House Committee on Government Reform.

In the meetings with the Saudis, which included Adel Jubeir, Nail Jubeir, Michael Petruzzello (managing partner of Qorvis Communications), and representatives from Patton-Boggs, the committee staff made it very clear that my case was very high-profile and that one of the purposes of the trip to Saudi Arabia was to ask the most senior Saudi authority for the release of my daughters.

The Saudis and their handlers continued to push very hard for Burton and the CODEL to meet with my daughters inside the kingdom. They were very sure of the outcome of that meeting. One of Burton's staff told me, "If I was not thoroughly convinced about what they were up to regarding this meeting, I am now. They are pushing it very hard."

Monica Stowers's daughter, Amjad, was also a high priority for the CODEL, and the Saudis were told they wanted her to return to the U.S. Just a few days before the delegation departed, the *Wall Street Journal* printed an article requesting that the president ask Prince Bandar while he was visiting the ranch in Crawford, Texas, that week for Amjad's release—Bush complied.

We surprisedly found out the day before Burton left on the trip that nineteen-year-old Amjad had been secretly married to a friend of her father, a forty-five-year-old married Saudi Air Force pilot with a wife and five children. (The marriage the girl underwent at age twelve was dissolved only because Monica was able to retrieve the girl from the man and took her daughter and son into hiding.) Someone had clandestinely picked up Amjad in the middle of the night at her mother's residence and we didn't know her whereabouts. This was to be an omen of how the events of the week ahead would unravel.

Raven

Once Burton and his staff landed in the kingdom of Saudi Arabia, they immediately began meeting with American women and children who were able to make the personal contact with them. They met them anywhere they could—hotels, coffee shops, the American embassy. Some women were too afraid to take a chance on meeting with them but were able to have notes passed on to the members and staff.

It soon became clear that the numbers the State Department had released were far too few. Just as I had suspected, hundreds of American women were being held inside the kingdom and were not able to leave. They were afraid of their Saudi husbands and the Saudi government. One woman told Dan Burton that she wanted him to put her and her children in a box, place them in the belly of the military plane, and take them home to America. Another woman relayed the message that her Saudi husband had threatened to bury her alive in the desert and would force her children to watch her die. (The details of this threat have been changed to protect the woman; if the specific threat were mentioned the husband might know his wife had talked to Burton—and the real threat was even worse.)

It was Saturday morning, August 31, 2002. I called the American embassy and asked for the contact number for Jim Wilson, chief counsel for the Government Reform Committee, who was traveling with Burton. During our telephone call I asked Jim for an update on the trip and spoke with Dan Burton, who said they were going to try to get my daughters back. "Pat, we're right in the middle of a powder keg here. I can't believe this place." The CODEL and staff were shocked by the entire experience in Saudi Arabia.

Within thirty minutes of speaking to Jim Wilson and Dan Burton the phone rang again. It was the State Department in Washington: "Ms. Roush, this is Randy Carlino from American Citizens Services at the Department of State. I am calling to inform you that your daughters are in Europe and we want to ask you if we can send a consular services officer to meet with them and take a statement from them."

I was speechless and couldn't figure out what was going on. "Where are they? What country are they in?"

"I am not able to give you that information. We just want to know if you want us to take a statement from them and if you have any message for us to give to them."

"I just spoke to Congressman Dan Burton in Saudi Arabia and he didn't mention anything like this. What's going on here? This is not what we asked. Is this some kind of trick? Where are my daughters? No—no statements. Do you hear me? No statements."

"Thank you, Ms. Roush. Good-bye."

I called Jim Wilson back. He knew nothing about it.

That evening Bill McGurn from the *Wall Street Journal* called. He had received a telephone call from Adel Jubeir, gloating that my daughters were in London. He said they were on vacation and that there were other relatives with them. Then he bragged that my daughters had said that I was embarrassing them and they hated me and didn't want to come home. Mr. McGurn asked what they were going to be doing in London and Jubeir replied, "Going to Big Ben and the cinema." Then McGurn warned Jubeir that this was not a good move on their part. Jubeir laughed.

It was beginning to look like the State Department was working hand in glove with the Saudi government even after a Congressional delegation had arrived in the kingdom of Saudi Arabia to ask for the return of my daughters. The Saudi princes deliberately snubbed the six members of Congress that had journeyed so far for so many. The only prince that met with the CODEL and his delegation was the Saudi Foreign Minister, Prince Saud Bin Faisal. The same prince who had dealt with Mabus on my case so many times. He told them that the Saudi government didn't recognize U.S. law. He then made a statement that any American women living inside Saudi Arabia that wanted to leave, could leave. But no one left. Saud refused to allow his representatives to meet with Burton's staff lawyers to try to resolve all these tragedies case by case. Then in an effort to discredit Burton, he accused Burton of offering Amjad Radwan one million dollars to return to the United States with the CODEL. He brought up this "million dollar bribe" three times during his meeting with Burton

A Prayer for Alia and Aisha

Burton and the CODEL didn't have further information about my daughters. They knew less than I did. Apparently, Robert Jordan, the U.S. ambassador to the kingdom, told them later that evening that Alia and Aisha were in London.

The next day was Sunday, September 1, and the CODEL left Riyadh and flew in a military aircraft to Jeddah on the Red Sea. As soon as they arrived they were quickly whisked to the U.S. consulate for a reception. When they were all assembled in the large meeting room—there were more than twenty people involved with the delegation, which included six congressmen and their staff—Bush political appointee, Robert Jordan (Dallas attorney and Bush family friend)—abruptly got their attention and stated he had an announcement to make:

> We can confirm that, at their request, a consular officer in Europe met alone
> with Patricia Roush's adult daughters, Alia and Aisha Gheshyan. They are in
> Europe on vacation. The consular officer reports that they are well, and they
> do not wish to travel to the United States at this time. When we learned of
> the possibility of a meeting, an official of the Bureau of Consular Affairs
> informed Ms. Roush. We have no further comment at this time.

There was no sense of propriety or privacy on the part of Robert Jordan. It was as though he couldn't wait to make the announcement before this group who had gone to Saudi Arabia to try to bring these young women back to the United States after seventeen years of confinement. Instead of taking Dan Burton aside and quietly telling him what had happened, he publicly blurted it out with no qualms.

But Dan Burton didn't blink. He never showed any defeat and instead stood up and pulled a letter out of his pocket. It was from a wealthy Saudi woman whom he had met on the trip at some function—he did not reveal her name. She was asking for his help because she, too, was afraid of her husband and the authorities and couldn't speak freely. Burton read the letter aloud and said that if this Saudi woman couldn't speak freely and was asking for help, can we just imagine the situation that my daughters were in. He then asked the delegation for a moment of silence and prayer for Alia and Aisha.

Just before I went to church that same day, I received a telephone call from Randy Carlino of American Citizens Services at the State Department. He couldn't wait to inform me that my daughters said they didn't want to come home to the United States. He never told me they were in London—just somewhere in Europe. This was due to the Privacy Act—the State Department was concerned with protecting my daughters' privacy now that they had reached the age of maturity. This absurdity is like protecting the privacy rights of hostages—no info to the families. They gave me no further details about my daughters, just the official State Department statement that was being released as Jordan had read it.

I informed Carlino that the State Department had gone against my wishes and that this was contrary to what we had discussed many times before. I asked him why he had asked my permission for the statement to be taken if they were going to do it anyway. He denied ever asking for my permission. I told him to tell Colin Powell that it was not over and that the American people would not be fooled by this.

Later in the day I spoke with Jim Wilson. He was horrified by what had happened and said that Dan Burton felt this was totally unacceptable. They had work to do when they got back to Washington. He gave me assurances that Burton would continue the fight.

I thought that the girls and I had suffered enough those two days, but Labor Day weekend 2002 was one of the toughest periods of time I have gone through. I kept thinking about the girls. They must have been so scared. What a cruel game to play with them. They hadn't been allowed out-side that living hell known as Saudi Arabia since they were little girls—sev-enteen years! Then Adel Jubeir decided to play games and made it possible for them to leave, but only under his circumstances—in a little Saudi hot-house controlled environment in a London hotel—a brutal manipulation of two young woman who had been oppressed for almost two decades.

That same Sunday night I received an email from an Arab Associated Press reporter based in Cairo—Donna Abu-Nasr. It turned out that she also had inter-viewed my daughters. She stated, "I know it is going to be very painful for you to hear this, but your youngest daughter, Aisha, stated, 'We will not rest until she dies.'" In her article Abu-Nasr noted that Alia had dark circles under her eyes, and that in the London hotel room where they were interviewed there was strain show-ing on the faces of Alia and Aisha. "Throughout the interview the sisters were rest-less and shifted constantly in their seats. They both jumped when they heard knocks on the door—one time it was room service, the other housekeeping."

This Saudi friendly Associated Press reporter went on: "The Saudi gov-ernment urged the sisters to tell their story, according to Saudi officials who arranged their meeting with AP on Sunday. Saud [Saudi Foreign Minister Prince Saud] said Saudi officials also had urged the women to visit their mother, but they refused, saying they feared they would not be allowed to leave the United States."

Then Abu-Nasr wanted a comment from me. I told her that my daugh-ters loved me and I loved them. This same female, Arab reporter just hap-pened to be someone who has written an incredible amount of articles that are very favorable to the Saudi government. It is interesting to note that she was their reporter of choice for this most particular assignment.

The Blowhard Zone

Just when I thought it was all over, I received another phone call the day after Labor Day from Bill O'Reilly's producer, Kristine Kotta. She told me that they had sent one of their producers from San Diego to London to interview my daughters on the weekend and they wanted me on the show that evening.

I couldn't believe it! He did it. I had asked O'Reilly not to do it and told him it would hurt my daughters, but there was that carrot Jubeir was hanging in front of him—an exclusive interview with Pat Roush's daughters.

Kotta quickly told me that the show would be favorable to me. She stated that the producer told her that she felt the girls' father was there with them. There were also many other Saudi men besides the husbands.

The producer who interviewed my daughters told Kotta that the whole thing looked like it was rehearsed. There was even a "Saudi Media Specialist" present in the room "minding" my girls and giving them head signals as to how to answer the questions posed by the FOX producer. This was an employee of Qorvis Communications—Shareen Soghier from their Washington office.

Kristine Kotta also told me that my daughters were nervous and afraid. She said that Aisha appeared confused about why they were taken to London and why all those people were brought into the hotel room to ask them questions. When asked what they were going to do in London, Aisha answered, "See Big Ben and go to the cinema." This was the exact same line that Jubeir had told Bill McGurn. This confirmed that they had a script to follow. Jubeir even knew the lines.

Alia knew what was going on. No wonder she had black circles under her eyes. I could imagine Alia staying awake all night in London surrounded by her father, his brothers, the husbands, and God knows who else. She knew she was in a free country but she never had a chance for freedom. It must have tormented her.

Both Associated Press and FOX television reported that Alia had a four-month-old baby girl whose name was Basma. I wondered if I would ever hold my new granddaughter or even get to know her.

When I appeared on O'Reilly's television program that night the whole tone changed. I knew it was a setup when I heard the producer state, through the microphone in my ear, that my girls hated me. O'Reilly launched right into me and then proceeded to berate my daughter Aisha for saying that she thought Osama Bin Laden was a "clean, peaceful man."

He went into a diatribe about how brainwashed my daughters were and that he was sorry for me but that I had to face it—my daughters didn't want to see me again and did not want anything to do with the United States. He said he did all that he could to help me. If my daughters had said they wanted to come home, he, personally would have done everything to rescue them. But my daughters were just too far gone. They were never coming home. When I tried to explain what the Saudis were doing, O'Reilly ordered the director to "Cut Ms. Roush's mike off. She is too emotional."

For seven straight television programs Bill O'Reilly mentioned my story and brought up my name. He discussed it on his radio program and wrote a commentary about it for WorldNetDaily.com, later published across the country through Creators Syndicate. He bragged about how he successfully pressured Jubeir into producing the girls in London. Then he referred to that statement Aisha made about Bin Laden. "That sealed it. If two American citizens are that far gone—for whatever reason—there is little anyone can do."

O'Reilly continued, "They are not going to fight for their freedom. They are going to stay where they are . . . My job is to find the truth . . . But freedom cannot be imposed . . . But there was no hint. Only the praise of Allah. And of Osama Bin Laden."

Yes, Bill O'Reilly was the judge, jury, and executioner of my innocent daughters. He knew he was wrong but wouldn't admit it so every chance he got, he tried to justify what he did before millions of people who watch his television show, listen to his radio program, or read his column. He used my daughters for ten minutes of video on a television show. He was duped by Jubeir, who used him to get what he couldn't get from others. It was a conspiracy of three—the Saudi government, the State Department, and Bill O'Reilly. A *fait accompli*.

Hearing No. 2: Burton Strikes Back

One month after Dan Burton returned from Saudi Arabia, another hearing was held by his Committee for Government Reform: "Americans Kidnapped to Saudi Arabia: Is the Saudi government responsible?"

The hearing involved testimony from four other parents with children in Saudi Arabia and two American teenagers who had recently escaped from Saudi Arabia. Ray Mabus accepted an invitation to testify and the State Department again sent Ryan Crocker and Diane Andruch, who I later found out had personally given the order for the consular officer at the American Embassy in London to meet with Alia and Aisha.

Two days before the hearing *60 Minutes* had aired a segment involving an American woman who was able to be reunited with her sixteen-year-old daughter who had been detained in Saudi Arabia for eight years. Adel Jubeir had complained that he had not been invited to the first hearing so Burton extended an invitation for him to testify at the second hearing. But Jubeir didn't really want to come. Under his diplomatic status he could not be subpoenaed, so Burton got the next best thing—Michael Petruzzello from Qorvis Communications, who came only under subpoena.

Members of the committee were being lobbied by Saudi retainers who were calling Burton's staff liars. A green folder with the Saudi government insignia was passed around on Capitol Hill and to the State Department. It contained the AP article written by Abu-Nasr, a letter to the *Wall Street Journal* from Prince Bandar entitled, "We Are Not Holding Americans Captives," a letter to Colin Powell from Prince Saud, a letter to Dan Burton from Prince Bandar, and a "fact sheet" entitled, "The Kingdom of Saudi Arabia Is Fully Committed to Resolving Parental/Child Abduction Cases," which stated that my case had been solved.

I arrived in Washington for the two-day hearing and was told that I might be called upon to answer questions. Before the second day of the hearing began I approached Petruzzello and introduced myself. "Mr. Petruzzello, I'm Pat Roush. I just want you to know that this is a real flesh-and-blood issue here—these are my daughters."

This graduate of the Catholic University looked me straight in the eyes and smirked. "I'm so sorry about your daughters."

On one side of Petruzzello—a large, squarely built man with a thick mass of salt-and-pepper hair and heavy jowls—was his lawyer, Leslie Kiernan, from the Washington law firm of Zuckerman-Spaeder, LLP. She was strikingly pretty with her white, impeccably flawless complexion with faint freckles and red hair pulled back into a ponytail. Ms. Kiernan positioned herself in the front row of the hearing room directly behind Mr. Petruzzello's left shoulder. He was also accompanied by one of his partners from Qorvis, Judy Smith, a former White House deputy press secretary who became the spokeswoman for Monica Lewinsky during President Clinton's impeachment proceedings. This tall, stately black woman with long, flowing black hair sat next to Kiernan.

Burton began, "The Saudi Ambassador, Prince Bandar, wrote a letter to the *Wall Street Journal* dated September 12 stating that no Americans are being held against their will in Saudi Arabia. We know after yesterday's hearing that his statement is false. He lied. And after being in Saudi Arabia with five of my colleagues, both Republicans and Democrats as well as Independents, we all know that that's not true because we talked to women who are being held against their will and their children as well."

Burton went on to say that he had hoped the Saudi Arabian government would be able to work with them but that hadn't happened. "In public they say and do all the right things. In private they do everything to undermine our efforts . . . Once again we are given misinformation and disinformation from the Saudi government, and we are not the only ones.

"Two of President Clinton's top anti-terrorism aides just wrote a book. They said that Prince Bandar, who has lied to the media and to this committee through the media, repeatedly lied to the FBI about the Khobar Tower bombing . . . now with these kidnapping cases we've been given misinformation again and that's not acceptable."

He continued, "Adel Al-Jubeir complained to *60 Minutes* that he was not invited to our other hearing so we asked him if he wanted to come to this hearing. But he didn't want to come so we subpoenaed their top lobbyist, Michael Petruzzello, who has been called the leader of the Saudi's efforts to deal with our committee. Mr. Petruzzello heads Qorvis Communications and is paid $200,000 per month—$2,400,000 per year by the Saudi government."

Congressman Doug Ose (R-Calif.) immediately asked Petruzzello, "Were you aware before Chairman Burton left the United States that the Al-Gheshayan daughters were going to London for an interview with O'Reilly?"

Petruzzello replied, "I was aware of this two days before the Gheshayan sisters arrived in London."

Ose continued, "Who advised you of that?"

"Adel Jubeir."

Ose: "Apparently, at some point within the embassy a decision was made to have the Al-Gheshayan girls go to London for the purpose of the interview."

Petruzzello explained, "It is my understanding that the trip to London was inspired by Adel Jubeir's appearance on the FOX O'Reilly show some weeks before where he made a commitment to work to have the girls meet with U.S. government officials and the media outside of Saudi Arabia."

Ose: "It's a remarkable coincidence. Is there anybody here that you recognize in the audience that's otherwise here on behalf of the Saudi government?"

Petruzello turned around and immediately identified two heavyset men seated several rows behind him as employees of Patton-Boggs. Jamie Gallagher from The Gallagher Group—another Washington lobbyist hired by the Saudi government—was acknowledged, as well as another attorney from Zuckerman-Spaeder. Very few people are aware of this "shadow crowd" that does the bidding of the Saudi government behind the scenes. They are paid a handsome price for these maneuvers and are responsible for many of the underhanded, dirty games that the Saudis have played on me and others over the years.

Constance Morella (R-Md.) continued questioning Petruzello: "Qorvis played a significant role in the visit of the Roush girls to London last month. In fact, I understand a Qorvis employee was actually present during at least one of the interviews. Did the Qorvis employee meet up with the traveling party in Europe or in Saudi Arabia?"

Petruzello: "The Qorvis employee met with the sisters in London."

Morella: "Have the two Roush daughters ever been subject to coercion or duress?"

Petruzello: "Not that I'm aware of, but I have never spoken to the sisters . . . But I promise when I say that the Saudi government has been very clear in saying that they have never coerced the sisters to say or do anything that they didn't want to do."

Burton interjected, "Those women that went to London—their husbands were with them. We believe there was an entourage of other Saudi men with them. We don't know if their children were with them or not, which would have been another inducement to say what needed to be said . . . How do you know there was no coercion? When asked to sign a statement saying that the statements they made could be released to the public, they said that we can't sign those, that we have to ask our husbands first. Then they put their abayas back on and went and sat in the corner of the room. The husbands came, looked at the document, and said, well, we'll have to give this some thought. Do you think maybe there might have been some coercion there? . . . One girl after she got out said, 'My father said he threatened to kill me if I didn't say what I was told to say.' Do you think there might have been some coercion there?"

Petruzzello: "Mr. Chairman, the government has been diligent in trying to get the Al-Gheshayan sisters to come to the United States because they have been told by the committee and by the media any interview with the sisters in Saudi Arabia would be suspect."

Burton: "That's right. So they didn't come to the United States. They took them to England when I went with my delegation to Saudi Arabia at the very same time. And so they did not see their mother or go to the United States. They were not unattended by other Saudi men and we are not sure if they had their children with them. And you are not sure they were coerced?"

Petruzzello: "It is our understanding that the sisters have one child and the child was with them on the trip."

Burton: "Were you there with them?"

Petruzzello: "No, I was not."

Burton: "Who on your staff was there with them?"

Petruzzello: "Her name is Shareen Soghier."

Burton: "What was her purpose?"

Petruzzello: "When the sisters went to London they felt nervous about meeting with the American media and they wanted to have a woman just to be there when they did the interview. Shareen is an Arab-American who speaks Arabic and for obvious reasons, the Saudi government didn't want a government official there."

Qorvis and the Saudis were sure about the outcome of the meetings in London between my daughters and the American State Department and the Arab Associated Press reporter, but FOX television could be a loose wire if the interview was not monitored more closely—thus, the "minder" from Qorvis.

Burton: "I think that the coercion factor is very real. I've talked to so many women who were trembling, crying, scared to death that their husbands might even find out that they were even talking to U.S. congressmen or talking to someone in the media . . . The only way to know whether or not those ladies were coerced is to let them come to the United States, unencumbered, and let them talk to their mother and the media here. If they want to go back to Saudi Arabia, I don't think the United States would ever hold them. So would you convey to the Saudi government that the best way to make sure is to let them come to California? Let them come to the United States and let them talk to their mother—without their husbands—without an entourage of men and without threats."

Petruzzello: "The government has said that they have been working diligently to have the girls come to the United States . . ."

Burton chuckled. "Okay."

Petruzzello: "I think their trip to London wouldn't preclude that opportunity in the future and I will certainly relay that message."

Burton: "Yeah, well, I think they're probably gonna get it anyhow."

Congressman Chris Shays (R-Conn.): "My subcommittee . . . has held forty hearings on terrorism and periodically this government that you work for shows up in this scenario. Fifteen of the nineteen suicide terrorists were Saudi citizens. And that is imbedded in my thoughts. I had seventy families who lost loved ones from what fifteen Saudi citizens did. The Wahhabi form of Islam showed up continuously in my hearings as militant, fund-raising, sympathetic to terrorism. The teaching of Islam in Saudi Arabia showed up continuously as being hateful, vengeful, and creating an environment in which terrorism would flourish. You are working for a government that is holding Americans against their will. You are also working for a government whose phenomenal wealth has gone primarily to 30,000 royal family members while at the same time the per capita income of the average Saudi citizen has gone from $24,000 to $7,000. I don't really have good feelings about the government you work for. But it has intensified immensely at the hearings our chairman has conducted . . . I view you as working for a very corrupt government that has a lot of oil—and we depend on a lot of oil—but I hope that we're willing to just allow them to take their oil somewhere else and if we have to every day wait in line—so be it."

Burton: "In the seventies we got 50 to 65 percent of our oil from the Saudis and their balance of payment situation was good. Now we get 15 percent of our oil from them and their balance of payment deficit is not good. If they don't start working with the United States with these issues, they're going to have big problems. This is totally bipartisan—all agree. We will beat the drum. We're going to beat the hell out of them until they do something about these kids and bring these kids home. I promise you that."

Congressman Brian Kearns (R-Ind.): "Because of this issue and because of the refusal of the Saudis to cooperate we are now looking at many, many issues involving our relationship with Saudi Arabia. This might be the first time we are examining our relationship with Saudi Arabia. And these hearings and this issue has been in part the catalyst. It's not going away . . . we have a phrase 'opening a can of worms'—well that's what it's done."

Delegate Eleanor Holmes Norton (D-D.C.): "The only polite way to describe our relationship with Saudi Arabia is of course, schizophrenic. Perhaps the best way to describe it is hypocritical. These people believe in nothing we believe in! And yet what we have seen is their law trump our law . . . the notion that a country with whom we supposedly have friendly relationships can have law that trumps our law on the most fundamental rights such as access to your child to whom you gave birth to, kidnapping, child abuse, spousal abuse—that those can be trumped by a so-called ally while our State Department says you've got to understand this is how diplomacy works—that is simply outrageous, shocking, won't be accepted. Isn't accepted by anyone in the Congress or this committee. It is the State Department's job to find a way to a solution here. This is our government bending to their outrageous laws—inconsistent with international law . . . The complicity of our own government angers me more than the paid representative of Saudi

Arabia. Unless the State Department finds some way on its own to thread the eye of this needle, essentially what you're asking for is congressional intervention . . . I want to make sure that both the State Department and the Saudi representative understand what I'm sure the parents already understand—that this is an issue that animates this entire Congress. It shakes us at the core of what we all put first—our own families . . . This is an issue of huge concern and the State Department better find a way to do something about it or the Congress will."

Congressman William Clay (D-Mo.): "What about these families sitting here in this room—the families that have been impacted . . . How do we handle that emotional strain?"

Petruzzello: "Congressman, I don't think anyone could not feel great sympathy for the families that are involved in these issues and it's not lost on the Saudi government how important this is both to the families and to Saudi-U.S. relations."

Burton: "It's lost on the Saudi government and I know you're their PR guy and you gotta make them look good, but I gotta tell you, and I looked them right in the eye when I was over there—it's lost on 'em. It's lost on 'em. They don't care. They'll give you lip service and they'll pay you $200,000 per month to make them look good, but they don't care. They don't care about these women and their kids. They don't care.

"The men rule. If you're a woman and the man says you don't go to the bathroom, you don't go to the bathroom. If your husband says you don't go out the front door, you don't go out the front door. They say to the kids, you do this and if you don't, they tie you up and beat you up . . .

"I mean, come on. To make it look like they have a human face regarding the people whose kids have been kidnapped and taken away from them is just a doggone lie. It's just a lie. They don't care and if they did care, they'd do something about it."

I was sworn in at the very end of the hearing to testify concerning the visa-hold issue and the events surrounding the trip to London. And then the hearing concluded with the very powerful words of Congressman Chris Shays: "Mr. Petruzzello, I would like for you to pass on to your client that there is only one way you resolve these cases and that is by returning the abducted children . . . I would say to the chairman—keep pushing, to the staff—thank you for your good work, to the very precious parents—the way you reach us is to remind us of our own children. Our hearts bleed for you. We don't intend to bring you any more pain by the questions we ask or add to your tears. But you have a right to expect that your government will speak up for you. You have a right to know that embassy employees will work on your behalf for justice. You have all those rights of expectations. And to Ms. Roush, you have waited the longest and your wait has to be even more painful. But I do know that you will never, never, never give up."

15

❧

FREEDOM AND LIBERTY

The only sure bulwark of continuing
liberty is a . . . people strong enough and well informed
to maintain its sovereign control over its government.
—Franklin Delano Roosevelt, April 14, 1938

America: The Great Experiment

It could be said that the highest calling is to be free: Individual freedom, political liberty, and freedom from bondage of the soul are at the very core of our humanity. In America we tend to take our freedom and liberty for granted. We forget to remind ourselves that the price for these privileges has been quite high. The liberation that we enjoy is the result of the efforts of our Founders—Washington, Jefferson, Madison—of great leadership that had the vision, knowledge, and conviction to draw from the lessons of history to put together this great experiment in freedom and liberty known as the United States of America.

The true principles of the United States are liberty and equality for all men. It is the dedication to these moral principles that makes the United States unique in history, the bearer of freedom to the world. A true test of a free society should be if it is producing leaders of ability, vision, and moral character.

The men who founded America and fought for their freedom from a tyrannical empire were of a moral distinction and political capability unsurpassed in world history. The American cause was in the hands of statesmen, not politicians, men who led their fellow countrymen rather than being guided by public opinion polls. These statesmen had a bedrock of principles—truth, character, and integrity—and a devotion to democratic liberty, a vision, a grand and noble vision, of mankind moving toward ever-greater freedom.

In contrast, nowadays, there seems to be a pervasive Machiavellian attitude among politicians, business executives, and corporate America. Increasingly it seems as if success or money is the only criterion by which to judge a leader or his actions.

Today's politicians have their antennae up and don't speak till they know what you want to hear. We tolerate leaders that display no morality in their personal lives and then put our full trust in these same people to make the most critical decisions for our own lives. You can't separate the personal life from the professional life—the same soul rules the man. Scandals involving our leaders that men of honor would never participate in are laughed at and joked about on late-night television and at the office. This should not be acceptable behavior in our free society. It's a disgrace that these men are not removed from office and are still paid by the taxpayers to make decisions for them.

Men like Pericles, Cicero, Jefferson, Lincoln, Franklin Roosevelt, and Churchill were great statesman. We have none today. This lack of great leadership and moral decay has left us without direction and with only politicians at the helm. The political system itself fosters dishonesty and corruption. Even the most well-intentioned man of conscience may find it difficult or impossible, once elected, to maintain his values due to pressure to appease special-interest groups, obligations to financial supporters, and the arena of politics.

Herman Melville wrote, "We Americans are a chosen people, who bear the ark of the liberties of the world." It could be said the United States, its foundations and history, is the most important single event in the history of freedom. And yet those very same ideals and principles that we have held so dear to us are now being threatened.

A Storm of Change

The foundation and fiber of America are undergoing dramatic change, unforeseen by the Founders: erosion of morality; media-manufactured leadership; lack of ethics and values in leadership; rampant consumerism and materialism; sexual licentiousness and saturation; portrayal of harsh violence and sex in films, television, magazines, and books; child pornography; Internet pornography; drug and alcohol abuse; increased use of antidepressant and antianxiety medications; the removal of God from our culture, society, and schools; lack of a spiritual community; scandals in our churches; youth with an attitude of purposelessness; loss of respect for each other and ourselves; a decline in the standards of our educational system; political apathy and distrust of political leaders; and an undermining current of "hubris" or arrogance that we are the best in everything around the world.

I don't think anyone can deny that we are all involved in a global storm with just one nuclear explosion separating us from the other side of the world. The fact is that America, and the world as we baby boomers knew it, has changed. It's no longer the world of the 1950s that I grew up in and longed to go back to all my life. The nostalgic memories of apple pie and a simpler, cleaner life are face-to-face with the cold, hard facts on the evening news. And now a new kind of "war" seems to be lurking around every corner, each letter we open, and every airplane we board. We all know that our lives and our country will never be the same.

The cities no longer consist of the Irish neighborhoods, the Italian neighborhoods, and the ethnic identities that made America the great experience it once was. There is a new type of immigration taking place from the Third World that is changing the core values of America as well as the language, ideals, and culture. This is coupled with the rotting of the inner cities of New York, Chicago, Los Angeles, San Francisco, and other areas that are now filled with pollution, violence, filth, poverty, homelessness, congestion, and more and more concrete. These are only symptoms of the moral blight that is covering us as a society.

This cloud of political apathy that shrouds America today is partially the result of a feeling of helplessness in the realm of world events, media hype, and corruption among politicians. People are overwhelmed and disempowered. They don't know how to get back what has been stolen from them. Where do we begin?

The seeds should be planted in our schools, which have now become battlefields with armed twelve-year-olds coming on campus with blazing guns. If we can make it into the classroom the importance of subjects like civics and history must be stressed. Civics—the study of citizenship and the rights and responsibilities it entails—is barely, certainly not adequately, being taught in our schools any longer. We don't have a sense of responsibility with this great freedom that we are heir to. Without accountability, individual freedom becomes license—a product of modern society.

Our entire history as human beings has been outlined through the ages by oral tradition and myths and legends of great leaders and warriors. It is part of our spirit. How wonderful it would be to have dedicated, inspired teachers that could earn a decent living by instilling the joy of learning into the hearts and minds of our young. History and our great heritage could come alive for our children and they would have a sense of identity, of who they are, why laws exist and what a great privilege it is to be able to participate in a free nation. We should emphasize to our children that a single individual can change the course of history for the better and make of life a blessed and noble thing, despite all public and private trials and difficulties too many to name.

As an individual I struggled with my own personal identity and my identity as an American. I grew up in post–World War II America when television was new and kids could go out trick-or-treating until ten at night without their parents ever entertaining a thought that they would be harmed. My teen years in a single-parent household were rocked by the 1960s: Vietnam, friends being brought home in body bags exhibited on the evening news, bra burning, students killed at Kent State University, civil rights, assassinations of three powerful leaders, "Flower Power," slogans such as "Question authority," "Don't trust anyone over thirty," and songs with lyrics like "You say you want a revolution."

I longed for that Italian culture of Bella Papa and the godfathers who would put me on their laps and sing to me in Italian—the boisterous family that would gather around the simple table and eat pasta and drink wine. I couldn't get those moments or that culture back; it was a different world as I grew up in the socially torn sixties, and then once I reached San Francisco when I was twenty-two, I totally didn't know who I was.

But I was not alone. Most of America was in the same turmoil and went through the same search. I was an idealist and wanted to save the earth, stop the war, work for peace and justice for all, be a missionary, be a nun, be a humanitarian and go off to strange, new lands and study antiquity. I met a man from a different culture and religion who was very dangerous and I became entrapped in a cycle with him and couldn't get out. It cost me the rest of my life, and it cost my daughters a lifetime sentence in a medieval madness with the worst gender apartheid in the world.

Only Truth Shall Set You Free

Despite all this and through all this I have found my identity both personally and spiritually—something that is truly a gift from God. During this search for self, I discovered that I have a rich heritage on both sides of the family, but the Roushes have something very special to contribute. Just before my father died, one of his relatives told me about a Dr. Lester L. Roush, who wrote the *History of the Roush Family in America* in three volumes. Another family history book by Dr. Roush was *Military Service of Nine Brothers in the Cause of American Independence*, an authentic record outlining the story of nine sons of our founder, John Rausch, who all served in the Continental Army.

Dr. Roush, who personally visited and took pictures of the grave markers of these nine brothers, writes:

> These brothers have all left their mark in the world. All generations benefit by their contribution to civilization in the following special ways:
>
> They were God-fearing men of high moral character, the noblest contribution which any man can make for the benefit of posterity.
>
> They were men of vision who foresaw how America could benefit the world, and contributed much to its founding.
>
> They influenced the establishment of the public school system for America, often beginning in their own home, "for their own and their neighbor's children."
>
> They believed that religion as well as education was necessary to "good government of mankind." All helped to establish schools and churches in their respective communities, many of which still flourish today.
>
> Their dreams, their activities, the causes they promoted have received the approbation of succeeding generations.

The irony is that all my life I wanted my father's love or some thing, some part of him, and he was not able to give it to me. I searched for a replacement for that love for fifty years when the best and only enduring gift he could ever have given me, besides his love, was this rich heritage of the Roush family. I never knew it but it was always a part of me.

My spirit flowed from these God-loving fighters for liberty from the Blue Ridge Mountains who died in the Shenandoah against British tyranny. And now I am engaged in a battle for the freedom of my daughters and others like them against an illegitimate, totalitarian government and the corrupt leaders of my own country. My ancestors gave up their lives for the sake of liberty and freedom, and now it has become my mission also.

The loss of basic morals by U.S. government leaders and the kowtowing to a petty, foreign, despotic government like Saudi Arabia by Washington has cost me the lives of my daughters and has put the United States in grave jeopardy. For what has happened to me is happening to America on a larger scale. This courting of Saudi Arabia by Washington and refusal to "draw a line in the sand" with that regime is one of the reasons that we lost three thousand innocent Americans on September 11 to hate-driven fanatics incubated and supported by the kingdom.

The two-path system continues with the Saudi princes and wealthy businessmen investing in the U.S. and exchanging high powered business deals with the corporate world, politicians, former U.S. ambassadors, former U.S. presidents, and State Department personnel while back home the mullahs preach anti-American homilies to the local population.

There has never been an official U.S. investigation concerning what is going on inside Saudi Arabia with Al-Qaida and who is funding these "charities" that allow this terrorist organization to continue its deeds and plots against the Western world. This "special" relationship between Saudi Arabia and the United States is a plague on our land. Americans do not fully comprehend the extent of this disease or its possible consequences.

What did all the Roush brothers and the GI Joe's in the trenches die for? Certainly not for America's sons and daughters to be sacrificed to a foreign government for the sake of cheap oil and corrupt business deals.

I summon my blue-eyed slaves anytime it pleases me. I command the Americans to send me their bravest soldiers to die for me. Anytime I clap my hands a stupid genie called the American ambassador appears to do my bidding. When the Americans die in my service their bodies are frozen in metal boxes by the U.S. Embassy and American airplanes carry them away, as if they never existed. Truly, America is my favorite slave.

—King Fahd Bin Abdul-Aziz, Jeddah, 1993
(Herb Mallard, Sauduction.com, corroborated
by anonymous State Department employee)

Mahatma Gandhi and Martin Luther King Jr., believers in freedom who led their people from civil disobedience into freedom, were paradigms of how an individual can change the course of history. Gandhi believed in the supreme importance of truth. Truth is God. In order to conquer untruth you must first conquer yourself. Gandhi equated liberty with truth. Gandhi's words offer one of the most enduring statements of the ideal of freedom as truth and of our duty to struggle for both:

God is, even though the world deny Him. Truth stands, even though there be no public support. Truth is self-sustained. Truth is, perhaps, the most important name of God. It is more important to say that truth is God than to say God is truth. I shall not fear anyone on earth. I shall not bear ill will towards anyone. I shall not submit to injustice from anyone. I shall conquer untruth by truth, and in resisting untruth I shall put up with all suffering.

16

❧

THE JOURNEY

Stand at the crossroads, and look, ask for the ancient paths: which was the good way? Take it and you will find rest for yourselves.
—Jeremiah 6:16

The Unexplainable

When people ask me how I have been able to sustain myself through almost two decades of grief, loss, and misery, and continue to be able to work, write, and maintain the composure to continue this struggle for the release of my daughters, I give them the short answer—my faith in God and my love for my children. But to expound on the lessons I have learned and spiritual growth that has transformed me I would have to give a much more detailed response.

274

From almost the beginning of this journey God revealed Himself to me in the most mystical, intimate ways. I was not prepared for the signs, and in the beginning they both astonished and frightened me. At first, I sought explanations from various clergy, but most of them were not familiar with mysticism, miracles, or the power of the Holy Spirit and had only basic, traditional seminary backgrounds. It wasn't until I met Peter Aragon and began reading the mystics that I discovered that what was happening to me had also happened to them and was a very special gift from God.

I knew that I was being called by God and kept trying to get closer and closer but was frustrated because although He was telling me He was with me, I was still here on earth in such pain and still separated from my daughters. I was glad God loved me and wanted me but I kept questioning Him about the girls. Why couldn't we be together? Wasn't I trying to do His will? Wasn't I trying to be righteous? Wasn't I walking through that "narrow gate"? What did my innocent daughters ever do to deserve this fate?

The world we live in is not a fairy tale. There is no happily-ever-after ending but an enormous amount of pain, misery, and suffering. Too much. I couldn't get relief: All the things I tried to do to get my girls back failed. I didn't know what more I could do to bring about the result I wanted—the return of my daughters. I thought it all rested with me; if I did x, y, and z, I could make it happen. If I could only convince one more congressman or connect with one more mercenary, then they would come home and this nightmare would end.

I desperately wanted to rescue my daughters, and for thirteen years I breathlessly ran from one thing to the other until I finally collapsed and my house of cards came down. I had to face fifty years of living and stand naked before God. Nothing from the past worked for me any longer. God had to take away all the debris and I had to become a new creation.

The signs that were given to me allowed me one foot in heaven, but the other foot bound me to this earth. At first I thought these special messages meant that my girls were coming home to me soon. But God was not on my timetable. The slap on the shoulder, the presence on the tennis court, the personal messages from individuals, the St. Jude medal phenomena, auditory visions, out-of-body raptures, the message from my mother after her death, numbers and dates and names that were more than coincidences, and lately physical changes that keep occurring to the Medugorje rosaries were all nudges from God to let me know I was not alone.

The day before I began to write this book I found my rosaries on my nightstand with the crucifix tied to the top of the rosary. The next morning, after sleeping with the rosary in my hands, the crucifix was totally gone from the chain. Then several weeks later while I was holding the rosaries in my hand—they changed into two complete circles, three decades of beads in one circle and two decades in the other. Within fifteen minutes the rosary changed back into one complete five decade chain. [When that happened, I fell to my knees in prostration—I knew I was in His presence.]

And then on the Feast of our Lady of Guadelupe, after listening to the mass on the radio, I put my hand in my bathrobe pocket and felt something— the crucifix was returned.

Swimology

But it is impossible to get out of the presence of God. His presence is with everyone at all times. How easily we forget this while we spend our lifetime looking and searching for meaning and purpose. As St. Augustine stated, "We were created for Thee and our hearts will not rest, until they rest with Thee." I had experienced a turbulent life and nothing I did brought me the peace I so desired until I stopped confusing the peace of the world with the peace only the Lord could give me.

Modern society is neurotic and involved in constant strife, competition, and restlessness. Contemporary culture has no message, and true spirituality is not emphasized. On the one hand, science has become our God; if you start talking about God, and especially Jesus, people look at you a little differently and think you're strange. On the other, if psychic power, cosmic energy, or "the stars" are mentioned, it's quite all right.

We spend money on counselors, psychiatrists, gurus, therapists, psychics, and "life trainers" to help us find the way, the key to fulfillment—happiness. I was astounded when I read an article in the newspaper about a woman who calls herself a "personal coach" and makes a living traveling around the world hosting seminars teaching people how to manage what she calls "the six forms of energy"—money, time, physical vitality, creativity, enjoyment, and relationship. We've turned to consulting, counseling, and now coaching to find out how to live. We've given away our dignity to "experts" and institutions when the answer is already inside us. We tune in TV gurus to give us answers to common sense living.

I was on a retreat one time and heard a story about a professor who took an ocean voyage in a cargo ship. He spent every evening in his cabin studying and reading. An old sailor, curious about the professor, went down to talk to him. The first night the old sailor asked the professor what he was studying.

The professor stated, "Geography. Haven't you ever studied geography?"

And the old sailor said, "No, sir. Never heard about that."

The professor responded, "You haven't studied geography? Then you have wasted one quarter of your life."

The next night the old sailor went down the stairs to the professor's cabin and asked, "What you are doing, sir?"

The professor answered, "I'm studying oceanography. Haven't you ever studied oceanography?"

And the old sailor replied "No, sir. Never."

"You haven't heard about oceanography? Then you have wasted one quarter of your life."

On the third night the old sailor went to the professor's cabin and asked him what he is doing.

"Studying meteorology. Don't tell me you haven't studied about meteorology? It's the study of the weather. If you haven't studied meteorology then you just wasted another half of your life."

The next night the boat was swaying and the wind was blowing. The old sailor crept down to the professor's cabin. "Professor, have you ever studied swimology?"

"Swimology? What's that? I never heard of that before."

"Well, sir, swimology is knowing how to swim. If you don't know how to do that, then you have just wasted your whole life because there's a hole in the boat and we're sinking."

The ultimate test is with ourselves. No one can live our lives for us. It's not a matter of reason or knowledge but the real experience of living. You must get in the water and do it yourself—swim.

An interesting side note: After I starting becoming whole, all kinds of wonderful secondary pluses began to happen to me and I could do things with ease that I could never master before. I tried all my life to swim and even took lessons when I was a child but I could never "get it." Then one day while in the pool, I just started to swim—now I swim for one hour every day. I did it! I passed Swimology 101!

Unknowing Gift

The signs God gave me edified my faith and renewed my spirit. I realized the power involved in the Spirit and that Spirit was who we really are: These fragile bodies are merely the covering for something far more wonderful and enduring. We have to learn how to identify with Spirit, our true self, our authentic self. Spirit is because Spirit is of God. We have as much Spirit now as we ever had because Spirit doesn't grow, die, or go away. God is nontemporal. Spiritual growth is our ability to participate, to cooperate with that Spirit. With every sign or miracle I wanted to go deeper into the mystery. Once I received these "glimpses of glory" and tasted the water I wanted more. I thirsted for God. I didn't want to stay here in this dimension any longer and hungered for that "mystical marriage," the ultimate union with God that the great mystics spoke of.

But that was not God's plan. I had work to do here—it was not yet my time to leave. I had many lessons to learn before I traveled to the next world. I didn't understand the blessings of pain and suffering. I often questioned God about why I had to suffer such losses. I likened myself to my cancer patients and would often say that I had terminal cancer of the heart but never died. No one could cure me. There was nothing I could do to take away the pain of the loss of my daughters.

I finally realized that what I was truly involved in was not what was seen but the unseen spirit of evil. And over the years I learned a great deal about evil in men's hearts—especially those closest to me whom I trusted and loved. Everyone seemed to have had an agenda with me—including the only two men I ever loved, my father, David Roush, and David Baioni.

There, again, was one of those "strange coincidences." Both had the same name and a problem with their optical nerve. And both betrayed me in the end and caused me untoward pain and misery. But it was through this pain and the pain of losing my daughters, which worked as a double-edged sword—both hurting me and healing me—that I was able to walk through my trials and come out on the other side intact, transformed, and whole.

David Baioni "found" the medal and gave it to me on the anniversary of the date it was given to me by Joyce. His finding the medal and giving it to me was symbolic of the great gift he inadvertently gave me: the incredible spiritual conversion I underwent when he betrayed me. This final deception and loss caused me to go into a spin that none of my survival techniques could bail me out of. I had no one to go to except God.

I had very good coping skills that I'd used from childhood and prided myself on my strength and courage, but God wanted more of me. He wanted me to go back to the hurts that I never dealt with and the abuse that I never totally acknowledged and bring it all into the light. St. Ignatius, the great retreat director, emphasized that we must begin at the foundation, not the second floor. Compounded pain, covered up with fifty years of following my old story line, had to be exposed. And you cannot put "new wine into old wineskins." I had to become a new person from the inside out, for it is only when we find the depths of ourselves that we find our dignity and our soul: We then know that we are more than this body, this psyche.

Peter Aragon was my spiritual director, my consel, who was there to guide me through that storm and point me in the direction of truth. But each journey is individual and the journey was mine. I had to find the right path.

Usually when we are going to a place we have never been to, we like to have a map. There are many signposts but it is an individual journey. Some people seeing the same signposts still take different routes. And so it is on our spiritual journey back to God, to our home from whence we came. We are all going to the same place but each on our separate journeys with different paths.

Another World

My pain and suffering opened up the whole world of inner life to me and an experience of "another world"—the real world—that I had searched for all my life. The existence of an alternative reality has always been known to native and aboriginal peoples, who have been in touch with their bodies and spirits from primitive times. And in the course of God's salvation history the knowledge of this other world has been revealed to us in many ways. It is an infinite world not held within the finite boundaries of time and space. It is free of the illusions of this life.

My struggle with suffering and longing to be released from it has pushed my search for its meaning even further, but it was only through suffering and sacrifice that my real spiritual growth occurred. This interior experience of the paschal mystery is something everyone, sooner or later, will have to undergo, for no discipline or effort can offer you immunization. It is a gift we are rooted in.

The concept of sacrifice is not culturally embraced. The culture teaches us to get what we want, no matter what. The message of sacrifice is foolishness to the world. But truth is that nothing lives without sacrifice. A seed is planted in the ground so a tree will be born. The seed doesn't know that when it dies, it will be a tree. It never sees the tree.

Life is change. You can never put your feet in the same river twice. You aren't even completely the same person you were this morning. Deep and rich spiritual truths can be revealed by this suffering, death, and resurrection, but what you learn from it totally depends on your cooperation with the Spirit within you.

Our lives are cycles of dying (loss), healing, and resurrection (rising).

Something is taken away from us, we grieve, and go on to adjust to a new life. It requires that we constantly let go of what we were before.

If we fail to enter into this dying and rising process there is bitterness, restlessness, and anger, which rob us of our precious life time. It is impossible to cooperate with this ebb and flow of natural order if we try to block divine providence. It requires total surrender. If we don't do it, life has a way of doing it to us.

In my case I had a death of my wholeness (the loss of my children), and many other fractured areas of my life that were never healed. I couldn't accept that loss because the girls were not dead, but beyond my reach. I couldn't bury them, grieve, and go on with a new life. It was like an endless funeral on top of the constant struggles, disappointments, and betrayals. The revelation that my own government was going through great lengths not only to keep my daughters away from me, but to appease a foreign government and a foreign national involved in kidnapping them, made the whole process very difficult for me to handle.

I knew I couldn't continue to slug it out with these forces the way I used to. It proceeded to destroy me until I became able to detach myself from what was happening. I couldn't change what they were doing or get my daughters back, but I could change me. They had physical control over my loved ones, but I wasn't going to give them power to hurt me any longer. I decided not to give them that gift. They figuratively burned me at the stake—but like Joan of Arc, my heart did not burn.

The next step was to deal with my anger.

"My Foe Outstretched Beneath the Tree"

There is a poem by William Blake, "The Poison Tree," about how when we hold things in, anger can yield a bitter and poisonous fruit. I saw what it was doing to me. I knew that I could never be the person I wanted to be until I let the anger go. The key was forgiveness. The Lord asks us to forgive but it is *the* way into the paschal mystery.

I wanted to be free, but keeping the hurt and anger alive was placing me in spiritual bondage. As St. John of the Cross stated, "If a bird is tied by a chain or a thread, he is still bound." I had to learn that by forgiving the person I was not condoning the actions or crimes and not excusing what was done. In forgiving the person and not the action, there is some justice. I had to learn to let things go and bless those responsible. Once it was done, it was done. It was a transforming experience for me and was part of the process of becoming whole.

Everything about me started to change. I started reading the mystics, the Bible, and the lives of the saints. I prayed, went to monasteries on retreats, became a vegetarian again, and removed myself from the secular life as much as I could. I discovered myself. I discovered the deliciousness of being alone—of the silence. Then I discovered that you cannot be alone. God is with you at all times. Fourteenth-century mystic Julian of Norwich stated, "Between me and God, there is no between."

I discovered Julian when I began to read the mystics (we don't know her real name). She was the first woman to write a book in the English language and her family probably died in the great plague of the times. She was an anchorite and lived in a one-room hut attached to a church. This hut had two windows: One faced the marketplace and the other the church. Her life was poised between these two windows. The marketplace symbolized the temporal world that doesn't last, and the window to the church was the innermost world, life of the spirit that will never die.

The window to the marketplace, the one we spend most of our time at, distracts us and prevents us from looking at God within. We have to close the door to the marketplace in order to look more deeply and seek more deeply the God within. I think most people believe that "real life happens outside of me" with connections to people. But there are rich, wonderful happenings going on inside us—*sine qua non*.

An unknown fourteenth-century mystic wrote in *The Cloud of Unknowing* that all thoughts and concepts must be buried beneath a "cloud of forgetting," while our love must rise toward God hidden in the "cloud of unknowing."

The paradox is that nearly all the mystics acknowledge they cannot even speak about their ineffable experiences, but they all want to write about it and tell us about what is the unspeakable, the unexplainable. They hope that the silence will speak to us between the words.

Perhaps it is expressed simply by a zen koan:

> Sitting quietly, doing nothing
> spring comes . . .
> the grass grows by itself

The Art of Living

I couldn't find God in a church, monastery, or religion. I found Him in my aloneness and my pain. It is the experience of God that I was always after, not the traditions, rites, and rituals. There are no great contemporary spiritual teachers and priests; gurus and self-help books are unable to give us the answers we seek. But God has not left us alone. Our teachers are the great mystics and saints with Holy Scripture to guide us and the Holy Spirit to protect us.

There is no more running away to a cloister or a mountaintop. The world has grown small and urban life is a reality. As Thomas Merton stated, "The new deserts are concrete," referring to the desert fathers in the early church that left society and went off to live in isolated communities. We're all searching for that "connection" and the churches are not meeting our needs. I believe we have moved into another era where the laity, the people, are being called to an inner conversion as were the early Christians. Everyone must be a mystic and find that secret wisdom of God. For spirituality is not something added on to life. It is life—the art of living.

We can trace the tapestry of our lives and see what God was trying to tell us only after the passage of time—with the changes that have taken place in our souls. While we are involved in the struggle we can only pray for the guidance and grace of God. Life is constantly reminding us that we are fallible. We do make mistakes, but God doesn't make mistakes. We have much to learn from things that do not turn out as we plan. It teaches us humility and that we are not "in charge" here. God uses us as vessels for His own purpose. As I have grown spiritually, I have learned to cooperate with the Spirit and not to try to control it. The word is *surrender*. The Twelfth Station of the Cross in Medugorje—the Crucifixion—where I placed my Pound Puppy photo of Alia and Aisha, was to be my salvation. And maybe theirs.

A few years ago I bought an antique painting of *The Agony in the Garden* and keep it near to remind myself of how many times I have asked God to "let this cup pass over." But I didn't know where all these crosses were leading—to oneness, wholeness, holiness. God sees the beginning and the end of the parade; we are only caught moment by moment in time and space. I've come to accept that what has happened in my life with my daughters is similar to the story of Joseph in the Bible.

Going Home

Joseph was the favorite of the twelve sons of Jacob and was sold by his jealous brothers. He won the favor of the Egyptian pharaoh and was later placed into a position of authority. Later in the story he was able to redeem not only his family but his nation from starvation brought about by famine across the land. It was only because he was betrayed and sold into slavery that he was able to redeem his people. I believe that somehow the enslavement of my daughters and my work on this issue will bring about the freedom of many others and that Alia and Aisha will be able to come home at last. God has told me this in so many ways. And He always keeps his promises.

As Thomas Merton states in *No Man Is an Island:*

Each one of us has some kind of vocation. We are all called by God to share in His life and in His Kingdom. Each one of us is called to a special place in the Kingdom. If we find that place we will be happy. If we do not find it, we can never be completely happy. For each one of us, there is only one thing necessary: to fulfill our own destiny, according to God's will, to be what God wants us to be.

I have known for some time that my work in this arena is my vocation. It began as the kidnapping of my children, which brought me to the brink of international politics and then into the exposure of human rights abuses and government corruption. My story is everyone's story. It is the story of America, and what can happen to us as a nation, as a free people, if there is not a change.

As part of my ongoing process of becoming whole and holy I decided to get in touch with my Italian roots even further and took a trip to Italy. I had been there briefly many years ago, but last year's trip was my journey to the land of Bella Papa—Calabria. After renting a car in Rome, I spent one month traveling to the most precious places of antiquity and Christianity.

After I left the Amalfi coast and etched my way along the *autostrada* toward the southern provinces, my heart sang when I saw the sign "Piani Crati" near the city of Cosenza. Although my uncle Alphonso had written a book about our family's beginnings in the poor village on the rolling hills of Calabria, no one had ever been back to retrace their steps. I walked in the shadow of these simple Italian peasants who had left their land to go to America to find a better life. I even visited the church of Santa Barbara where they were baptized. I had come home.

I completed the "arc"—the transformation from Esther's daughter, to a young woman caught in a milieu of social and cultural changes, to young motherhood, to a student, to a battered woman, to a single working mother, to a victim of an international crime, to a leader in an immense movement for freedom and justice.

Everyone wants to go home—Odysseus, Dorothy, E.T., and Alia and Aisha. But we all long to go home to our final destiny—to our God.

And God, I'm sure, is keeping with the old Italian tradition of saving the best wine for last.

And so, my darling Flowers,
this is my very special gift to you—with grace and in truth.

Love,
Mom

AFTERWORD

After the October 2002 hearing before the House Committee for Government Reform, Dan Burton subpoenaed all documents relating to Pat Roush's case and other American victims of Saudi abductions from the three U.S. lobbyist/PR specialists involved in the London scheme: Qorvis Communications, Patton Boggs LLP, and The Gallagher Group. All three refused to turn over the material and stated that the Saudi Embassy had given them instructions not to do so, citing diplomatic exemption under the Vienna Convention for Diplomatic Relations. Burton then tried to subpoena the three executives from each of those firms: Michael Petruzzello, Jack Deschauer, and Jamie Gallagher to appear as witnesses at a hearing. All three avoided service from U.S. Marshalls until great pressure was exerted from Burton's office and the media.

During the time that the subpoenas were requested for the documents, three partners of Qorvis Communications left the firm, including Judy Smith.

Another hearing was held on December 4 and 11, 2002: "The Saudi Claim of Privilege: Must Saudi Lobbyists Comply with Subpoenas in the

Committee's Investigation of Child Abduction Cases?" Pat Roush, Margaret McClain, Michael Petruzzello, Jack Deschauer, Jamie Gallagher, Saudi embassy attorney Maureen Mahoney, along with the foremost world expert on the Vienna Convention, Professor Eileen Denza, testified.

The Saudis and their retainers still refuse to comply with the congressional subpoena to turn over these documents, and angry members of Congress vowed to pursue the matter during the next congressional session.

Pat Roush continues her efforts to free her daughters and other American women and children from Saudi Arabia and bring them home to America. As a result of her work with Dan Burton and the Committee for Government Reform, two pieces of legislation have been introduced in the U.S. Congress that will both protect American citizens that seek assistance and sanctuary in U.S. Embassies worldwide and will also deny visas to the United States to the extended families and employers of individuals who kidnap U.S. citizens.

Pat has extensive plans for this issue and will travel extensively during the coming years to take this matter to the highest levels of international forums and worldwide political levels. She is committed to freeing her daughters and all American women and children abused, threatened, and held in Saudi Arabia against their will, as well as to the issue of international child abduction and human rights for women and children throughout the world.

About the Author

Patricia Roush has pioneered the issue of international child abduction and has been at the forefront of political issues and human rights abuses concerning Saudi Arabia for almost two decades. Her work continues to bring about many legislative changes concerning human rights, protection of American children and women in foreign countries, religious freedom, abduction prevention, and visa restrictions. She has testified before congressional committees on five occasions and makes frequent appearances on national television and other media.

WND BOOKS

A DIVISION OF THOMAS NELSON, INC.

The pen is indeed mightier than the sword. In an age where swords are being rattled all over the world, a new voice has emerged. An unprecedented partnership between WorldNetDaily, the leading independent Internet news site, and Thomas Nelson, Inc., one of the leading publishers in America, has brought about a new book-publishing venture—WND Books.

You can find WND Books at your favorite bookstore, or by visiting the Web site www.WorldNetDaily.com.

In *Center of the Storm: Practicing Principled Leadership in Times of Crisis,* former Florida Secretary of State Katherine Harris discusses the behind-the-scenes negotiations and backroom bartering that everyone suspected, but no one dared to disclose, during the infamous 2000 presidential election vote recount. Through never-before-revealed anecdotes, she explains twelve essential principles that helped her not just survive but thrive. She clearly illustrates how we, too, can learn these skills that help us in times of crisis. ISBN 0-7852-6443-4

The Savage Nation: Saving America from the Liberal Assault on our Borders, Language, and Culture warns that our country is losing its identity and becoming a victim of political correctness, unmonitored immigration, and socialistic ideals. Michael Savage, whose program is the fourth largest radio talk show and is heard on more than three hundred stations coast to coast, uses bold, biting, and hilarious straight talk to take aim at the sacred cows of our ever-eroding culture and wages war against the "group of psychopaths" known as PETA, the ACLU, and the liberal media. ISBN 0-7852-6353-5

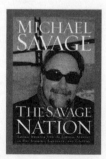